Approaches to Teaching
Woolf's *Mrs. Dalloway*

Approaches to Teaching
World Literature

Approaches to Teaching Woolf's *Mrs. Dalloway*

Edited by

Eileen Barrett

and

Ruth O. Saxton

The Modern Language Association of America
New York   2009

MLA and MODERN LANGUAGE ASSOCIATION are trademarks
owned by the Modern Language Association of America. For
information about obtaining permission to reprint material from
MLA book publications, send your request by mail (see address below),
e-mail (permissions@mla.org), or fax (646 458-0030).

Library of Congress Cataloging-in-Publication Data

Approaches to teaching Woolf's Mrs. Dalloway /
edited by Eileen Barrett and Ruth O. Saxton.
p. cm. — (Approaches to teaching world literature ; 112)
Includes bibliographical references and index.
ISBN 978-1-60329-058-6 (hardcover : alk. paper)
ISBN 978-1-60329-059-3 (pbk. : alk. paper)
1. Woolf, Virginia, 1882–1941. Mrs. Dalloway—Study and teaching.
I. Barrett, Eileen. II. Saxton, Ruth.
PR6045.O72M7335 2009
823'.912—dc22   2009019765

Approaches to Teaching World Literature 112
ISSN 1059-1133

Cover illustration of the paperback edition: *Flowers*, by Vanessa Bell. 1930s.
Oil on canvas. Government Art Collection, United Kingdom.
© Estate of Vanessa Bell, courtesy Henrietta Garnett

Printed on recycled paper

Published by The Modern Language Association of America
26 Broadway, New York, NY 10004-1789
www.mla.org

CONTENTS

PREFACE

Virginia Woolf's 1925 novel *Mrs. Dalloway* is a central modernist text and a celebrated work within the Woolf canon. Along with *To the Lighthouse*, it is not only one of the most widely read but also one of the most frequently analyzed and taught of Woolf's novels.

Mrs. Dalloway reflects and refracts the canonical tradition, illustrates modernist innovations, and anticipates postmodernist techniques. Situated in the historically pivotal era between the two world wars, it surveys the damage of empire and colonialism; analyzes the British class structure; and addresses key political, scientific, sexual, and psychological issues of the twentieth century. The novel interrogates conventional marriage, portrays challenges for professional women, and illuminates varieties of lesbian passion. As an evocation of the residual effects of trauma and war, *Mrs. Dalloway* speaks to contemporary international conflicts. Through the juxtaposition of the lives of Septimus Warren Smith and Clarissa Dalloway on a Wednesday in June 1923, Woolf raises enduring questions about human frailty and connection, consumerism, class structure, same-sex passion, nationalism and war, solitude, depression, trauma, grief, and lasting friendship. It is a compelling work to those of us who attempt to explore its beauty, power, and insight with our students.

At the end of the twentieth century, Woolf's once obscure literary novel reentered popular consciousness in new ways. The 1998 film adaptation of *Mrs. Dalloway* directed by Marleen Gorris, starring Vanessa Redgrave in the title role, introduced Woolf's novel to the growing population of book clubs as well as to other common readers. In music, the Ashley Adams Trio produced a compact disc called *Flowers for Mrs. Dalloway*, and the Indigo Girls included the song "Virginia Woolf" on their *Rites of Passage* compact disc. Michael Cunningham's Pulitzer Prize–winning tribute to Woolf and the novel, *The Hours*, pairs well with *Mrs. Dalloway* in classroom teaching. The well-reviewed 2002 film based on Cunningham's novel shifts the popular reference point for Woolf from Edward Albee's *Who's Afraid of Virginia Woolf?* to Nicole Kidman's Oscar-winning performance. This kind of public and popular visibility brings new readers to Woolf's novel. It also results in the expansion of the already rich materials available to aid teachers in making Woolf's novel accessible to twenty-first-century students.

Whether we teach *Mrs. Dalloway* to undergraduate or graduate students, in literature, theory, women's studies, composition, or interdisciplinary courses, this novel challenges readers with its many allusions, unusual structure and plot, and innovative narrative form. The internal monologues, temporal shifts, and literary and historical references often make the text difficult for first-time readers. Thus we include essays that acknowledge this difficulty and that offer practical strategies for the classroom teacher who must, for example, explain to a confused student that, yes, on page 11, Clarissa is still on her way to buy the flowers for her party.

The body of scholarly criticism on *Mrs. Dalloway* speaks to the novel's complexity and richness. We come to our classes and our readings of the novel informed by the diversity of excellent theoretically grounded close readings of Woolf's text. Current critical work on *Mrs. Dalloway* is often informed by cultural, postmodern, and postcolonial studies. While some critics place *Mrs. Dalloway* in the context of Woolf's other writings, others locate their interpretations in, for example, lesbian, queer, feminist, psychological, or trauma theories. Grounded in the historical and material conditions of the twentieth century, many readings stress the importance of race, class, and economics in Woolf's work. Critics attend to Woolf's engagement with the popular culture of her time, provide narrative analyses informed by poststructuralism and Continental philosophies, and discuss her relation to other literary works.

In this volume we recommend from among this vast body of work the critical materials that complement teaching and that illuminate *Mrs. Dalloway* for students. We include essays by teachers who represent a range of theoretical approaches and who are at the same time aware of the commonplace concerns that arise in the classroom.

We would like to thank Joseph Gibaldi for his early encouragement of this project. We especially appreciate the guidance and support we received from Sonia Kane, assistant director of book publications of the Modern Language Association; in particular, we thank her for supporting the distribution of the student survey, which proved invaluable for measuring student responses to the text and to various teaching methods. We appreciate the thoughtful comments from the peer reviewers of the manuscript, including those of the MLA Publications Committee.

We are grateful to the numerous colleagues who provided detailed responses to our questionnaires; their many proposals would fill three volumes. We thank our contributors for sharing their excellent scholarship and dedication to teaching. We thank Beth Rigel Daugherty and Mary Beth Pringle, editors of *Approaches to Teaching Woolf's* To the Lighthouse, for their generosity, especially during the preparation of our proposal. Thanks go as well to Mark Hussey, who readily shared his extensive knowledge of Woolf studies.

Our collaboration allowed us to pool strengths and fill in gaps for one another, reminding us from initial idea to finished manuscript of the benefits of interdependence and of the vitality of the community of Woolf scholars and readers.

Eileen acknowledges support she received from the Office of Faculty Development at California State University, East Bay, that enabled her to attend a workshop on the scholarship of teaching. She thanks her colleagues Julie Glass, Patricia Guthrie, Rita Liberti, and Gale Young for stimulating conversations about pedagogy and Jane Lilienfeld and J. J. Wilson for ongoing discussions about Woolf. Mary D'Alleva, Sue Fox, and Aline Soules provided insightful comments on the "Materials" section. Valuable help from her graduate assistant Samantha Tieu ensured that the final manuscript-preparation stage went smoothly. Elissa Dennis read, advised, and provided numerous "exquisite moments" throughout the project.

Ruth recognizes the support provided by Mills College through a sabbatical leave, two faculty-development research grants, and a grant from the Meg Quigley Women's Studies Program. Warm thanks to the graduate research assistants—Jeana Hrepich, Sophie Weeks, and Jessica Tanner—who provided invaluable assistance at each stage of the manuscript. Ruth also thanks her colleague and daughter, Kirsten T. Saxton, for reading drafts at every step in the process and the rest of her family—Paul, David, Katherine, and Karl—for helping her focus on the manuscript through a major home renovation and a car accident. They were always ready to remind her of Woolf's "spot the size of a shilling" on the back of her head and to help her maintain a sense of humor.

EB and ROS

Part One

MATERIALS

Editions

This volume cites and recommends for teaching the 2005 Harcourt paperback edition of *Mrs. Dalloway*, which is based on the first American edition, published in 1925. Bonnie Kime Scott's introduction, annotations, and supplemental materials make this edition the most useful for teachers and students. The general editor for Harcourt's annotated series of Woolf's works, Mark Hussey, provides a preface that discusses important aspects of Woolf's life: her early publications; her marriage to Leonard Woolf and their partnership in the Hogarth Press; and her feminism, pacifism, and lesbianism. He also considers her reception in the late twentieth and twenty-first centuries. Scott's introduction describes the genesis of the novel, parallels between Woolf's life and *Mrs. Dalloway*, and Woolf's relation to her modernist contemporaries. An annotated map of *Mrs. Dalloway*'s London allows readers to trace the characters' perambulations throughout the city. Annotations at the end of the novel are thorough and unobtrusive. A focused bibliography and suggestions for further reading provide ample information for curious readers.

The 1981 Harcourt edition with a foreword by the novelist Maureen Howard is used by many instructors. Howard admires Woolf as a writer; suggests the influence of Woolf's reading Greek tragedies, Marcel Proust, and James Joyce while composing the novel; and describes the complex design of *Mrs. Dalloway*. Recent printings include a reading-group guide that covers narrative, character, spatial and temporal design, literary references and cultural history, and themes of disorder, death, and sanity. While the apparatus adds value, a few errors mar this edition. Howard implies that the novel is set in 1922, a year earlier than the critical consensus. The biographical note also errs when it claims that the Hogarth Press published works by Joyce: although the Woolfs were asked to publish Joyce, they never did.

Alternatively, United States instructors may select *The* Mrs. Dalloway *Reader*, edited by Francine Prose, also based on the 1925 American edition. We recommend the 2004 edition of the *Reader*, which features a foreword by Hussey that explains the connection between Woolf's novel and the posthumously published short-story collection *Mrs. Dalloway's Party*. In addition to the novel, this volume includes "Mrs. Dalloway in Bond Street," several other Woolf stories, Woolf's 1928 introduction to *Mrs. Dalloway*, selected diary entries, a letter Woolf wrote about the novel, and a map of 1923 London. Katherine Mansfield's "The Garden-Party" and E. M. Forster's "The Early Novels of Virginia Woolf" enrich the context for Woolf's novel, and essays by the writers Deborah Eisenberg, Margo Jefferson, Daniel Mendelsohn, Elissa Schappell, Elaine Showalter, Michael Cunningham, Mary Gordon, Sigrid Nunez, Francine Prose, and James Wood provide an array of responses to *Mrs. Dalloway* and Woolf's other works.

For instructors who teach Woolf in survey or period classes, *The Longman Anthology of British Literature: The Twentieth Century*, edited by Kevin Dettmar and Jennifer Wicke, contains the complete novel along with "The Lady in the Looking-Glass: A Reflection," excerpts from Woolf's *A Room of One's Own*, *Three Guineas*, and *The Diary*, and Woolf's letter to Gerald Brenan about *Mrs. Dalloway*. The "Regendering Modernism" section juxtaposes sections from *Orlando* with pieces by Vita Sackville-West, E. M. Forster, Rebecca West, Mansfield, Jean Rhys, and Angela Carter.

The Longman and all Harcourt printings of *Mrs. Dalloway* are based on the American edition of the novel, published by Harcourt on 14 May 1925, the same day that the Woolfs' Hogarth Press published the British edition. In 1928, Random House published a Modern Library edition, based on the American edition, for which Woolf wrote an introduction. Since then, Harcourt has been and is likely to remain the primary United States publisher of *Mrs. Dalloway*. In 1998, the Sonny Bono Copyright Term Extension Act extended copyright from seventy-five to ninety-five years from first publication for works (such as *Mrs. Dalloway*) whose copyright was in a renewal term (United States [Copyright Office]). Woolf's *The Voyage Out* (1915), *Night and Day* (1919), and *Jacob's Room* (1922) came out of copyright respectively in 1990, 1994, and 1997; thus they are available from several United States publishers. *Mrs. Dalloway*, however, will not be in the public domain until 2020. Since copyright laws differ, Woolf's novels are widely available in paperback in Great Britain, Canada, and Australia. Electronic versions of the novel based on the British edition, which differs from the American edition, are accessible on the Internet. Stuart N. Clarke offers a list of recommended United Kingdom paperback editions of *Mrs. Dalloway*.

Instructors interested in Woolf's manuscript preparation, the publishing history of *Mrs. Dalloway*, and the differences between the British and American editions should consult G. Patton Wright's "Note on Editorial Method" in Hogarth's 1990 Definitive Collected Edition of *Mrs. Dalloway* and Morris Beja's "Text and Counter-text: Trying to Recover *Mrs. Dalloway*." Both essays explain how Woolf corrected three sets of proofs: one for Hogarth's British edition; a second for Harcourt's American edition; and a third, private set that she sent to her dying friend Jacques-Pierre Raverat. The Harcourt proofs are now in the Lilly Library at Indiana University, Bloomington, and the Raverat proofs are in the University Research Library at the University of California, Los Angeles. The Hogarth proofs were lost, presumably destroyed during World War II. Woolf's niece Angelica Garnett poignantly introduces Wright's edition of the novel, which is based on the first British edition and contains Wright's detailed notes and lists of textual variants and emendations. Beja questions Wright's use of the first British edition, for which there are no available proofs, and illustrates how seemingly minor changes affect the novel's meaning. Beja's essay as well as his 1996 Shakespeare Head edition of *Mrs. Dalloway*, based on the corrected proofs for the first American edition, are extremely helpful to scholars; unfortunately, because of copyright issues discussed above, neither the Wright nor the Beja edition is readily available in the United States.

In 1996, Helen Wussow transcribed and edited *Virginia Woolf The Hours: The British Museum Manuscript of* Mrs. Dalloway. Wussow describes the materials available in the Berg Collection of the New York Public Library and argues that *The Hours* is the first full-length draft of *Mrs. Dalloway*. She analyzes Woolf's writing notebooks, the manuscript of *The Hours*, and the stories in which Woolf introduced the characters of Clarissa and Septimus, "Mrs. Dalloway in Bond Street" and "The Prime Minister." Brenda Silver's *Virginia Woolf's Reading Notebooks* describes the Monk's House papers at Sussex University, with detailed notes about what Woolf was reading during the composition of *Mrs. Dalloway*. For further discussion of Woolf's process of composing *Mrs. Dalloway*, the following sources are recommended: Susan Dick's "Building It Round One: *Mrs. Dalloway*," Suzette A. Henke's "'The Prime Minister': A Key to *Mrs. Dalloway*," Charles G. Hoffman's "From Short Story to Novel: The Manuscript Revisions of Virginia Woolf's *Mrs. Dalloway*," Jacqueline Latham's "The Manuscript Revisions of Virginia Woolf's *Mrs. Dalloway*: A Postscript," and E. F. Shields's "The American Edition of *Mrs. Dalloway*." Those who plan to use source materials should consult the regularly updated "Guide to Library Special Collections" in *Woolf Studies Annual*.

London Maps and Walks

In her introduction to *Mrs. Dalloway*, Angelica Garnett recalls the thrill of walking London streets with her aunt, suggesting, "As we read *Mrs. Dalloway* we feel the whole of London, from Westminster to Greenwich and from Regent's Park to Saint Paul's, is held in the hollow of Virginia's hand" (vii–viii). Several instructors advise using a map to appreciate Woolf's urban landscape and to follow the journeys of her characters through London. Recommended are the map in the Harcourt annotated edition of *Mrs. Dalloway* and Morris Beja's "The London of *Mrs. Dalloway*," a hand-drawn map with twenty-one annotations. David Daiches and John Flower's chapter "Virginia Woolf's London," in *Literary Landscapes of the British Isles: A Narrative Atlas*, includes a map; photographs of London during the Blitz and of the Strand in 1923; and descriptions of the walks of Clarissa, Septimus and Rezia, Peter, Elizabeth, and Doris Kilman. David Dowling's Mrs. Dalloway: *Mapping Streams of Consciousness*, a book frequently cited by instructors, contains a map of Westminster as well as five separate maps that trace the movements of Septimus, Clarissa, Elizabeth, Peter, and Richard. Elisa Kay Sparks maintains an excellent Woolf Web site with a vivid, detailed map of *Mrs. Dalloway*'s London. Colored lines illustrate each character's path through the London streets and parks, allowing for

[handwritten margin note: present? Still guided walks?]

comparisons. The Virginia Woolf Society of Great Britain's Web site maintains Stuart N. Clarke's "A *Mrs. Dalloway* Walk in London," a thorough, scholarly tour for experts as well as common readers. Mirslav Beker's "London as a Principle of Structure in *Mrs. Dalloway*," Susan Merrill Squier's "The Carnival and Funeral of *Mrs. Dalloway*'s London" (*Virginia Woolf* 91–121), and Andelys Wood's "Walking the Web in the Lost London of *Mrs. Dalloway*" discuss the significance of the walks in the novel. London visitors can benefit from "A Mrs. Dalloway Walk (from Westminster to Regent's Park)," the fourth of seven Virginia Woolf walks that Jean Moorcroft Wilson recommends in *Virginia Woolf, Life and London: A Biography of Place* (194–206). Laura Doan and Terry Brown's "Being There: Woolf's London and the Politics of Location" discusses teaching *Mrs. Dalloway* to United States students in London.

Reference Works

Every instructor's bookshelf should include Mark Hussey's *Virginia Woolf A to Z*. With deft cross-references, Hussey transcends the alphabetical organization prescribed by the A to Z series and produces an accessible, informative work. Edward Bishop's useful *A Virginia Woolf Chronology* lists Woolf's reading and writing and provides an abbreviated view of her professional and social activities. Although it is no longer available for purchase, *Major Authors on CD-ROM: Virginia Woolf* is owned by many institutions. Edited by Hussey, the compact disc features Woolf's complete works, including variant and rare editions; Hussey's *A to Z*; and other source material—all in a searchable format. Beverly Ann Schlack's *Continuing Presences: Virginia Woolf's Use of Literary Allusion* contains a chapter on Woolf's mythological and literary references in *Mrs. Dalloway*.

B. J. Kirkpatrick and Stuart N. Clarke's *A Bibliography of Virginia Woolf* is a thorough, reliable source. Instructors might also consult bibliographies by Maurice Beebe, Barbara Weiser, Laura Sue Fuderer, and Justine Dymond; Laura Moss Gottlieb's *Index to the Virginia Woolf Miscellany*; and the *Annual Bibliography of Woolf Studies*, published since 1996 on the Web site of the International Virginia Woolf Society.

Since 1973, the *Virginia Woolf Miscellany* has been publishing short articles and reviews of books focused on Woolf and related studies. The International Virginia Woolf Society maintains a Web site, organizes panels at the MLA conventions, and sponsors an e-mail discussion list that general readers and scholars can use to exchange information and ideas about Woolf. In addition to supporting its exceptional Web site, the Virginia Woolf Society of Great Britain publishes the *Virginia Woolf Bulletin*. Instructors also recommend *Woolf Studies Annual*, a journal published by Pace University Press, and the volumes of selected papers from the annual conferences on Virginia Woolf. Those interested in attending the annual Woolf conferences will find information on the International Virginia Woolf Society Web site.

Biographies

Quentin Bell's 1972 *Virginia Woolf* is a thoroughly researched, clearly written biography of his aunt. Also recommended is Hermione Lee's *Virginia Woolf*, which chronicles Woolf's political and personal passions, argues the centrality of feminism to her writing, and places Woolf in the artistic, political, and social context of her time. Julia Briggs's *Virginia Woolf: An Inner Life*, another meticulously researched biography, complements Lee's historical, cultural, and social context with detailed attention to Woolf's writing process. Biographies recommended by instructors and reflective of a North American perspective are James King's *Virginia Woolf*, Panthea Reid's *Art and Affection: A Life of Virginia Woolf*, and Phyllis Rose's *Woman of Letters: A Life of Virginia Woolf*. Mary Ann Caws's *Virginia Woolf* offers a brief, richly illustrated introduction to Woolf's life.

All these biographers value Woolf's capacity to transform personal suffering into art; they also respect her belief that "the connection between [life and fiction] is highly complicated" (Introduction 11). Studies that provide specific insights into the complex connection between Woolf's life and *Mrs. Dalloway* include Thomas Caramagno's *The Flight of the Mind: Virginia Woolf's Art and Manic-Depressive Illness*, Louise DeSalvo's *Virginia Woolf: The Impact of Childhood Sexual Abuse on Her Life and Work*, Roger Poole's *The Unknown Virginia Woolf*, and Stephen Trombley's *All That Summer She Was Mad*.

Mrs. Dalloway Basics

Instructors and students agree that Woolf's narrative style is the most difficult challenge to appreciating the novel. David Dowling's Mrs. Dalloway: *Mapping Streams of Consciousness* provides a thorough introduction to the novel's narrative style, theme, characters, and literary and historic context. In addition to detailed maps, Dowling includes photographs and graphic images that illustrate narrative time sequences and movements of characters. Richard Lane's Mrs. Dalloway is another excellent source. Lane includes study questions for each section of the novel and glossaries that define key literary terms and that explain unfamiliar references and historical figures. Photographs and quotations in graphic sidebars add to the volume's visual appeal. Excerpts from reviews, criticism from Woolf's contemporaries, and current analysis enhance Lane's commentary and chronicle the critical conversation. Nicholas Marsh's *Virginia Woolf*, part of the St. Martin's Analysing Texts series, models close reading of passages from *Mrs. Dalloway* to illustrate how the novice reader can unravel and appreciate Woolf's style. Jeremy Hawthorn's *Virginia Woolf's* Mrs. Dalloway: *A Study in Alienation* is a valuable book-length study.

Some short, readable essays on *Mrs. Dalloway* can assist instructors in achieving particular class goals or can be assigned to students. For practical ideas about how writing helps students read *Mrs. Dalloway*, instructors may consult Susan Kirschner and Paul Connolly's "Opening Questions: A Workshop in Writing to Read Virginia Woolf." Students can learn to appreciate connections among characters by reading Susan Searles's "'Accesses of Emotion—Bursting into Tears': Why All the Crying in Virginia Woolf's *Mrs. Dalloway*?" To focus students on a comparison with a familiar fairy tale, instructors may assign Ann Martin's "Sleeping Beauty in a Green Dress: *Mrs. Dalloway* and Fairy Tale Configurations of Desire." Students can gain an understanding of narrative events and time with the visual diagrams in Wendy Patrice Williams's "Falling through the Cone: The Shape of *Mrs. Dalloway* Makes Its Point." Discussion about Septimus's suicide and the meaning with which Clarissa imbues his death can be provoked by Deborah Guth's "'What a Lark! What a Plunge!': Fiction as Self-Evasion in *Mrs. Dalloway*." To help frame classroom discussions of the ending, instructors may refer to Edward Mendelson's "The Death of Mrs. Dalloway: Two Readings." Responses to the novel from high school students are described in Geneviève Sanchis Morgan's "Elizabeth Dalloway Talks Back: Students and the *Mrs. Dalloway* Experience."

Woolf's Own Writing

Woolf's introduction to *Mrs. Dalloway* provides a brilliant pedagogical pathway into the novel. Woolf describes the author's relationship to her work ("once a book is printed and published it ceases to be the property of the author" [10]), grants authority of interpretation to her reader ("it would still be for the reader to decide what was relevant and what not" [11]), and explains her original intention (that "in the first version Septimus, who later is intended to be [Clarissa's] double, had no existence . . . and that Mrs. Dalloway was originally to kill herself, or perhaps merely to die at the end of the party" [11]). The diaries and letters shed light on these intentions; reading these works, students can trace Woolf's concerns about Clarissa's superficial personality, the development of Peter Walsh, and Woolf's personal connection to Septimus's mad scenes. Students will sense Woolf's excitement when she realizes that "Mrs. Dalloway has branched into a book; & I adumbrate here a study of insanity & suicide: the world seen by the sane & the insane side by side—something like that" (*Diary* 2: 207). They will also detect the passion underlying her purpose: "I want to give life & death, sanity & insanity; I want to criticise the social system, & to show it at work, at its most intense" (2: 248). Finally, students will see the discoveries Woolf makes through writing: "It took me a year's groping to discover what I call my tunnelling process, by which I tell the past by instalments, as I have need of it" (2: 272). Survey instructors either provide relevant excerpts or assign *A Writer's Diary*, which in Leonard Woolf's words includes "practically everything which referred to her own writing" (L. Woolf viii). Volume 2 of *The Diary of Virginia Woolf* focuses on the period when Woolf was writing *Mrs. Dalloway*; volume 3 of *The Letters of Virginia Woolf* contains discussions about the novel with friends, critics, and other readers.

Instructors regularly use Woolf's essays to illuminate *Mrs. Dalloway*. After all, she worked simultaneously on fiction and essays, publishing the first *Common Reader* a month before and the revised American edition at the same time as *Mrs. Dalloway*. Moreover, through the course of several essays, Woolf articulates her emerging narrative theories. Thanks to Andrew McNeillie's meticulously anno-tated edition of *The Common Reader* and *The Essays of Virginia Woolf*, we can follow how Woolf revised and developed these theories from "Modern Novels" (1919) to "Modern Fiction" (1925) and from "On Re-reading Novels" (1922) to "Mr. Bennett and Mrs. Brown" (1923) to "Character in Fiction" (1924).

Useful discussions of Woolf's essays are in Melba Cuddy-Keane's *Virginia Woolf, the Intellectual, and the Public Sphere*, Jeanne Dubino's "Creating 'the Conditions of Life': Virginia Woolf and the Common Reader," Suzette Hen-ke's "Virginia Woolf: The Modern Tradition," and Beth Carole Rosenberg and Jeanne Dubino's *Virginia Woolf and the Essay*. The essays can be successfully taught with the aid of Beth Rigel Daugherty's "'Readin', Writin', and Revisin'": Virginia Woolf's 'How Should One Read a Book?'" and "Taking a Leaf from Virginia Woolf's Book: Empowering the Student."

Instructors also assign Woolf's shorter fiction to complement and assist stu-dents' understanding of Woolf's novel. In addition to the essays by Susan Dick, Suzette Henke, and Charles G. Hoffman already cited, useful sources are Dean R. Baldwin's *Virginia Woolf: A Study of the Short Fiction*, Kathryn N. Ben-zel and Ruth Hoberman's collection *Trespassing Boundaries: Virginia Woolf's Short Fiction*, Avrom Fleishman's "Forms of the Woolfian Short Story," and Kathryn Simpson's "The Paradox of the Gift: Gift-Giving as a Disruptive Force in 'Mrs. Dalloway in Bond Street.'"

Of Woolf's major novels, *To the Lighthouse* is most often taught with *Mrs. Dalloway*. A volume that includes important criticism on both novels is Su Reid's collection Mrs. Dalloway *and* To the Lighthouse. Readers of Beth Rigel Daugherty and Mary Beth Pringle's *Approaches to Teaching* To the Lighthouse will find not only solid pedagogy but also extensive recommendations in theory and context for Woolf's work.

Critical Reception and Changing Perspectives

Instructors who teach *Mrs. Dalloway* in theory, criticism, and cultural studies courses note how diverse scholarly interpretations of the novel enhance student understanding. Although this huge outpouring of critical and theoretical approaches is a tremendous asset to classroom instruction, it can be daunting even for the teacher familiar with Woolf's work. A useful place to begin reading is Laura A. Smith's "Who Do We Think Clarissa Dalloway Is Anyway? Re-search into Seventy Years of Woolf Criticism," an overview that helps students and instructors wade through shifting interpretations of the novel.

The novel's early reception is discussed in Robin Majumdar and Allen McLaurin's *Virginia Woolf: The Critical Heritage*, which includes reviews and articles by E. M. Forster from the *New Criterion*, Arnold Bennett from the *Evening Standard*, and T. S. Eliot from the *Nouvelle Revue Française*. Volume 3 of *Virginia Woolf: Critical Assessments*, edited by Eleanor McNees, includes five reviews from Woolf's time and sixteen critical essays spanning the years from 1951 to 1989. Instructors can also consult Harold Bloom's edited collection *Clarissa Dalloway* for a rich selection of critical approaches that focus on Woolf's modernist heroine. The volume includes selections from Woolf; early reviews by Forster and Wyndham Lewis; extracts from longer critical works by Morris Beja, Joan Bennett, David Daiches, Edward A. Hungerford, and Jane Marcus; as well as significant portions from important essays by Lee R. Edwards, Blanche H. Gelfant, and Geoffrey Hartman. John Mepham's *Criticism in Focus: Virginia Woolf* provides a framework for critical perspectives of all Woolf's major works.

Narrative, Philosophical, and Psychological

Nathalia Wright's 1944 essay "*Mrs. Dalloway*: A Study in Composition" provides an excellent commentary on Woolf's narrative. J. Hillis Miller's frequently anthologized "*Mrs. Dalloway*: Repetition as the Raising of the Dead" illustrates how Woolf extends the traditional narrator of English fiction to represent a form of memory. Edward Bishop's "*Mrs. Dalloway*: Writing, Speech, and Silence" analyzes the quality of Woolf's discourse, and Anna Snaith's " 'I Wobble': Narrative Strategies" explains her use of free indirect speech. Pamela Caughie's *Virginia Woolf and Postmodernism: Literature in Quest and Question of Itself* illuminates postmodernist elements of Woolf's narrative, and Makiko Minow-Pinkney's *Virginia Woolf and the Problem of the Subject: Feminine Writing in the Major Novels* uses linguistic and French feminist theory to shed light on *Mrs. Dalloway*. An often mentioned collection is Kathy Mezei's *Ambiguous Discourse: Feminist Narratology and British Women Writers*. Philosophical approaches are offered in Mark Hussey's *The Singing of the Real World: The Philosophy of Virginia Woolf's Fiction* and Lucio Ruotolo's *The Interrupted Moment: A View of Virginia Woolf's Novels*.

Elizabeth Abel's regularly cited "Narrative Structure(s) and Female Development: The Case of *Mrs. Dalloway*" analyzes the novel's female psychological development. Woolf's intellectual response to Sigmund Freud is examined in Abel's "Between the Acts of *Mrs. Dalloway*." In addition, Jane Lilienfeld's "Accident, Incident, and Meaning: Traces of Trauma in Virginia Woolf's Narrativity" draws on the latest developments in narrative and trauma theory; Mark Spilka's "On Mrs. Dalloway's Absent Grief: A Psycho-Literary Speculation" discusses repression of grief; Jeremy Tambling's "Repression in *Mrs. Dalloway*'s London" provides a historically informed discussion of how Woolf connects state, community, and individual forms of political, psychological, and sexual repression; and Ban Wang's "'I' on the Run: Crisis of Identity in *Mrs. Dalloway*" investigates symbolic power, the constitutions of the subject, and psychic resistance.

Feminist, Lesbian, and Queer

Selected articles that represent significant feminist contributions to the study of *Mrs. Dalloway* include Rachel Bowlby's "Thinking Forward through Mrs. Dalloway's Daughter," Lee Edwards's "War and Roses: The Politics of *Mrs. Dalloway*," Blanche Gelfant's "Love and Conversion in *Mrs. Dalloway*," Johanna X. K. Garvey's "Difference and Continuity: The Voices of *Mrs. Dalloway*," Suzette A. Henke's "*Mrs. Dalloway*: The Communion of Saints," and Emily Jensen's "Clarissa Dalloway's Respectable Suicide."

Lesbian criticism articulates how some of Woolf's narratives celebrate the lesbian and homoerotic as well as how they resist the narrative of heterosexuality; expose the repression of sexual identity; and challenge the social, political, and historical discourses. Works such as Patricia Cramer's "Notes from the Underground: Lesbian Ritual in the Writings of Virginia Woolf," Toni A. H. McNaron's "'The Albanians, or Was It the Armenians?': Virginia Woolf's Lesbianism as Gloss on Her Modernism," and Judith Roof's "The Match in the Crocus: Representations of Lesbian Sexuality" explore Woolf's encoding of the lesbian erotic, address the complexities of Woolf's sexual history, and provide theoretical and textual analysis. Lesbian narrative, themes, and discourse in *Mrs. Dalloway* are thoughtfully discussed in Julie Abraham's *Are Girls Necessary? Lesbian Writing and Modern Histories*; Tuzyline Jita Allan's "The Death of Sex and the Soul in *Mrs. Dalloway* and Nella Larsen's *Passing*," Eileen Barrett's "Unmasking Lesbian Passion: The Inverted World of *Mrs. Dalloway*," Kathryn Simpson's "'Queer Fish': Woolf's Writing of Desire between Women," Patricia Juliana Smith's *Lesbian Panic: Homoeroticism in Modern British Women's Fiction*, and Gay Wachman's *Lesbian Empire: Radical Crosswriting in the Twenties*. The application of queer theory to Woolf's novel is addressed in Thomas Peele's "Queering *Mrs. Dalloway*," and Judith Roof's "Hocus Crocus" and Cramer's "Response" articulate relevant theoretical and political differences among poststructuralist, queer, and lesbian-feminist readings.

Cultural, Historical, and Postcolonial

With its emphasis on Woolf's critique of the social system, Alex Zwerdling's *Virginia Woolf and the Real World* marks another change in Woolf studies. His essay "Mrs. Dalloway and the Social System" discusses how historical forces and social institutions influence Woolf's characters. Criticism that examines class, material conditions, and consumer culture in the novel includes Reginald Abbott's "What Miss Kilman's Petticoat Means: Virginia Woolf, Shopping, and Spectacle," Sharon O'Dair's "Beyond Necessity: The Consumption of Class, the Production of Status, and the Persistence of Inequality," Leena Kore Schröder's "Mrs. Dalloway and the Female Vagrant," and Jennifer Wicke's "Mrs. Dalloway Goes to Market: Woolf, Keynes, and Modern Markets."

Gillian Beer's *Virginia Woolf: The Common Ground* covers a range of topics of interest to teachers of Woolf—prehistory, philosophy, science, industry, and community. Chapters that focus on *Mrs. Dalloway* are "The Body of the People: *Mrs. Dalloway* to *The Waves*" and "The Island and the Aeroplane: The Case of Virginia Woolf." Donald Childs's "Boers, Whores, and Mongols in *Mrs. Dalloway*" discusses how eugenics discourse is embedded in the novel. Also of note are Elizabeth Lambert's "Proportion Is in the Mind of the Beholder: *Mrs. Dalloway*'s Critique of Science" and Michael Whitworth's discussion of scientific and medical contexts in *Virginia Woolf*.

Frequently recommended by those who teach courses on war literature is Paul Fussell's *The Great War and Modern Memory*. Allyson Booth's *Postcards from the Trenches: Negotiating the Space between Modernism and the First World War*, Mark Hussey's collection of essays *Virginia Woolf and War*, and Karen Levenback's *Virginia Woolf and the Great War* include illuminating discussions of *Mrs. Dalloway*. Marlene A. Briggs's "Veterans and Civilians: The Mediation of Traumatic Knowledge in *Mrs. Dalloway*," Karen DeMeester's "Trauma, Post-traumatic Stress Disorder, and Obstacles to Postwar Recovery in *Mrs. Dalloway*," and Sue Thomas's "Virginia Woolf's Septimus Smith and Contemporary Perceptions of Shell Shock" provide valuable information and analysis. Trudi Tate's *Modernism, History, and the First World War* is highly recommended for its emphasis on women and war and its discussion of *Mrs. Dalloway*. Also recommended are Claire M. Tylee's *The Great War and Women's Consciousness: Images of Militarism and Womanhood in Women's Writing, 1914–1964*; Kathy Phillips's *Virginia Woolf against Empire*, which traces Woolf's critique of imperialism, war, and gender in *Mrs. Dalloway*; and Scott Cohen's "The Empire from the Street: Virginia Woolf, Wembley, and Imperial Monuments."

Christine Froula's *Virginia Woolf and the Bloomsbury Avant-Garde: War, Civilization, Modernity* reveals how Woolf's intellectual and political relationships shaped her pacifist, feminist, and aesthetic vision of civilization. Her chapter "*Mrs. Dalloway*'s Postwar Elegy: Women, War, and the Art of Mourning" considers how Woolf uses her art to confront the devastating violence of war.

Mrs. Dalloway is considered in the context of the Bloomsbury art movements in Jennie-Rebecca Falcetta's "Geometries of Space and Time: The Cubist London of *Mrs. Dalloway*." The novel's relation to the emerging art of cinema is explored in Leslie K. Hankins's "The Doctor and the Woolf: Reel Challenges—*The Cabinet of Dr. Caligari* and *Mrs. Dalloway*" and in Elizabeth Lambert's discussion of Fritz Lang's *Metropolis*, "Mrs. Dalloway Meets the Robot Maria."

Woolf and Other Writers

"For books continue each other, in spite of our habit of judging them separately," Woolf famously wrote in *A Room of One's Own* (80). With its rich, allusive language, *Mrs. Dalloway* invites comparison with its literary precursors and contemporaries as well as discussion of its influence on twentieth- and twenty-first-century works. Alice Fox's *Virginia Woolf and the Literature of the English Renaissance* provides an overview of Woolf's Elizabethan allusions. For a discussion of Shakespearean influence on *Mrs. Dalloway*, instructors may wish to consult "Something Central Which Permeated: Virginia Woolf and *Mrs. Dalloway*," an influential essay in which Reuben Arthur Brower argues that "[t]he best preparation for understanding *Mrs. Dalloway* is to read *The Tempest*, or *Cymbeline*, or, better still *The Winter's Tale*" (123). Steven Monte's "Ancients and Moderns in *Mrs. Dalloway*" takes up influences from Vergil to Katherine Mansfield. Molly Hoff's essays on *Mrs. Dalloway* in *Explicator* and Jean Wyatt's "*Mrs. Dalloway*: Literary Allusion as Structural Metaphor" include comprehensive discussions of *Mrs. Dalloway*'s relation to literary tradition.

Jocelyn Harris's "Clarissa Lives! Reading Richardson through Rewritings" provides thoughtful suggestions for teaching *Mrs. Dalloway* with its main character's eponymous precursor. Chella Courington's "From *Clarissa* to *Mrs. Dalloway*: Woolf's (Re)Vision of Richardson" analyzes how Woolf's Clarissa resurrects subversive elements in Richardson's *Clarissa*. Kenneth J. Ames's "Elements of Mock-Heroic in Virginia Woolf's *Mrs. Dalloway*" examines allusions to Alexander Pope in the novel. Beth Carole Rosenberg's *Virginia Woolf and Samuel Johnson: Common Readers* includes analysis of *Mrs. Dalloway* in the light of Johnson's influence; Perry Meisel's *The Absent Father: Virginia Woolf and Walter Pater* traces Woolf's response to Pater and other absent fathers. Alison Booth's *Greatness Engendered: George Eliot and Virginia Woolf* offers a thorough, informed discussion of Woolf's relation to George Eliot.

Several works address Woolf's relation to Thomas Hardy, Joseph Conrad, and her modernist contemporaries E. M. Forster, D. H. Lawrence, and Katherine Mansfield. Rosemary Sumner's *A Route to Modernism: Hardy, Lawrence, Woolf*; Shirley Neuman's "*Heart of Darkness*, Virginia Woolf, and the Spectre of Domination"; Elizabeth Heine's "The Significance of Structure in the Novels of E. M. Forster and Virginia Woolf"; Helen Wussow's *The Nightmare of History: The Fictions of Virginia Woolf and D. H. Lawrence*; and Patricia Moran's *Word of Mouth: Body Language in Katherine Mansfield and Virginia Woolf* all focus on *Mrs. Dalloway*. Instructors who teach *Mrs. Dalloway* with *Ulysses* should read Maria DiBattista's "Joyce, Woolf, and the Modern Mind," Molly Hoff's "The Pseudo-Homeric World of *Mrs. Dalloway*," Teresa Fulker's "Virginia Woolf's Daily Drama of the Body," and Harvena Richter's "The *Ulysses* Connection: Clarissa Dalloway's Bloomsday."

Jane Marcus's *Hearts of Darkness: White Women Write Race* draws parallels between *Mrs. Dalloway* and Mulk Raj Anand's *Coolie*, a novel that Marcus describes as "*Mrs. Dalloway* turned upside down, with its main text recording the destruction of the body and soul of a 'subaltern subject'" (174). Margot Gayle Backus's "Exploring the Ethical Implications of Narrative in a Sophomore-Level Course on Same-Sex Love: *Mrs. Dalloway* and *The Last September*" recounts teaching Woolf with Elizabeth Bowen in her course on gay and lesbian literature. Critics also compare *Mrs. Dalloway* with novels by Doris Lessing. Comparisons with Lessing's work can be found in Theresa Crater's "Septimus and Charles Watkins: The Phallic Suppression of Masculine Subjectivity," Ruth Saxton's "The Female Body Veiled: From Crocus to Clitoris," Claire Sprague's "Multipersonal and Dialogic Modes in *Mrs. Dalloway* and *The Golden Notebook*," and Christine Wick Sizemore's "The 'Outsider-Within': Virginia Woolf and Doris Lessing as Urban Novelists in *Mrs. Dalloway* and *The Four-Gated City*."

Margaret Diane Stetz's "*Quartet in Autumn*: New Light on Barbara Pym as Modernist" compares Pym's novel with *Mrs. Dalloway*. Suzan Harrison's "Playing with Fire: Women's Sexuality and Artistry in Virginia Woolf's *Mrs. Dalloway* and Eudora Welty's *The Golden Apples*" and Christy L. Burns's "Powerful Differences: Critique and Eros in Jeanette Winterson and Virginia Woolf" contain discussions of sexuality in Woolf, Eudora Welty, and Jeanette Winterson. Josephine O'Brien Schaefer's "The Great War and 'This Late Age of World's Experience' in Cather and Woolf" pairs Septimus with Claude Wheeler from Willa Cather's *One of Ours*. Laurie Vickroy's "A Legacy of Pacifism: Virginia Woolf and Pat Barker" sheds light on *Mrs. Dalloway* and Barker's World War I trilogy. Beth Rigel Daugherty's "Teaching *Mrs. Dalloway* and *Praisesong for the Widow* as a Pair" and Jennifer Unter's "Virginia Woolf's Clarissa and Zora Neale Hurston's Janie: Images of Women in Literature" offer suggestions about teaching Woolf with Paule Marshall and Zora Neale Hurston.

Toni Morrison devotes a chapter of her master's thesis, "Virginia Woolf's and William Faulkner's Treatment of the Alienated," to *Mrs. Dalloway*. Criticism that examines the Woolf-Morrison connection includes Eileen Barrett's "Septimus and Shadrack: Woolf and Morrison Envision the Madness of War," Barbara Christian's "Layered Rhythms: Virginia Woolf and Toni Morrison," Lorie Watkins Fulton's "'A Direction of One's Own': Alienation in *Mrs. Dalloway* and *Sula*," and Lisa Williams's *The Artist as Outsider in the Novels of Toni Morrison and Virginia Woolf*. Finally, Michael Cunningham's *The Hours* has inspired a great deal of critical discussion. Recommended are Mary Joe Hughes's "Michael Cunningham's *The Hours* and Postmodern Artistic Re-Presentation" and Birgit Spengler's "Michael Cunningham Rewriting Virginia Woolf: Pragmatist vs. Modernist Aesthetics."

Multimedia and Popular Culture

Any discussion of Woolf and popular culture should begin with Brenda Silver's *Virginia Woolf: Icon*, an incisive analysis of the extensive visual and verbal representations of Woolf in popular culture. Michael Whitworth's chapter "Recontextualizing and Reconstructing Woolf" in his book *Virginia Woolf* and Hermione Lee's *Virginia Woolf's Nose* are also helpful. In addition to teaching *Mrs. Dalloway* with Michael Cunningham's *The Hours*, instructors might select Robin Lippincott's *Mr. Dalloway*, a fictional sequel to Woolf's novel. Henry Alley's "*Mrs. Dalloway* and Three of Its Contemporary Children" discusses *Mrs. Dalloway*'s progeny.

Woolf's iconic status results, in part, from recent adaptations that along with documentary films can be helpful tools for teaching. Instructors recommend both Marleen Gorris's *Mrs. Dalloway* and Stephen Daldry's *The Hours*. John Fuegi and Jo Francis's *The War Within: A Portrait of Virginia Woolf* provides a superb introduction to Woolf; the filmmakers' essay "The Making of *The War Within*" is particularly illuminating. *Virginia Woolf's* Mrs. Dalloway, directed by Kim Evans, includes reenactments of the novel starring Eileen Atkins and commentary by Hermione Lee. Diane F. Gillespie discusses this film in "'Human Nature Is on You': Septimus Smith, the Camera Eye, and the Classroom." Students may also listen to an unabridged audiocassette of *Mrs. Dalloway* read by Virginia Leishman or an abridged version by Atkins.

The Internet is a vast resource for visual images and materials on World War I, shell shock, and London in the aftermath of war. The *Imperial War Museum Collections Online* sheds light on all aspects of twentieth-century wars and conflicts; students can listen to firsthand accounts of trench warfare as well as see photographs and war propaganda from the period. Also recommended by instructors is the Emmy Award–winning eight-part PBS series *The Great War and the Shaping of the Twentieth Century*, produced in association with the Imperial War Museum. It covers political and military history of World War I as well as the social and cultural effects of the war; the companion Web site is also a marvelous teaching resource. For an excellent collection of London photographs in the 1920s, instructors may visit the online *Museum of London Picture Library*. Finally, the *New York Times* Web site archives articles and reviews relevant to Woolf.

Part Two

APPROACHES

Introduction

Ruth O. Saxton

> The first duty of a lecturer—to hand you after an hour's
> discourse a nugget of pure truth to wrap up between the
> pages of your notebooks and keep on the mantelpiece
> forever.
>
> —Virginia Woolf, *A Room of One's Own*

It was tempting, in the process of editing this volume, to look for essays that deliver a "nugget"—essays that immediately shift our angle of vision on a novel that is itself concerned with truth and with perception. But in putting together the collection, we avoided essays that focus on the writer's own scholarly visions, however brilliant. While one may find new ways of reading *Mrs. Dalloway* in this volume, our goal is not to engender revelatory scholarly insight. Rather, it is to prompt recognition of familiar ways of teaching, to provide seductive glimpses of unfamiliar techniques, and ultimately to contribute to students' enjoyment of the novel and ability to articulate their own readings of a text that too often intimidates them into turning to cheat sheets or parroting an instructor's insights uncritically.

We include essays whose primary concern is with the novel as it exists in the classroom. While differing in scope, methodology, theoretical perspective, and contextual grounding, they share a passionate investment in teaching. Whatever approach our contributors take, they offer specific teaching suggestions—ranging from in-class exercises, the presentation of archival materials and contextual readings, and the use of visual and technological tools to group projects and essay topics—that any teacher may adopt or adapt. In addition, each essay attends to the pedagogical processes and theoretical contexts that inform its suggestions.

In addition to the usual survey of instructors that is the foundation of volumes in the Approaches series, we carried out a survey of students. It revealed that students—from those in first-year writing seminars to those in upper-division literature courses and graduate theory courses—overwhelmingly found it hard to access the prose and to figure out who is speaking when and whose thoughts the prose in *Mrs. Dalloway* is expressing on any given page. Their responses reinforce our sense that students have difficulty with the actual text. The novel's lack of chapters or recognizable plot and the shifts in point of view and movement between present and past as well as between characters' minds often baffle students, who do not necessarily find helpful a definition of stream of consciousness or a biographical sketch of Woolf's life. Instructors who responded to our survey were primarily concerned with students' lack of specific historical and literary knowledge to bring to the novel. In this collection, we attend to both these intertwined areas of student need: a way into the text on the page and a contextual framework in which to make meaning of that text.

Contributors address the text's difficulties and provide prereading assignments, hands-on classroom activities, and proven exercises that can be adapted by teachers in multiple contexts. Essays also provide innovative ways to situate the novel in postwar London. Teachers will find useful suggestions for connecting modernist literary experiments to salient events of World War I and for discussing the still-powerful Victorian notion of the angel in the house, the rise of consumerism, and the effects of shell shock and trauma not only on returning soldiers but also on ordinary citizens in postwar London.

Whatever its focus—whether to view the novel as an exemplar of literary modernism, an articulation of postwar London, or an investigation into unexamined assumptions about femininity, masculinity, or empire—each essay is deeply engaged with and offers insights into how instructors can help students find their ways into *Mrs. Dalloway*, appreciate their discoveries, and perhaps even become the common readers so respected by Woolf.

The volume is meant to be suggestive rather than exhaustive; we hope that it will raise new questions and ideas about ways to approach *Mrs. Dalloway* in the classroom. We also hope it will lead instructors to push at the boundaries of these approaches and thus move the conversation into areas we have not imagined.

The essays are divided into four sections: "Approaching a Modernist Text," "Using the Context of War," "Reading Intertextually," and "Teaching in Multiple Settings." We find that the sections and their self-evident titles provide a useful organizational structure; we hope readers will enjoy how the essays also speak to one another across sections.

The first section, "Approaching a Modernist Text," addresses theoretical strategies and practical ways in which we can usefully situate Woolf's novel within its modernist context. The essays here provide students with a way into reading a modernist text, a task students from freshmen to graduates reported as their central problem with the novel. These essays suggest concrete methods to use when teaching critical issues associated with social and literary modernism. While they are specific to *Mrs. Dalloway*, they are easily adaptable to teaching any modernist literature, since they address the sea changes just burgeoning at the beginning of the twentieth century in such fundamental notions as the nature of time, space, consciousness, selfhood, and nation.

James Knapp provides students key terms—such as *collage, commodification, urban*, and *department store*—to help them understand the emerging conditions of modern life and offers a cultural studies context in which students draw connections between Woolf's setting and contemporary commodity culture. Lecia Rosenthal explains to students the formal and historical developments of modernism by situating the novel in conversation with Woolf's essays "Mr. Bennett and Mrs. Brown" and "Modern Fiction." Victoria Rosner describes teaching *Mrs. Dalloway* as a city novel and illustrates how Woolf's vision of the urban demonstrates the aesthetic techniques and social realities of her era as it simultaneously provides students a way to connect with the text. In contrast, Nick Smart explores how students may find the text's lyric rhythm and tone soporific and distanced from their hectic lives. He has students write essays entitled "On Not Knowing Woolf" modeled on Woolf's "On Not Knowing Greek." Using theories by Henri Lefebvre and Gillian Rose, Antonia Losano introduces students to the role of space in the constitution of social orders by having them draw maps of their own days and using these maps as a means to discuss how characters experience Woolf's London differently according to their social positioning.

The essays in the second section, "Using the Context of War," introduce students to the geopolitical, social, and economic world Woolf's characters inhabit. The first two essays discuss ways to use archival materials to enhance understanding of the novel. Meg Albrinck shows how analyzing recruiting posters provides her class with a context for examining the rhetoric that shapes Septimus's decision to enlist in the army. To enable comprehension of the far-reaching effects of World War I, Marlene Briggs provides her students with a kit of archival materials from the Imperial War Museum as a way to discuss why the war looms large in a novel written after the armistice. With an emphasis on empire, she helps students pursue Woolf's ethical inquiry into spectatorship and suffering at home and abroad. Margot Norris uses World War I poetry, theories of trauma studies, and the historian Paul Fussell's chapter on trench warfare to ground Woolf's technical innovations in speaking the unspeakable in a larger historical and poetic context. Finally, Anne Fernald moves the focus from Septimus's shell shock to an exploration of the impact of war on women. Placing the novel in context with contemporary writings, she illustrates how approaching *Mrs. Dalloway* as a war novel decenters the assumption that war is mainly about men and battles.

The third section, "Reading Intertextually," explores methods for teaching the novel in the context of other texts, ranging from the poetry of Horace to *The Hours*. Starting from Woolf's essay "The Strange Elizabethans," David Leon Higdon presents *Mrs. Dalloway* as part of an ancient carpe diem tradition, a reading that enables students to examine, for example, Clarissa's and their concerns with time, love of life, and fear of extinction. Reading the novel at the end of a semester's course on British women writers of the long nineteenth century, Judith Seaboyer invites students to see how the novel complicates their readings of Victorian literature, just as their readings of Victorian women writers enrich their understanding of *Mrs. Dalloway*'s female characters. Mary Beth Pringle's essay provides an account of a summer course in which Harold Bloom's theories of retelling and Annette Kolodny's counterarguments create an intellectual context in which to interrogate notions of modernism by reading *Mrs. Dalloway* with selected chapters of James Joyce's *Ulysses*, Michael Cunningham's *The Hours*, and Judith Kitchen's *House on Eccles Road*.

Leslie Hankins's recognition of students' visual literacy combines an equal focus on the novel and the cinema. Her essay provides a step-by-step overview of the ways in which she uses Woolf's accessible essay "The Cinema" as a starting point for helping students develop a vocabulary and technique to engage in close readings of fictional text and film. Madelyn Detloff continues the discussion of film in an essay that explores the discourses held in common by texts of different genres and time periods, reading the novel in conjunction with, for example, Hanif Kureishi's *Sammy and Rosie Get Laid*.

The final section, "Teaching in Multiple Settings," considers the challenge of teaching *Mrs. Dalloway* in specific venues, including a community college in Wisconsin, a state university in Illinois, liberal arts colleges in Ohio and Georgia, a women's prison in North Carolina, and a medical humanities program in Virginia. In her essay on narration, Karen McLeer expects her two-year college students to have difficulty comprehending Woolf's narrative style and thus provides a writing exercise that prepares them for the collective unconsciousness that Woolf introduces throughout the novel (the exercise involves interrupting a freewrite by dropping a book and turning off the lights). Ruth Hoberman appeals to the visual skills of non–English majors in her literary masterworks course, using a drawing exercise to help students distinguish speaker from speaker and thoughts from utterances. Inspired by her own reading of Woolf's "How Should One Read a Book?" Beth Rigel Daugherty creates a book club out of her general education classroom in an attempt to create lifelong readers.

Christine Sizemore explains that students at the historically black women's liberal arts college at which she teaches often bring to *Mrs. Dalloway* a discomfort with a lesbian reading of the text; she discusses how she prepares them to read the novel through a lesbian lens by first assigning them a contemporary lesbian text, *The Threshing Floor*, as well as theoretical readings. Martha Eads discusses the empathy for Clarissa she discovered not only among traditional students but also among women prisoners, upending notions that one must share Clarissa's class status to appreciate the novel. Using quotations from a survey of her students conducted three years after they completed the course, Eads illustrates how the novel helped them develop both a love for reading and a sense of empathy and connection to others. The section concludes with Marcia Day Childress's essay on teaching the novel to doctors as well as to graduate students in a course on professional values in medicine and law. Childress describes ways in which *Mrs. Dalloway* fosters conversations about recovery, self-knowledge, trauma, and the connections between illness and creativity.

We hope these essays challenge easy notions about which students can and cannot relate to Woolf and provide inspiration and practical help in making *Mrs. Dalloway* accessible to all students.

Experiencing Modernity in *Mrs. Dalloway*

James F. Knapp

When students begin to read *Mrs. Dalloway*, they are often dazzled by its style but at the same time puzzled. Everything that happens is located in a vividly present subjectivity, and yet that subjectivity is shifting, volatile. The book is filled with details of the everyday—typewriters, shopwindows, telephones, and bus stops—but everyday things seem to exist in a myriad of separate worlds, crowding the consciousness of the reader while remaining isolated, somehow radically different from one another. Characters are intensely aware of their surroundings while remembering moments of the past. They think about how much has changed, and yet they seem obsessed with continuity. Emotions are ephemeral, swinging from exhilaration to despair and back again. Students tend to be intrigued but also frustrated. If they are intrigued enough to read on and frustrated enough to talk about it in class, then as a teacher I have my starting place.

I generally teach *Mrs. Dalloway* about halfway through an upper-level course on modernism. The course examines some major texts (by figures like Woolf, T. S. Eliot, and Eugene O'Neill) along with work by writers who were situated differently to the high modernist tradition (Willa Cather, Ben Hecht, Jean Toomer, and Langston Hughes). Although the aesthetic innovations of modernist literature (and modern art) are central to our discussions, the course presents modernist art as part of an emerging social, economic, and urban modernity that was transforming the lives of men and women around the globe. The work my students do when they turn to Woolf's representation of London in the years following the First World War prepares the ground for me to ask the question that drives the course: So what is modernist art anyway? I do not ask this question at the beginning of the course, but only after we have developed a shared vocabulary and defined some of the issues that *Mrs. Dalloway* engages so clearly.

After an initial discussion of two essays that introduce the class to the critical and intellectual history of modernism—Michael Levenson's introduction to the *Cambridge Companion to Modernism* and Michael Bell's "The Metaphysics of Modernism" from the same volume—we begin with *A Lost Lady*, by Willa Cather. Although the book is not set in a large city, as most of the other works in the course are, Cather's novel about the decline of a frontier town on the Great Plains is in many ways a precursor to those works. Made possible by the extension westward of the railroad, and later of the telephone, her frontier village begins as the creation of heroic individuals guided by an ethos of communal responsibility. But the railroad was feared as well as welcomed in the nineteenth century; it was the sign of industrial modernity's intrusion into and destruction of traditional ways of life. The telephone may likewise have been seen to enable what Anthony Giddens calls "disembedding," the " 'lifting out' of social relations from local contexts of interaction and their restructuring across indefinite spans of time-space" (21). As a more complex capitalist economy begins to touch their frontier village, while at the same time leaving it to die economically, Cather's characters feel a disorienting transformation of all they know. The disquietude caused by change, depicted in Cather's novel, is explored even more deeply in Woolf's novel.

We move next to Ben Hecht's *Thousand and One Afternoons in Chicago*, a collection of brief sketches of urban life in the first two decades of the twentieth century. Hecht gives us a mix of lives different from Woolf's (entrepreneurs rather than aristocrats, working stiffs rather than servants) but useful similarities as well. Both novels employ collage as a fundamental structuring principle, and though Woolf's units might be seen as threads in a tapestry and Hecht's as discrete tiles in a mosaic, both collages ask the students to leave their narrative expectations behind and read in an active way. The pressure placed on traditional notions of art by a growing mass culture, subtly present throughout *Mrs. Dalloway*, is also prefigured by Hecht, whose sketches were originally written for newspaper publication. This issue of high art versus low, central in many discussions of modernism, is extended later in the course, as we read Eliot's *Waste Land*, and culminates in our study of the blues lyrics of Hughes.

Although a number of motifs recur as we move from one writer to the next, students might need more than the clues in my syllabus and in my occasional minilectures in order to take control of their reading and build a sense of continuity. In the hope of giving them some useful tools, I assign each student a keyword at the beginning of the course. The words are quite various, but each carries important resonance within the period. The words (or phrases) are *arts and crafts, cinema, city, civilization, class, collage, commodification, country, crowd, department store, design, form, gender, high culture / low culture, history, immigrant, imperialism, labor, language, little magazine, manifesto, mass, memory, modern, myth, nation, newspaper, popular, primitive, progress, race, tradition, unconscious, war, woman, work,* and *world's fair.*

The keyword list provides the basis for a range of activities. On the informal side, students are asked to jump into a discussion when it touches on their particular word, and they do so willingly. The significance of the words changes and deepens as the course progresses and allows the students to feel that when they come to Woolf's novel, they already have ways to talk about it. More formally, one of the three required papers asks them to reflect on the significance of their words for modernist art. The essays tend to be unusually thoughtful, in part because they are, of necessity, carefully focused.

Initially, our discussion of the keywords tends to focus on the emerging conditions of modern life. When we turn to *Mrs. Dalloway,* I ask students to reflect on how their words might also be helpful in discussing the features of a literary text. I tell the class that my agenda is to work toward an understanding of historical representation, to see how the past comes to us in the form of text. *Mrs. Dalloway* is particularly interesting in this light because it represents not only the present but also the past of its characters. Moreover, because the novel deals with the emergence of the new, readers can imagine their own present to be the future of these characters.

Confronting the disruptions of emerging modernity in terms of their own lives is exciting to students but not always easy to understand, so we turn to the details of the book to try to make sense of this idea. The continuity of tradition is strongly visible in the novel, often in images that represent other images: Saint Paul's, for example, is depicted by Woolf as a monumental repository for social memory. As such, it is an image of continuity, inviting viewers to membership in a stable and traditional society. A "seedy-looking nondescript man" hesitates on its steps: "the cathedral offers company, he thought, invites you to membership of a society; great men belong to it; martyrs have died for it; why not enter in, he thought . . ." (27–28). And yet when Richard Dalloway stops to look at a shopwindow with Hugh Whitbread, the antiques in the window seem to represent history as "wreckage," a heap of fragments without any possibility of coherence (110). In images such as these, Woolf warns the reader away from identifying the past with some lost coherence, which many of the characters, like Clarissa, are tempted to do: "Then came the most exquisite moment of her whole life passing a stone urn with flowers in it. Sally stopped; picked a flower; kissed her on the lips" (35).

The characters in *Mrs. Dalloway* experience a sense of fragmentation and discontinuity more often than the reassuring coherence offered by Saint Paul's monumental tombs and banners. When my class discusses this prevailing sense of fragmentation, a keyword that proves useful is *commodification.* The British Empire is always present to the novel, whether in Peter's personal history or in the more public sites of memory. A regimental battle flag in Saint Paul's only gathers more strongly the aura of permanence around it as its material fabric fades and tatters. But the empire is also represented in the scene in which Doris

Kilman, blundering around the Army and Navy Stores, finds herself "hemmed in by trunks specially prepared for taking to India" (130). The trunks appear in a paragraph in which Woolf describes "all the commodities of the world, perishable and permanent, hams, drugs, flowers, stationery, variously smelling, now sweet, now sour. . . ." (130). The department store, that sensational innovation of the nineteenth century, epitomizes discontinuity, as everything can be reduced to a commodity and placed side by side to be sold. Empire, no longer figured as an organizing set of values (e.g., civilization, sacrifice), is swallowed up by a vast and bewildering array of interchangeable commodities.

Central to the appeal of the department store at the time of the novel was its value as spectacle, as a place where all was to be seen but where all that was seen was constantly changing. The commodity was necessarily ephemeral. Nowhere in the novel is this ephemeral quality more strikingly represented than in the scene of the skywriter, when individuals, as members of the urban crowd, all become the same, look up, and watch. The plane is offering nothing tangible, only a brand name, and the name literally blows away like the cloud that it is. This spectacle is more surprising to Woolf's characters than it is to the students, who know that money is made from information in the twentieth century. But the students also understand that the crowd's delight at this spectacle of modernity is, like the experience of the city itself, double-edged. Woolf represents the exhilaration of walking the city streets perhaps most tellingly when Elizabeth, riding on the top of the bus, feels that her identity is almost entirely in her hands, that she could be anything. The anonymity of the street allows her to feel a sense of liberation from the constraints of tradition, as Marshall Berman has argued in his book *All That Is Solid Melts into Air*. But though students can easily identify with Elizabeth's hopefulness, they also relate to the anxiety of entering a world where nothing stays the same. Peter understands Clarissa's anachronistic yearning for a time when identity was fixed and essential: ". . . and these great swells, these Duchesses, these hoary old Countesses one met in her drawing room, unspeakably remote as he felt them to be from anything that mattered a straw, stood for something real to her" (75). Rezia Warren Smith, on the other hand, seeing the beggar woman on the street and knowing how catastrophically the war has changed Septimus, fears the ruthlessness of modernity, which renders identity utterly transient and fleeting: "Suppose one's father, or somebody who had known one in better days had happened to pass, and saw one standing there in the gutter?" (81).

Peter, back from a failed career in India with no prospects, is potentially this poor woman in the gutter. Nevertheless, Woolf allows him a striking moment of realization of how deeply modernity has changed the world. Daylight saving time has been instituted since he was last in England, and he finds it "inspiriting" (158). He envies the young people their new summer time and senses that their lives are better, that there has been a "shift in the whole pyramidal accumulation," which had "weighed them down, the women especially" (158). For students, it is a short step to the realization that *Mrs. Dalloway* is a book about the lived experience of urban modernity, as men and women experience the new while remembering what they imagine to have been a more stable and coherent time. As students identify the features of emerging modernity in the book, they come to see that Woolf's novel does not try to describe the new transparently but rather to represent the structure of feeling of those who find themselves living through a time of rapid social and cultural change—a time much like their own.

"The Proper Stuff of Fiction":
Virginia Woolf and the Meaning of the Modern

Lecia Rosenthal

> Let us not take it for granted that life exists more fully in
> what is commonly thought big than in what is commonly
> thought small. . . . "The proper stuff of fiction" does not
> exist; everything is the proper stuff of fiction, every
> feeling, every thought; every quality of brain and spirit is
> drawn upon; no perception comes amiss.
> —Virginia Woolf, "Modern Fiction"

When teaching *Mrs. Dalloway*, I have often found that students who most resist
the novel pose questions that are the most useful to a discussion of it as a modernist text. Such responses include those that question the novel's engagement
with seemingly trivial, inconsequential, and even politically objectionable matters ("Who cares about an upper-class woman worried about throwing a party
for other uptight snobs?"); those that articulate an impatience with the novel's
diffuse, perspectivally shifting, or difficult style; and those that put pressure on
the ending of the novel and its incorporation of Septimus's death into Clarissa's
narrative. I rehearse these responses because they echo long-standing debates
over the meaning of modernism, indeed over the fate of the very possibility of
meaning in an aesthetic attuned to dissonance, discontinuity, and rupture.

I have taught *Mrs. Dalloway* in a variety of contexts: courses on modernist
literature and cultural theory, courses on trauma and twentieth-century British
literature, and seminars devoted entirely to Woolf's oeuvre. In what follows, I
offer an approach to teaching the modernism of *Mrs. Dalloway* drawn primarily
from an introductory course in which I focus on works by Joseph Conrad, E. M.
Forster, and Woolf. The approach places the novel in conversation with two of
Woolf's literary critical essays, "Mr. Bennett and Mrs. Brown" and "Modern
Fiction." Written in the years just before the publication of *Mrs. Dalloway*, the
essays elaborate some of Woolf's most condensed reflections on the problems
and promises of what she calls modern literature.[1]

Reading Woolf's essays enables students to situate their responses to the
novel, and to modernism more generally, within a context in which modernism
appears as an emergent discourse rather than as an established canon with a
fixed set of values. Thus, for example, Woolf's "confession" that she struggles
with the "obscurity" of T. S. Eliot's poetry provides a useful point of departure
for a discussion of the "difficulties" that beset and inhere within modernism as
it resists conventional expectations of narrative form and challenges its readers
to withstand—and even to value, if not merely tolerate or passively venerate—

what Woolf calls "the effort and strain of writing against the grain and the current of the times" ("Mr. Bennett" 116–17). As part of the introduction to the course, I assign excerpts from an essay by Judith Butler entitled "The Values of Difficulty," in which she theorizes the continued political relevance of the "aesthetics of difficulty" so often associated with modernism and with high modernism in particular.

Debates over the difficulty of modernist prose, over its ostensible incoherence, obscurity, and resistance to accepted norms of comprehensibility, constitute one of modernism's most enduring and important legacies. Reviews of Woolf's first novel, *The Voyage Out*, criticized it as "bewildering" and "disjointed" and lacking a "whole" (Majumdar and McLaurin 51); similarly, one reviewer faults *Jacob's Room* for having "no narrative, no design, above all, no perspective" (Majumdar and McLaurin 107). Although the critical response to *Mrs. Dalloway* was generally more laudatory, at least one reviewer acknowledges that for "those who desire a static universe . . . [*Mrs. Dalloway's*] exhilarating deluge of impressions, will perhaps be unpleasing" (Majumdar and McLaurin 164). Such comments prefigure later debates in literary theory in which modernism is alternatively denounced or embraced for its resistance to established forms of meaning, or for what Woolf calls "the smashing and the crashing . . . the sound of breaking and falling, crashing and destruction" ("Mr. Bennett" 114–15) that characterize modernism's attempt to invent new, and indeed newly challenging, forms of literary representation.

In the classroom, I have found that while Woolf's prose does not tend to evoke the strident criticisms of difficulty and elitism that often attend discussions of James Joyce or of other canonical modernists such as Eliot (what one might call the Leavisite response; for F. R. Leavis's famous critique of Woolf, see McNees, "Colonizing" 43–50), student responses to her work, including to *Mrs. Dalloway*, frequently echo long-standing arguments about modernism's threat to interpretive stability. Thus when one student, as part of an assignment to write a brief response paper to the novel before class discussion, praises Woolf for "a way of writing that compels me to think and feel about a thousand things at once," she implicitly engages a line of criticism that has found modernism compelling precisely because it opens up unprecedented—if potentially overwhelming—possibilities for thought. Here I would include, along with Woolf's own elaborations of the modern, discussions such as Erich Auerbach's "The Brown Stocking" and Theodor Adorno's "The Position of the Narrator in the Contemporary Novel," as well as Jean-François Lyotard's "What Is Postmodernism?," which associates the modern with the aspect of the sublime suggested by the student's comment.

By contrast, when another student, referring to the aeroplane scene in the novel—or those passages in which a disappearing signifier in the sky calls attention to the narrative's questioning of transcendence as it attempts to write, to read and read into, and eventually perhaps to hold together the thoughts of its characters—asks, "Do these scattered thoughts add up to anything?," he anticipates a line of criticism that problematizes modernism's drift toward the subjective as being complicit with a wider, politically conservative ideology that consolidates rather than questions the "impossibility of understanding reality" from a stable and normative (for Georg Lukács, Marxian humanist) point of view (Lukács 25).[2]

While I do not necessarily require students to read the early reviews of Woolf's work or the above-mentioned criticism (I place them on reserve at the campus library so that students who are interested can access them), they inform my approach to teaching *Mrs. Dalloway*, allowing me to help students to question the implications of their initial responses and to situate them within a wider conversation about the charged stakes of the modernist experiment. More important, by assigning Woolf's essays, I am able to introduce students to some of the deeply political concerns that have motivated such discussions of difficulty and that continue to reveal the challenges of modernism to be more than a matter of technical innovation alone.

I teach the course as a discussion. Through close readings of the novels, students begin to make connections among them, focusing on concerns such as the decentering of authority, the breakdown in consensual or unitary perspective on reality, and the self-conscious foregrounding of storytelling and of competing, often irreconcilable narratives in the fractured representation of experience. At the same time, instead of working to consolidate an abstract or rigid definition of modernism as such, students are encouraged to attend to differences among the works. Contrasting, for example, Conrad's emphasis on persistent ambiguity and the failures of reconciliation (in *Heart of Darkness* and *Lord Jim* in particular) with Forster's emphasis on ideological closure and formal resolution (in *Howards End* and *A Passage to India*), students confront those rifts and incommensurabilities that have led critics to prefer the term *modernisms* to that of the misleadingly coherent heading of a singular *modernism*.

Out of our discussions of Conrad and Forster, students begin to understand modernism's formal developments—its self-referentiality, discontinuous temporalities, refusal of discreet and reliable omniscience, and pervasive irony that privileges ambiguity over certainty—not as aesthetic experiments occurring in a vacuum but rather as responses to a world seen as increasingly alienated from the fixities of tradition and skeptical of the ideological certainties of the present. Woolf's texts continue this conversation and introduce new concerns, including most notably an emphasis on the writing of "ordinary" experience and the "life" of the mind.

Many students will be aware that literary modernism shares its historical moment with the emergence of psychoanalysis and Sigmund Freud's discovery of the unconscious. The fruits of elaborating this connection in an introductory course come through focusing on Woolf's interest in and writing of what she calls, in "Modern Fiction," the "hitherto ignored" or that still "dark" rather than fully illuminated domain of the psychological. The novelist must, as Woolf writes, have the courage to say that what interests him is no longer "this" but "that." . . . For the moderns, "that," the point of interest, lies very likely in the dark places of psychology. At once, therefore, the accent falls a little differently; the emphasis is upon something hitherto ignored; at once a different outline of form becomes necessary, difficult for us to grasp, incomprehensible to our predecessors.   (152)

When discussing this passage, I ask students to consider the simultaneous precision and vagueness with which Woolf defines the impulse of the modern. Even as she names the psychological as its defining mark, she resists turning the depths of the mind into merely another known and fully realized object, just one more species of the reified world she finds so problematic in the work of her "materialist" contemporaries.

As part of Woolf's attempt to imagine a world that convention has not yet accounted for, "Modern Fiction" makes an appeal to its audience:

> Examine for a moment an ordinary mind on an ordinary day. The mind receives a myriad impressions—trivial, fantastic, evanescent, or engraved with the sharpness of steel. From all sides they come, an incessant shower of innumerable atoms. . . .   (149–50)

This passage helps students understand Woolf's psychological realism as a species of fiction, where fiction is understood not in opposition to truth but as part of that world of language and representation that imposes form onto reality, in this case a reality so expressly infinite ("an incessant shower of innumerable atoms") as to suggest an incompletion and arbitrariness in any attempt, including her own, to give it proper form. As she boldly asserts toward the essay's end, "'The proper stuff of fiction' does not exist" (154).

In "Mr. Bennett and Mrs. Brown," Woolf places a similar emphasis on a world in which the writer is confronted with social realities unaccounted for within precedent conventions. Like *A Room of One's Own* and *Three Guineas* after it, the essay deploys a mixture of the literary and the expository, highlighting the role of the imagination as necessary to a critique of the historically contingent yet seemingly inalterable limits of the possible, the thinkable, the representable. As opposed to those Edwardian writers she decries, Woolf sees a more modern literary ethos, to which she gives the name Mrs. Brown. Just as the figure of Shakespeare's sister, whom Woolf will have to "imagine, since facts are so hard to come by" (*Room* 46), will enable Woolf to critique the truth as it has been handed down by the masculine historians of the past, so Mrs. Brown points to the blind spots, lapses, and failures that haunt contemporary prose.

If the unfinished story of Mrs. Brown (and her traveling companion and oppressor, Mr. Smith) seems to strike a populist chord, an attempt to expand the limits of fiction to a class-inclusive ideal, the juxtaposition of the essay with

Mrs. Dalloway raises interesting questions about the politics of class in Woolf's work. Some students, citing Woolf's choice of an upper-class heroine, will question her commitment to the reality of Mrs. Brown. There is an opportunity here to discuss the novel's representation of class and to think about the way in which prejudice (national, colonial, racial, economic, social, philanthropic, gendered) is both upheld and criticized in the text. As recent scholarship has demonstrated, the novel is far from indifferent to the concerns of class, nationalism, and power (Zwerdling, "*Mrs. Dalloway*"), and the question of whether Woolf fulfills or betrays the promise of Mrs. Brown in *Mrs. Dalloway* enables students to consider how they understand that promise and what its arrival might look like.

Mrs. Brown is slippery and various. Bound up with Woolf's famous claim that "on or about December, 1910, human character changed" ("Mr. Bennett" 96), she appears to represent an argument for historical specificity, an attentiveness to the way in which character is ineluctably tied to context. At the same time, Woolf insists that what she is after is "character in itself" (97) and champions the ahistoricality of her imagined heroine, claiming, "Mrs. Brown is eternal, Mrs. Brown is human nature" (110). In this sense, Woolf's argument is not so much a call for inclusiveness as it is a rethinking of the conventions of literary realism. For all the character's marginality (she is "elderly" and evinces a state of "extreme poverty" [98]), Mrs. Brown fascinates Woolf not as a representative of a particular group or class but as an occasion to foreground the irreducible role of the artistic imagination in giving form to reality. One of the essay's most provocative sentences reads, "But, I ask myself, what is reality? And who are the judges of reality?" (103). With this question, one that can productively broach a discussion of the writing of reality in *Mrs. Dalloway*, Woolf demonstrates that her interest lies not in confirming dominant, agreed-on, or already verified versions of the world but in challenging the assumptions that would make any such narrative appear natural or inevitable. As wildly all-encompassing as "the spirit we live by, life itself" (119), Mrs. Brown opens rather than answers the question.

One seductive effect of reading Woolf's prose is the sense of being placed inside the minds of its characters, such that we, like Woolf's narrator, are given the boundary-crossing, telepathic ability to eavesdrop on interior monologues that would, in the lived world of the characters, remain unheard, unnoticed, forgotten. When I ask students to reflect upon how the narrative produces such a heightened effect of intimacy, I often turn to the moment in *Mrs. Dalloway* when Peter, sitting alone in Regent's Park, thinks "to himself":

> A terrible confession it was (he put his hat on again), but now, at the age of fifty-three one scarcely needed people any more. Life itself, every moment of it, every drop of it, here, this instant, now, in the sun, in Regent's Park, was enough. Too much indeed. A whole lifetime was too short to bring out, now that one had acquired the power, the full flavour; to extract

every ounce of pleasure, every shade of meaning. . . . For hours at a time (pray God that one might say these things without being overheard!), for hours and days he never thought of Daisy.   (77)

Several points of discussion emerge from this passage. How does Peter's desire to condense the totality of "life itself" into a single moment—a fantasy he thinks of as an acquired "power"—relate to his acknowledgment that "life itself" overflows, is "[t]oo much indeed"? How can the tensions suggested in the passage—between satisfaction and frustration, completion and incompletion, pleasure and suffering, power and fear—help us think about our interpretations of the novel, our desire to feel that we know these characters and that, through them, we have been granted access to something like "life itself"? Similarly, how does the parenthetical remind us of the presence of a narrator whose omniscience so often works through self-effacement? Here, by giving us access to thoughts Peter would prefer to keep secret, the narrator betrays its own mediating function, the stealth-like capacity to blur the thresholds between internality and externality, first- and third-person narration, subjectivity as self-contained interiority and subjectivity as requiring a witness to overhear and effect the self's autoarticulation.

Posing such concerns for discussion not only encourages students to reflect on the way character in the novel is effected through style and artifice but also reintroduces a conversation about modernism and the representation of subjective life. If one of the standard characterizations of modernism is that it privileges the subjective over the objective, the reality of individual mental experience over that of a consensual or neutral observer, *Mrs. Dalloway* often disturbs such oppositions by providing a representation of life itself in which events such as a kiss or a suicide are real and, at the same time, subject to the filters of memory, gossip, words unspoken, and words overheard. This representation may be disturbing; it does not add up to a theory or a definitive answer to Woolf's question "what is reality?" ("Mr. Bennett" 103). And yet, perhaps because of the difficulty of thinking this unanswered question, reading the novel can be very pleasurable, as many students have attested.

In "Modern Fiction" and "Mr. Bennett and Mrs. Brown," Woolf sketches an ideal of the modern without implying the existence of an already fulfilled teleology of progressive development. The endings of both essays are remarkable for their nod to an open-ended futurity, an appeal to the reader to resist the presumption of normative closure. These essays are useful reminders of the hesitation and nuance with which one of the exemplary writers of modernism imagined its present and future possibilities. As Woolf writes at the end of "Mr. Bennett and Mrs. Brown":

Tolerate the spasmodic, the obscure, the fragmentary, the failure. Your help is invoked in a good cause. For I will make one final and surpassingly rash prediction—we are trembling on the verge of one of the great ages of

English literature. But it can only be reached if we are determined never, never to desert Mrs. Brown.   (119)

Here, I like to ask my students what they think this "great age" might entail. Whether they think it has already arrived and vanished or remains to be ful- filled, they are certain to question Woolf's extravagant, hopeful prediction and, in my experience, to become enraptured with the possibilities of rethinking, critically and perhaps with an eye toward their own realities, the difficulties of modernism, the figure of Mrs. Brown.

NOTES

[1] The publication history of each of these essays deserves brief mention. "Mr. Bennett and Mrs. Brown" was published in an early form in 1923. In 1924, Woolf substantially revised, retitled (first as "Character in Fiction" and then again under its original title), lectured from, and republished the essay (*Essays*, vol. 3). In order to avoid confusion with the earlier draft (while McNeillie includes both drafts, the title "Mr. Bennett and Mrs. Brown" takes us to the earlier version), and because Leonard Woolf's edition of the *Collected Essays*, in which the essay also appears, can be difficult to find, I refer to the essay from the more widely available *"The Captain's Death Bed" and Other Essays*. The essay that became "Modern Fiction" was first published in 1919 under the title "Modern Novels" (which McNeillie includes in *Essays*, vol. 3). It was then revised and republished as "Modern Fiction" in *The Common Reader*, which was first issued in April 1925, just prior to the September publication of *Mrs. Dalloway* (Kirkpatrick). I refer to the version in McNeillie's 1984 edition of *The Common Reader*.

[2] Interestingly, Lukács's argument shares some of its tenets with the Leavisite conser- vatives, who criticize Woolf in particular for her apparent lack of "interest in the world 'out there'" (McNees, "Colonizing" 45) and modernism more generally for failing to provide moral clarity.

"Life Struck Straight through the Streets": *Mrs. Dalloway* as City Novel

Victoria Rosner

> In people's eyes, in the swing, tramp, and trudge; in the bellow and the uproar; the carriages, motor cars, omnibuses, vans, sandwich men shuffling and swinging; brass bands; barrel organs; in the triumph and the jingle and the strange high singing of some aeroplane overhead was what she loved; life; London; this moment of June.

This sentence, taken from the first pages of *Mrs. Dalloway*, may be one of the noisiest in all of Woolf's work (4). Clarissa Dalloway is joyfully overwhelmed by the city's uproar, the more so because of its contrast with the hush of her home. But the city is far more than a stimulating distraction for Clarissa and her fellow urban citizens. The city threads through the novel on many levels; my students come to see that all its major themes are articulated in relation to its metropolitan context. Further, many of the experimental modernist techniques of the novel that students can find difficult to grasp, such as its narrative organization, snap into clarity when examined in terms of the novel's urban milieu. In a number of ways, then, *Mrs. Dalloway* can be diversely and profitably taught as a city novel, a work that takes its shape and its story from the rhythms of London life.[1]

I organize the teaching of *Mrs. Dalloway* as a city novel into three interrelated sections, with a seventy-five minute class devoted to each: urban time and temporal structures, comparative discourses of modernist urbanism, and the experience of space in the city. I emphasize the following questions: How are *Mrs. Dalloway* and the city intertwined? How does Woolf's novel represent the rhythms of city life? How do her characters experience the space of the city? How does the urban setting of *Mrs. Dalloway* determine both the novel's form and meaning? These questions help the students explore the relation between the city and the novel on many levels and conceive the city simultaneously as an explanatory frame for interpreting the novel, a significant historical context, and a foundational dimension of literary modernism.

When teaching *Mrs. Dalloway* to undergraduates, I begin with a brief introduction to the novel's narrative style. This introduction is especially valuable in a course on modernism, but since many students find the novel's narration hard to follow, it is useful in any case. *Mrs. Dalloway*'s stream-of-consciousness style can be read as a response to the stimulation and abrupt juxtapositions of city life, a connection supported by close reading. I invite the students to analyze how the narrative travels from one character's mind to the next, and they quickly discern that the novel moves spatially, shifting on the basis of many factors. These factors include proximity, such as when we shift from Clarissa's mind to Scrope Purvis's and back again (4); coincidence, as when characters encounter each other unexpectedly; shared experience, as when the narration shifts from Mrs. Dempster to Mr. Bentley, both of whom, though miles apart, look at the same airplane (27); interruption, seen when Edgar J. Watkiss's words break into Septimus Smith's line of thought (14); and simultaneity, for example, when we enter the collective mind of the crowd (17). All these phenomena are especially characteristic of city life, as the class will come to see. I conclude the discussion by comparing Woolf's use of the Aristotelian dramatic unities with James Joyce's in *Ulysses*, forming a transition to our discussion of city time.

Students readily accept the idea that time is of central importance to understanding *Mrs. Dalloway*, especially when I tell them that Woolf's original title was *The Hours*. We explore city time as a distinct variety of temporal experience, one with only a tangential relation to natural time. City time is human-made, and as numerous historians of modernity have argued, it takes on particular features in the early twentieth century.[2] In *Mrs. Dalloway*, time functions as a collective organizing principle of duration, most conspicuously through the tolling of Big Ben. Set amid the continuous flow of experience in this novel without chapters, Big Ben organizes the text and serves as a collective point of reference, both visually (since in 1925 the clock tower was a far more visible part of the London landscape than it is today) and aurally. Other types of collective urban time experiences can be identified by students: coincidence, which is facilitated by population density; punctuality, mandated by the rush of events in city life; collective memory, produced when shared thoughts (as of the war) move through the crowd; and speed, a fascination of city dwellers that creates a compressed time experience and a desire for the thrill of dangerous, mechanized movement (as when the advertising plane passes over the park).

These kinds of city time are all group experiences, but the class can also identify temporal structures in *Mrs. Dalloway* that are more personal and subjective. Most important among these is the temporality of thought. The novel shows us that each character thinks distinctively, whether like Clarissa, whose mental monologue seamlessly joins past and present, or like Peter Walsh, whose thoughts tumble over one another in a rush of the present. Despite these important differences, the time of consciousness is always discontinuous and lacks linear transition. It can be argued that city thought has a staccato rhythm, created by the interruptions and stimulations of the urban environment. The time experience of the individual can also take the form of a pathology. Septimus, for example, can neither control his memories nor distinguish them from the present day. Hysteria like his was widely considered an urban disease exacerbated by the city; witness his doctor's desire to send him away to the country for quiet and rest and Septimus's own repeated desire to "get away from people" (24).

In the second class session, we discuss how the novel is shaped by contemporary emergent discourses of modern urbanism. As students make their way through *Mrs. Dalloway*, I also ask them to read early-twentieth-century essays about urban life. Two works that mesh most harmoniously with Woolf's novel are Georg Simmel's essay "The Metropolis and Mental Life" (1903) and Gustave Le Bon's *The Crowd* (1897).[3] Simmel's rich and prescient essay catalogs the many influences to which the metropolitan inhabitant is subject and shows how they produce specific personality types. I ask students to describe how Simmel thinks the city affects its inhabitants, and they quickly find examples of the phenomena he describes in Woolf. For instance, he discusses how the city renders individuals anonymous and encourages them to deal impersonally with one another (411–12). Students can see a correspondence in Septimus's experience; Woolf tells us that "London has swallowed up many millions of young men called Smith" (82), and Septimus's impersonal treatment by doctors is a cause of his suicide. Students are also interested in Simmel's theory of the extreme metropolitan personality, according to which individuals manifest "the utmost in uniqueness and particularization" (422) in order to stand out from the urban crowd. They see parallels in the trademark behavior of some characters (like Peter with his knife) as well as in Miss Kilman's outspokenness and Sally's repeated bragging about her sons. In like fashion, students are able to develop a deeper understanding of Woolf's portraits of crowd activity through Le Bon's early work on group psychology.

I also try to provide a richer cultural context for thinking about the city in relation to *Mrs. Dalloway* by assigning oral presentations to pairs of students. About ten to fifteen minutes in length, these presentations ask students to make connections between the novel and various topics in the history of modern urbanism. For this research assignment, I ask students to submit an annotated bibliography of sources together with a write-up of their presentation on the assigned day. I also ask them to imagine their presentation as a kind of performance (no note cards allowed) in which they give their fellow students some experience of the elements of modernist urbanism. Students have presented successfully on topics such as the rise of mass transportation (as illustrated in Clarissa's and Elizabeth's bus rides), advertising and consumer culture (the rise of the department store and ads in the urban landscape), and shell shock and its treatment, and they have employed techniques such as making films, decorating the classroom with advertisements, and writing and acting short scenes.

The topic of space in the novel allows us to consider how both the characters and the story arc take on substance and meaning through their relation to the city. I open discussion with my favorite classroom tool for *Mrs. Dalloway*, the maps of the central characters' city walks that David Dowling provides in Mrs. Dalloway: *Mapping Streams of Consciousness*.[4] Students are intrigued by the idea of using maps to interpret a novel and respond with a range of pertinent observations and interpretations. For example, they notice that the female characters cover less ground than the male characters and that they retrace their steps on the return trip, whereas the men come back by a different route, the difference indicating men's greater liberty in the city. (That both Clarissa and

Elizabeth go into the city only to shop points to the emergence of the woman middle-class consumer at that time and the female *flânerie* that this new role may have allowed. The significance of the urban female stroller in *Mrs. Dalloway* can be a productive sidebar in courses on literature and gender.)[5] Peter's path is longest and most peripatetic, suggesting his errant nature. Richard's and Peter's walks form complementary parallels, dramatizing their competition as a kind of wary border patrol over the turf of Clarissa. That Clarissa's route is exactly half of Richard's represents his relative freedom in comparison with her exclusion from public life. Elizabeth shows her adventurousness by going into a part of the city that no other character explores. Septimus's walk continues and extends Clarissa's, just as his leap from the window extends her contemplative trip to the window at the end of the book. Students are invariably amazed by the extent to which the themes of the novel can be derived from these maps and are inspired to think about literature in radically spatial terms.

The discussion of styles of pedestrianism leads to a consideration of urban place: What are the important locations in the novel, and why do characters visit them? Do all characters have equal access to all locations? What kinds of relationships and behaviors are enabled by particular locations? Two locations to consider are the shopping district and the park. The significance of women's entry into the world of commerce, so proudly announced in *Mrs. Dalloway's* first sentence, has been well described by feminist theorists.[6] Students may wish to compare Clarissa's shopping experience to Miss Kilman's in order to think about questions of social class, about how the florist Miss Pym caters to Clarissa as though they were intimates (13), while Miss Kilman's indifferent saleswoman "thought her mad" (127). Regent's Park in *Mrs. Dalloway* is a site of social mingling, of private behavior performed in public, and of serendipity, since people are more open to the unexpected while in the park. Londoners in the park will sleep, sing, cry, and hallucinate; they form ready impressions of one another and allow themselves the leisure to reminisce, play, and fantasize.

A suitable conclusion to the discussion of urban spaces can be found in the consideration of two important locations that are outside the city but in dialogue with it: the distant world of the British Empire and the pastoral world of Bourton, Clarissa's childhood home.[7] The imperial context enters *Mrs. Dalloway* in many ways, such as through the colonial monuments featured in the text, through Peter's thoughts about India and his career there, and through Lady Bruton's initiatives in foreign affairs. Peter's absurd adventure in pursuit of the "black but enchanting" young woman he follows across London (51) is an excellent example of the imperial self-importance that Woolf skewers as she shows how the colonies—financially, philosophically, politically—make London life possible. Bourton also has a complementary relation to London, for if the colonies represent exotic destinations that underline London's apparent centrality, Bourton's innocent pastoral throws into relief London's vitality and adventure. " 'I love walking in London,' said Mrs. Dalloway. 'Really it's better than walking in the country'" (5). Students will readily see that Clarissa's comment, like Peter's vanity, is in part a defensive self-justification, since it is at Bourton that Clarissa felt most alive to the possibilities of life.

As my brief sketches of these approaches indicate, teachers can accomplish a great deal by considering *Mrs. Dalloway* as a city novel. My students are consistently impressed by how much the form and content of the text can be extrapolated from its city setting. I find that this approach makes sense not only in courses on the city but also in broader surveys of modernism or twentieth-century literature. The urban subject is, quintessentially, the modernist subject, torn between an absorption into the hum of city living, with its distinct rhythms and routines, and a profound alienation brought on by the anomie of urban life.

NOTES

[1] Numerous critics have considered the role of the city in Woolf's work generally and in *Mrs. Dalloway* in particular. See Alter; Bowlby, "Walking"; Lord; Snaith, *Virginia Woolf*; Squier, *Virginia Woolf* and "Tradition"; and Wood.

[2] See, for example, Crary; Kern; Schnapp; and Virilio. I find it useful to juxtapose *Mrs. Dalloway* with films that also explore the transformation of time in the modern city, such as Fritz Lang's *Metropolis* (1927), Charlie Chaplin's *Modern Times* (1936), and Walter Ruttmann's *Berlin: Symphony of a Great City* (1927).

[3] For Le Bon, I give students the introduction ("The Era of Crowds") and part of book 1 ("The Mind of Crowds") from *The Crowd*.

[4] The advantage of Dowling's maps over the single map included in the Harcourt edition is that his maps make it simple to compare the shape, direction, and scope of the different characters' paths through the city.

[5] The idea of the female flâneur, a possible equivalent to the nineteenth-century male strollers who were connoisseurs of urban spectacle, has occasioned a great deal of critical commentary. See, for instance, Nord; Walkowitz; E. Wilson; and Wolff. Also see Woolf's essay "Street-Haunting: A London Adventure."

[6] See Bowlby, *Carried Away* and *Shopping*; Nava; Parsons, *Streetwalking*; and Wicke.

[7] For studies of Woolf's relation to empire, see Adams; Cohen; Marcus, "Registering"; Friedman; and Wollaeger. Also see Woolf's *Three Guineas*.

On Not Knowing Virginia Woolf

Nick Smart

> One must be able to pass easily into those ecstasies, those
> wild and apparently irrelevant utterances, those sometimes
> obvious and commonplace statements, to decide their
> relevance or irrelevance, and give them their relation to
> the play as a whole.
> We must "be able to pass easily"; but that of course is
> exactly what we cannot do.
> —Virginia Woolf, *Common Reader*

In a seminar on Virginia Woolf and modernism that I teach at a women's college in a suburb of New York City, I use the *Common Reader* essay "On Not Knowing Greek" to address resistance to the wild ecstasies of that prime example of modernism's puzzles and beauty, *Mrs. Dalloway*. The assignment helps me remember that some students will struggle with the novel, whose famous textual centerpiece—a puff of encrypted skywriting—might be an emblem of either the limitless pleasures of interpretation or the frustration such an ephemeral concept can cause.

My students, who live not under the halo of quaint messages written on the clouds but with the ceaseless digital-age push and pull of information, are mostly of the working and middle class. They are bent to careerist focus by need coupled with the mantra of professionalism they receive from so many sources and in search of social ties that will counteract the fragmenting effects of their overburdened schedules. Clarissa's pace does not seem hectic or her life much burdened when compared with their job-having, family-tending, double-majoring, club-joining existences. The lyric rhythm and tone of the novel can be a soporific to the overwrought consciousness. Some students sink into the text's seemingly undifferentiated texture, lamenting the absence of signs of progress—chapter breaks—that might refresh their spirits. Their reading process is not what they expected, and they form a resistance in response to frustration.

When students fear that a special vocabulary or sensibility is needed in order to get the value of a text, the defensive tendency to ignore these unknown elements and then get nothing from reading is understandable. An approach to teaching and learning in which the two pedagogical activities are models of each other seeks to tap unconscious resistance and blind spots to alert students to the ways in which the text could be of value to them. Shoshana Felman argues that blocks, sites of active unknowing, are the richest veins in the brain and can be opened by teachers whose frankness about their own lack of mastery introduces the technique of engaging unknowable subjects. With the complexity of *Mrs. Dalloway* and the potential curiosity of my students as subject matter, proving that I am no master is easy to do.

I teach *Mrs. Dalloway* in a seminar on Woolf and modernism that attracts students from English, history, women's studies, art, psychology, and other programs. Many participants lack experience with literary modernism, so we begin with a two-week module that establishes a baseline for discussion. During this minisurvey, students encounter Walter Pater's description of aesthetic criticism in the preface to *The Renaissance*, examples of Paul Cézanne's and Paul Gauguin's decadent postimpressionism, Woolf's analysis of materialist fiction's inadequacy in "Modern Fiction," and, as an example of imaginative prose both Edwardian and modernist in character, James Joyce's *Dubliners*. Finally, with aesthetic frenzy, revolutionary paintings, raw materialism, and robust decay a short train ride away, we take a class trip to Manhattan, where the city can be engaged as a modernist text. The goal of these framing activities is to arrive at a working definition of modernism that stresses formal experimentation and interest in the psychological and emotional conditions of existence. To introduce the "On Not Knowing" assignment, I explain that there is another aspect of modernism to be considered, one I know and love but cannot teach.

This statement is no mere device. The dialogistic nature of the modern novel makes unknowing a given. It would be impossible for me to describe beforehand the *Mrs. Dalloway* that will emerge from a student's unique engagement with and resistances to the text. The company we are in, we nonmasters of the art, is good, and once students have read "On Not Knowing Greek," they will be able to add Virginia Woolf to the professor as another model for the construction of knowledge at the site of its negation.

In her essay, Woolf addresses the shrouded remoteness of venerated writers: "Euripides was eaten by dogs; Aeschylus killed by a stone; Sappho leapt from a cliff. We know no more of them than that. We have their poetry, and that is all" ("On Not Knowing" 23). More than one student will read these words and think, "Virginia Woolf, looking a lot like Nicole Kidman, filled her pocket with stones and walked into the river. Is that the meaning of this literary subject, that its author committed suicide or was molested or was crazy?" But if the students turn to Woolf's fiction for their answer, we are on the path to a more sustaining kind of knowledge.

Woolf demonstrates this text-first approach to the unknowable intentions of ancient literature when she reads the first lines of *Electra* and asserts that "at once the mind begins to fashion the surroundings" (23). This immediate fashioning describes the inevitable response to the famous first line, "Mrs. Dalloway said she would buy the flowers herself," and the novel's paradigmatic conflation of Bourton and London (3). To read the first page of *Mrs. Dalloway* is to sort out emotional larks and plunges and map subtly juxtaposed temporal locales. Clarissa's surroundings can be fashioned only out of expressions of unknowing such as, Why is she making such a big deal out of a simple errand and the task of throwing a party? Is she shallow? Why are the flowers important enough to start with? Is she a woman my mother's age or a girl of eighteen? Why do the doors need to be taken off their hinges?

The answer to the last question is crucial: a widened portal of perception, a broadband imagination, is the necessary platform for reading the *Mrs. Dalloway* we are discussing here. My assignment is a hinge for joining text and reader in this ultrareceptive space.

For the first of three *Mrs. Dalloway* sessions, I assign just ten or twenty pages of the novel and "On Not Knowing Greek." I ask the class to pay attention to Woolf's description of impediments to her appreciation of Greek literature (a lesson in the articulation of the nature of obstacles) and to pay attention to how she perseveres by shining the light of personal response on what is initially shadowed by strangeness and obscurity. The writing assignment for the week is to apply her method in "On Not Knowing Greek" to seemingly unknowable aspects of *Mrs. Dalloway*.

Examples in the novel of unknowability occur on many levels, from vexing interpretive paradoxes to more elemental frustrations with the novel's form. Margaret Kelly, a junior English major, writes, "I also cannot always know that what I find to be Woolf's message was her message . . . this is most frustrating to me as a reader." Margaret is wishing for a clear authorial presence with which she can identify, even though she knows that presence to be something the disembodied narrative of *Mrs. Dalloway* does not fully deliver.

Although Margaret, already getting a message she seeks to confirm, does not count the semantic structure of the text an obstacle, others will. Whereas Woolf wonders whether the modern mind can grasp the essence of a dithyramb, my students doubt that the modern text's coterminous fragmentation and fluidity will be as immediately arresting as the postmodern smashups with which they are more familiar.

Modern literature is a more taxing pleasure than many of its alternatives (students who ate up a Jane Austen seminar were uneasy with Woolf). One student remembers switching to *CliffsNotes* after the first page of *To the Lighthouse* in high school. "Everybody knows *Sparksnotes.com* is free," she adds in her journal. "I heard the movie was better," says another participant, anticipating *Mrs. Dalloway* and referring to the film adaptation of Michael Cunningham's *The Hours*.

Lack of engagement creates anxiety over not only completion of the novel (which Austen provokes, too) but also comprehension of it. How many moments of resonance are squelched by this feeling that the novel contains tones and themes too remote or experimental to be understood or enjoyed?

This is the place in the course where "On Not Knowing Greek"—in which Woolf performs critical readings of both literature and her own limitations—will help students convert resistance into empowering direct experience as the voice of the author provides not the meaning of the novel but insight into its aesthetic foundations. Someone will locate in the essay Woolf's wonderment at the open-air, public nature of Greek speech and art as compared with the more insular, technologized means of communication in modern Britain (24, 34). This opportunity to consider the novel in terms of the modalities it portrays or replicates is something students will discover they are ready to do.

Discussions of what students find absorbing about the expressive arts focus on film, television, Web sites, blogs, podcasts, and more. Class becomes more animated and engaging as they discover that their lives and Woolf's, their moment in history and hers, are based on a set of common properties. Cinematic, musical, streaming, with a tendency to jump around, *Mrs. Dalloway* behaves very much like forms of information and entertainment with which those of us with lives spent flipping, clicking, surfing, and grooving (with headphones on) are familiar. I suggest that those having trouble staying with *Mrs. Dalloway's* linear thread try using the text as if it were a listening device on which one can switch from track to track. I advocate thumbing through, but with Paterian intensity, the same intensity with which the saturated text will reward the earnest but unfettered effort. I want them to pay attention to palpable atmosphere, rhythm or charge, the literariness dependent not on plot or character but on reader and language for its existence. I think this part of the assignment pleases my students' highly developed sense of the value of random experience while furthering the objective I have in mind.

What I ask them to find by flipping, scrolling, and sampling is any thought, description, or exclamation that intrigues them enough to inspire further investigation. With the fragment in hand, they must search the text for a second passage that matches, complements, or clashes. And so on. Thus the novel, which might have been an imposing, antique book, becomes a field of potential meanings—a text!—that students organize on the basis of their responses, just as Clarissa attempts to bring order and meaning to her day. A modernist imagination begins to emerge; the reader is in the text. Now, students find reading *Mrs. Dalloway* sequentially a rewarding experience, because its dislocations and indeterminacy have become familiar artistic terrain. "No longer do I see one character, one Dalloway, one Walsh, one Septimus," Christina Simpson writes in her journal. "Now I see them in multiple perspectives—no longer is there a truth but a variety of truths as the reader chooses to make them, or as other characters make them." When the text emerges, students takes pride in their role in making it happen, and their notion of Woolf changes from a remote to an intimate one. "Woolf is a writer, and I am a reader," observes Dana Mamone, "so that connects us."

By encouraging such personal engagement, we devalue the kind of rote information about Woolf, or any other subject, that can be too easily learned and substituted for authentic response. I mean not the legitimate research students will do for their seminar papers but the pat responses cribbed with increasing frequency from a variety of dot-coms, the submission of which must leave a student feeling fraudulent. "On Not Knowing," like modernism's ineffability, has the virtue of calling for a response that can only be earned.

I reserve the last *Mrs. Dalloway* session for students' favorite passages. Each participant in the seminar reads her excerpt aloud, analyzes style and structure, and establishes the fragment's relation to the definition of modernism under which we are working. Clarissa's philosophic "here was one room, there another.

Did religion solve that, or love?" comes up (125). So does Peter's "escapade with the girl" (53), and he is let off the hook, no longer branded a stalker. The image of a "match burning in a crocus" is contemplated with pleasure (31). A reverie by Septimus, whose violent suicide is of special interest to those fascinated by Woolf's life and death, is usually among the favorite fragments. It is he, after all, who tells us of the beauty we can know, "for nothing, for ever, for looking . . ." (21).

Students begin to understand the significant contribution of modernist fiction's convention-altering aesthetic when they have participated in the creation of its unexpected beauty. This assignment helps them develop a learning strategy they will be able to use throughout their careers, whenever the knowing gets rough.

A Space of Her Own:
Women, Spatial Practices, and *Mrs. Dalloway*

Antonia Losano

From the opening delineation of Clarissa's walk through London to the description of her bedchamber, *Mrs. Dalloway* dramatizes the effects of space on people. To help students understand the importance of space in Woolf's work, I teach a unit on Woolf in a first-year writing-intensive seminar on gender and space in which we examine how space constitutes and constrains the lives of girls and women. In addition to *A Room of One's Own* and *Mrs. Dalloway*, we read Sandra Cisneros's *The House on Mango Street*, Susanna Kaysen's *Girl, Interrupted*, numerous children's books, and a few young-adult novels.

We start the course with spatial theory. We read Henri Lefebvre's "Plan of the Present Work," from *The Production of Space*, and David Harvey's helpful afterword to that text to introduce the idea that in Western philosophy space has been neglected as a category of thought. Lefebvre teaches us to examine the role of space in the constitution of the social order and the materialization of ideology. Next, selections from *Feminism and Geography*, by the feminist cultural geographer Gillian Rose, introduce us to the central notion that gender matters in the organization of social space. Rose's chapter "Women and Everyday Spaces" discusses theories of daily spatial existence and provides students with some vocabulary and methodologies with which to understand how gender influences women's experience of social space, giving us greater insight into Peter's comment that women "attach themselves to places" (54). Essays from Linda McDowell and Joanne Sharp's collection *Space, Gender, Knowledge* also introduce the theory and praxis of the gendering of space. A chapter from Mark Girouard's *Life in the English Country House* on the way gender ideology influenced the very structuring of houses in the past has proved useful as well, particularly in thinking through Clarissa's experiences at Bourton or the layout of the Dalloway home. We also read Fredric Jameson's piece on the Bonaventure Hotel (*Postmodernism*) to introduce the idea that social class likewise makes its mark on our spatial existence. This reading encourages students to pay more attention to submerged class dynamics in *Mrs. Dalloway*, as represented spatially—such as Doris Kilman's discomfort in the Dalloway home and later in a public café or Septimus Smith's experiences with upper-class doctors who invade his domestic space and somehow necessitate his flinging himself out the window.

I begin the unit on Woolf by asking students to choose a representative day in their school week and to keep a record of every place they go. They must map, in text or visually, each footstep they take during the day; many choose to use one of the mapping methods discussed in Rose or McDowell and Sharp. In addition, I ask them to keep rough notes of how their mental state correlates to their physical position, how they feel in different locations and why. During class, we share our maps and discuss the rules and barriers students note in their spatial experience. They are stunned and often outraged when they realize just how spatially constructed and constricted their lives are. (We always have the great bathroom debate: which gender gets better toilets and why, and why men's and women's bathrooms are located where they are located, and so on.) Even though the course is ostensibly about gender, someone always raises the equally pertinent issue of class; we discuss the material barriers in dining halls between staff members and students or the physically manifested divisions between faculty members and staff members or faculty members and students. Students know, of course, that these divisions exist; what is new for them is the realization that the divisions are spatially and materially instantiated. Someone structures them into their lives. Students always ask, "Whose fault is this?" We harness that righteous energy for the next assignment, in which they are asked to write a letter to the college administration exposing some spatial practices as problematic and suggesting changes.

We then read *A Room of One's Own* and map the narrator's day as Woolf describes it in chapter 1. As with the maps of their own days, students must keep a close watch on how the narrator's mental travels correspond with her physical travels. This analysis generates much discussion about the spaces allotted to knowledge and how women have historically been kept out of these places. The inaccessible library, the forbidden grass, the crossroad at which Shakespeare's sister is buried—all these become focal points for our class discussion.

We then turn to *Mrs. Dalloway*, attuned now to numerous issues of space and gender. The significance of Clarissa's attic bedroom or of Bourton is more clearly accessed if students have a lexicon borrowed from spatial theorists. In class discussions, we tackle a series of passages in which space figures prominently. We start with Clarissa's walk, which naturally we map. In reading this scene from a spatial perspective, students often discover the idea of Woolfian synchrony, with a spatial twist rather than the usual temporal one: that is, they notice that for every point in space there is an enormous flood of thought. Standing on the "kerb" for ten seconds, Clarissa nevertheless is represented as having two long pages of mental experience (4). Stream of consciousness makes more sense to students, I find, if they are encouraged to map it. They can see then that thoughts and events are connected in tentative and tenuous ways and sometimes not at all. Such lack of connection becomes increasingly easy to cope with as they realize that their own physical and mental paths are not always logically linked. They begin to see the novel as a spatial journey that begins with a plunge and ends with the dramatic arrival of Clarissa, sounding a kind of crescendo.

We then shift to the Dalloway home. When Clarissa returns from her flower shopping,

> [t]he hall of the house was cool as a vault. Mrs. Dalloway raised her hand to her eyes . . . she felt like a nun who has left the world and feels fold

round her the familiar veils and the response to old devotions. The cook whistled in the kitchen. She heard the click of the typewriter. It was her life, and, bending her head over the hall table, she bowed beneath the influence, felt blessed and purified. . . .   (28)

The Dalloway home is immediately both vault and blessed chamber—and, critically, "It was her life." That is, Clarissa perceives the domestic space as somehow representative of her existence. The nun imagery is continued in the famous description of Clarissa's bedchamber:

> Like a nun withdrawing, or a child exploring a tower, she went upstairs, paused at the window, came to the bathroom. There was the green linoleum and a tap dripping. There was an emptiness about the heart of life; an attic room. . . . The sheets were clean, tight stretched in a broad white band from side to side. Narrower and narrower would her bed be.   (30)

The single sentence "There was an emptiness about the heart of life; an attic room" sums up nicely the power of space: the attic room becomes a symbol for that emptiness, a record of it, but it is also a producer of that emptiness and so not just a symbol. Not that there is anything wrong with symbolism, of course, but students tend to rely too heavily on it, and here it is too easy an answer. The room seems in some way to have caused the emptiness; the narrowing of Clarissa's bed is not just an innocent image of her increasing physical coldness; it is also heavy with active effects. Students often have difficulty comprehending how space can constitute us by habituation, how ideology can become instantiated in space over time. *Mrs. Dalloway* makes this idea more comprehensible, an idea that is, I suggest to my students, a key component of Woolf's beliefs regarding gender.

After discussing Clarissa's walk and house, we branch out into other spaces in the novel: Bourton (inside and out), Peter's India, the small alcove room in which Clarissa has her epiphany about Septimus during the party, London itself. In talking about the space of the city, we tackle our last theoretical material: Michel de Certeau's *The Practice of Everyday Life*, specifically the chapters "Walking in the City" and "Spatial Stories." Certeau insists, "Every story is a travel story" (115); he compares the pedestrian with an enunciator, creating meaning with feet rather than voice. In *Mrs. Dalloway*, Clarissa, Peter, Elizabeth, and Rezia and Septimus Smith travel through the city, creating it and being created by it as they walk. Reading Certeau alongside *Mrs. Dalloway* allows students to move away from the simplistic model of space, in which social space influences mental space like a short-term trigger, toward a more complex one, in which social space constitutes mental space over time.

I ask students to trace, in their written assignments, various characters' experience in the same spatial way as they did with *A Room of One's Own*. They write an essay on one passage from *Mrs. Dalloway* that they feel contains particularly rich connections between space and internal thought or feeling. Left to themselves, they most often choose the description of Clarissa's bedroom and write of its metaphoric connection to her body: virginal, narrowed, aloof (in the sense of lofty, like an attic). Since we talk about that passage so extensively in class, I have found it helpful to forbid students to use it for their essays. When they branch out into the rest of the novel, the connections between space and consciousness become much more complex. Students discover that space does not always have an easy and direct impact on characters' thoughts; Mrs. Dalloway might be standing on the "kerb" in the opening pages, ready to take a plunge, but can her thoughts be described as plunging?

Take this passage:

> How much she wanted it—that people should look pleased as she came in, Clarissa thought and *turned and walked back towards Bond Street*, annoyed. . . . Much rather would she have been one of those people like Richard who did things for themselves, whereas, she thought, *waiting to cross*, half the time she did things not simply, not for themselves; but to make people think this or that; perfect idiocy she knew (*and now the policeman held up his hand*) for no one was ever for a second taken in. Oh if she could have had her life over again! she thought, *stepping on to the pavement*, could have looked even differently!   (10; emphasis added)

If we tackle this passage in class, it is easy to weed out the markers of place or movement in space—"turned and walked back towards Bond Street," "waiting to cross," "stepping on to the pavement," and even "and now the policeman held up his hand." Are these tags irrelevant, as students often wishfully claim? I argue that we must attend to them, but not only because they offer reflection on Clarissa's thoughts. Certainly there are some links to be made—she is waiting to cross at a moment of great psychological import for her; a policeman is holding her back at the moment she labels her personal characteristics "perfect idiocy." But there is something else going on in this passage: a metacritical commentary emerges in the interaction between physical space and mental travels. It is almost as if the spatial tags are marks not just of Clarissa's physical location (for do we really need to know that she is "stepping on to the pavement"?) but also of the fact that certain spatial experiences are inextricably tied to certain thoughts. In other words, nothing can be done "for itself, simply," as Clarissa seems to desire, because everything is linked—a feature of the novel most famously represented by the strange connection between Clarissa and Septimus. Such linking permeates all *Mrs. Dalloway* and arguably much of Woolf's oeuvre.

"Are *YOU* in This?" Using British Recruiting Posters to Teach *Mrs. Dalloway*

Meg Albrinck

My students are skeptical. They live in an era in which war is a regular topic on the evening news and special reports show acts of terrorism at home and abroad. They have few illusions about the physical brutality of life, and many of them have considered military service or know someone who is enlisted. When they encounter Septimus Warren Smith, his patriotism is somewhat familiar. However, few of them share his idealism. When they learn that he "went to France to save an England which consisted almost entirely of Shakespeare's plays and Miss Isabel Pole in a green dress walking in a square" (84), they are bewildered and sometimes dismissive. They do not believe one can (or should) protect a favorite teacher through military service, nor can they understand why Septimus would go to war to protect a dead man's plays.

To help my students enter Septimus's very different worldview, I build on one thing that they share with Septimus—immersion in visual culture. Visual texts surround us and shape our attitudes and beliefs. The key difference between Septimus and my students in their encounters with these texts is that my students have greater exposure to and facility with the myriad images that bombard them. While they may not consciously analyze the media they see, many find it less daunting to interpret visual texts than written ones. Thus I devote a portion of my unit on *Mrs. Dalloway* to the analysis of recruiting posters from the First World War. This focus helps students understand not only Septimus's motivation for enlistment but also the gender codes of the war years.

After examining the themes and characters of *Mrs. Dalloway*, I turn to the novel's connections to the events and images of the First World War. Unlike the environment today, where recruiting images are vastly outnumbered by other types of advertisements, calls to military service were the dominant form of advertisement during the war's early years. Indeed, almost twelve million recruiting posters were printed and distributed by the Parliamentary Recruiting Committee, and images blanketed kiosks, fences, storefronts, and even taxicabs throughout London (Great Britain 6). As the *Daily Chronicle* noted in 1915:

> In every street, on every hoarding, at every railway station, all the art and artifice of the poster-designer and publicity-agent have been enlisted in the national cause. Everywhere striking placards, plain or coloured, as you please, emphasise and illustrate the urgent necessity of the call to arms.
>
> ("2,500,000 Posters" 3)

Woolf would have seen such materials in her ambulations around the city and in her visits to the recruiting offices with Leonard in the autumn of 1917. Examples for classroom use are readily available online.[1]

Once the pervasiveness of these images is established, the next step is to discuss the way that poster artists are using form and content to promote cultural ideals and make arguments about the moral value of military service. (This type of analysis should also work well in a lecture format.) My students and I spend time talking about how the eye moves around visual images, how the figures are gendered, and how patriotism is embodied in actors and actions. I prefer *PowerPoint* slides to handouts, for the slides can be manipulated for size and number to approximate the historical experience of viewing an entire wall full of posters. Furthermore, using a central visual focal point gets students to look up from their texts and brings us together in a Woolfian fashion: "looking together unite[s] them," so to speak (Woolf, *To the Lighthouse* [1989] 97). This kind of conversation draws in students who are typically more reticent or who find literature dull and helps build a context of believability for those struggling to understand Septimus's values.

First and foremost in Septimus's conception of military service is a notion of protecting English culture, represented, by way of the lecturer Isabel Pole, as Shakespeare's plays. The academy and the culture it preserves are conflated to some degree in Septimus's mind, resulting in a vision of service that involves protecting both people and literature. Such ideas are not idiosyncratically produced by Woolf's character, but represent arguments that were circulating through recruiting posters of the time. In fact, the promotion of humanitarian masculinity was one of the first and most successful recruiting techniques in the government campaigns.

This ideal is captured in the phrase "Remember Belgium," which served as the dominant theme in early recruiting materials. Respected papers like the *Times*, more sensational tabloids, and government offices all portrayed small and defenseless Belgium in feminine terms, while representing Germany as a barbarian male nation. Emphasizing again and again that the Huns were brutalizing an innocent and virginal country, the press encouraged British men to correct the bestial activities of German soldiers through honorable intervention. Posters with this slogan encouraged British citizens to see German attacks on Belgium as precursors to attacks on British citizens and soil. In one poster titled "Remember Belgium" (Imperial War Museum, PRC 16), a fighting man in khaki looks toward the viewer, his rifle resting on the ground.[2] To his left, fire is destroying a village, with black smoke billowing across the sky. To his right, a woman flees with two children—one infant, one toddler. She is looking back over her shoulder, but the toddler is looking forward and reaching a small hand toward the soldier. The message is clear: to remember Belgium is to remember women and children displaced by the German armies.

As we look together at this poster, I ask students to consider how its structural elements visually support the poster's slogan and call to arms. We talk about the size and placement of the soldier in the center, about the lines of his figure and face, and about the poster's representation of military service as humanitarian intervention rather than brutal combat. Standing as a barrier between the fire on the left and the fleeing family on the right, this image of the fighting man encourages male viewers to recognize that their service will be primarily protective. Just as the soldier in the poster stands between the family and the fire raging behind it, so the viewer, through enlistment, will be able to stand between other innocents and German barbarism. Viewing such a poster, Septimus could easily translate his military service into direct protection of Miss Isabel Pole and the culture she represents.

A variation of this poster with the heading "Your Country's Call" (Imperial War Museum, PRC 87) makes this link even clearer by positioning the British landscape as the potential victim of German aggression. Here, the soldier gestures toward a pastoral scene of rolling hills and thatched cottages. Such an appeal highlights the Shakespearean element of the British landscape, referencing not only a more general Cotswoldsian scene but also Anne Hathaway's cottage, a new tourist site in Septimus's time. The Birthplace Trust had purchased the cottage and other Shakespearean properties in the area at the turn of the century and was busy restoring them to promote tourism. In a poster such as this one, therefore, Septimus would be able to interpolate himself as a defender of Shakespeare's England.

Septimus may also have been influenced by another genre of recruiting posters that surfaced in early 1915, after initial recruiting efforts failed to produce the required number of volunteers. These posters, manipulating images of masculinity to coerce and shame men into enlistment, help explain the feelings of inadequacy and guilt that haunt Septimus throughout the novel.

In contrast to the novel's more traditionally masculine characters like Sir William Bradshaw, Dr. Holmes, and Richard Dalloway, Septimus is seen as "a border case"—mostly because of his lack of physical strength, his sensitivity, and his romantic ideals (82). Characters respond to his gender performance in different ways; whereas Rezia finds him intriguing, his employer believes he is "weakly" and should play football (that is, soccer) (143, 84). Thus Septimus would have been the perfect target for recruiting posters that shamed unenlisted men into service.

One set of posters, produced by private regional recruiting offices, emphasizes the similarity between sport and war. Football held great significance as a sport that could inculcate the ideals of masculinity and team spirit needed for victory (see, e.g., Fussell 26–28; Showalter, *Female Malady* 169). These recruiting posters encouraged men to join the army so that they could be allied with members of their favorite football teams. One such poster encourages the "MEN OF MILLWALL" to "Join and be in at / THE FINAL / and give them a / KICK OFF THE EARTH" (Imperial War Museum, PST 0970); other posters encourage viewers to see the war as "the Greater Game" being played across the sea, on the "ONE FIELD TODAY WHERE YOU CAN GET HONOUR" (Imperial War Museum, PST 0830). Together these posters insisted that sport was manly and that war was a sport. That his employer advises football for Septimus before the war suggests that our hero, even before the war begins, does not adhere to his culture's ideals of masculinity.

Septimus is encouraged to step up to the demands placed on him and to take his place in the military machine. Posters such as "Are *YOU* in This?" (Imperial War Museum, PRC 112) can lead to some wonderful discussions of definitions of patriotism and gender. First, I ask students to map out the structural relationships among the various figures in the poster. They identify the pyramidal composition of the poster by tracing the chain of gestures, and we discuss whether the vertical arrangement of the figures implies a cultural hierarchy that privileges military men. A discussion of gender roles naturally follows as students attempt to position women in the national endeavor.

After examining the larger design of the poster, we turn our attention to the specific figures represented within. We look for commonalities among those involved in the chain of distribution along the poster's left side. Students notice that the military men and industrial worker are all hypermasculinized, having square jaws, broad shoulders, and muscular builds, and that all are actively participating in the work of war. The women are also working hard—their hands are engaged with bandages or bullets—but their slimmer shoulders imply a slighter build. All are dressed in uniforms of some kind, showing that their labor is not individual but part of a group.

We then turn our gaze to the man on the right, the one in civilian or professional attire, and I ask students to compare him with the other figures in the poster in activity, apparel, and appearance. They see a number of differences in this figure. First, the chain of gestures excludes him; no one hands him anything or makes eye contact with him. Second, unlike the others, he is not wearing a uniform of any kind; his clothing marks him as an individual, not as a team player. Third, his hands are passive, thrust deeply in his pockets and therefore not contributing to the national effort. Finally, the poster suggests, his lack of participation in the scene marks him as effeminate. In build, he is much closer to the size of the women than the men; his shoulders are narrower, his face thinner, and his chin and muscles less prominent. The poster thus insinuates that the unenlisted man is feminized by his civilian role. This poster and others like it were designed to shame unenlisted men—or "border cases"—into service. To be respected by Miss Isabel Pole, Septimus needed not only to protect her but also to be seen as masculine. Thus he needed to enlist.

The final piece we discuss is a poster entitled "Step into Your Place" (Imperial War Museum, PRC 104). Identified by their clothing and possessions, men of different classes and occupations step into their places in the procession marching to the horizon. The figural investigation of the previous poster allows students to read the arguments of this one confidently. They may not recognize the particular occupations of each character but can see that the distinguishable uniforms of civilian life fade into the indistinguishable khaki uniform of the military, and they understand the poster's suggestion that all are equal in the military effort. We discuss whether such a poster would have appealed to Septimus, who is excluded academically, economically, and aesthetically from the best his culture has to offer. Some students argue that this representation of service allows him to redirect his energies, moving him away from "drawing pictures of [his co-workers] naked at their antics" to performing his love of England in a sanctioned way (88). Others suggest that this ideal of equality leads to his downfall. As it forces him into a specific articulation of masculinity—a version that Peter Walsh also witnesses as he joins a group of schoolboys marching through Whitehall (50–51)—it also suppresses his individuality in ways that contribute to his psychological collapse.

I have focused primarily on the visual materials that help students understand Septimus's enlistment and the context of war that surrounds the novel. However, examination of other examples of recruiting rhetoric in popular poetry or wartime trends in advertising may also illuminate Septimus's character or the novel's representation of gender. *Mrs. Dalloway* is a difficult text for my students to fathom, not only because of its stylistic challenges but also because many feel distant from the perspectives and worldviews of its characters. Using recruiting posters to introduce students to this world reduces this sense of difference and encourages them to evaluate critically the links between the images Septimus encounters in 1923 and the ones they see today.

NOTES

[1] See, for example, posters at *Trenches on the Web* (Hanlon), *First World War.com* (Duffy), and "Posters and Art of WWI." A *Google* search of "poster 'first world war'" yields more sites, some that specialize in American posters and others that specialize in Canadian or French ones. Originals can be seen by appointment at the Imperial War Museum, London, which also allows nonflash photography of archival materials.

[2] All posters are referenced by their Parliamentary Recruiting Committee (PRC) number or that assigned by the Imperial War Museum, London (PST). PRC posters were produced by the British government; PST posters were privately issued.

Circling the Cenotaph: *Mrs. Dalloway*, Historical Trauma, and the Archive

Marlene A. Briggs

Mrs. Dalloway is a core component of a senior undergraduate English course that I teach at the University of British Columbia. This class explores British and Irish literature on the First World War by authors ranging from Wilfred Owen to Sebastian Barry. In this context, I teach *Mrs. Dalloway* as a modernist work of fiction on the unresolved aftermath of historical trauma. Trauma studies, an eclectic discourse that emerged in the 1990s to address issues such as conflict, genocide, and their long-term political and social legacies, inspires the exercises and strategies that I use in the classroom.[1] More specifically, I raise questions about the past and present reception of collective crisis by combining literary study with cultural, military, and social history. Newspaper advertisements, archival photographs, and recruiting posters sensitize students to the pervasive effects of the Great War in *Mrs. Dalloway*. Local memorials and annual traditions also illuminate Virginia Woolf's complex characters and concerns. As the educator Lisa Farley observes, archival materials may promote "an emotional and ethical engagement with traumatic histories": "At issue here is not the naïve and neutral question of 'what happened,' but how meaning develops from the conflicts, ambivalences, ambiguities, and investments in coming to know" (70, 82). By investigating the rituals of public commemoration and the imperatives of total mobilization, lively discussion forges a classroom culture that moves beyond stark chronologies and appalling abstractions to more embodied ways of engaging with massive violence.

Circling the Cenotaph

The 1918 armistice has profound significance in Woolf's novel. As Peter Walsh muses, "Those five years—1918 to 1923—had been, he suspected, somehow very important" (70). Yet the origins of Remembrance Day (Canada) and Veterans' Day (United States) have subsequently faded from view. Thus I invite members of the class to reflect on the meanings and memorial practices they associate with November 11. Why do we mark this date on the calendar? How can people remember an event that took place before they were born? Do other countries also honor this anniversary? What does this traditional day of observance mean to you? Drawing on examinations of conflict and memory, I outline the advent of familiar ceremonies and symbols: the armistice (11 November 1918), Peace Day (19 July 1919), the temporary Cenotaph in London (11 November 1919), the permanent London Cenotaph and the Burial of the Unknown Warrior (11 November 1920), and the Poppy Fund for disabled ex-servicemen (1921).[2]

With a digital projector, I then display topical newspaper headlines on the declaration of the peace alongside advertisements from the postwar period (1918–24). Excerpts from *Punch* or the *Times*, the daily journal that dominates the public sphere in *Mrs. Dalloway*, foster a multifaceted appreciation of the cease-fire in context. For example, makers of Bovril apologize to consumers in the *Times* for a bottle shortage during the devastating influenza pandemic (1918–19) that debilitates Clarissa Dalloway.[3] Furthermore, *Punch* features an advertisement for Glaxo, a dairy substitute for "invalids, the aged and those of delicate digestion" that Mrs. Coates invokes in the skywriting scene (20). These and other intersections between fiction and history and between art and ephemera reveal Woolf's intensive and extensive immersion in her specific time and place.

Some students, however, cite Clarissa's belief that the war "was over; thank Heaven—over" with keen approval (5). After all, they protest, five years—almost one-quarter of the life span of many young people in my classes—should be long enough to absorb the shock of any trauma. To disrupt this linear model of temporality, I initiate a brainstorming exercise at the blackboard about the governing role of circles in the novel, encompassing preoccupations, rhythms, spaces, and specters. Neither the signing of the truce, for instance, nor the burial of the dead dispels the ghost that haunts Septimus Smith. Why, moreover, does he suffer from "sudden thunder-claps of fear" five years after the armistice (85)? Conversations about the circle motif enable students to overcome their timidity with a difficult text. Simultaneously, they become attuned to the recursive style of modernist prose as well as the dynamic repetition that marks the deferred assimilation of historical trauma.

As students ponder the circle motif in *Mrs. Dalloway*, they begin to complicate official interpretations of the Great War. To this end, photographs from the Hulton Archive of Getty Images afford the class an opportunity to inspect the construction, formal design, triumphal inscription ("The Glorious Dead"), and changing reception of the London Cenotaph since 1919.[4] Peter salutes young boys who place a ceremonial wreath at the empty tomb: "One had to respect it; one might laugh; but one had to respect it, he thought" (50). Why, I inquire, does this gesture garner his support? Do the boys pause to reflect on the meaning of their tribute? More generally, does public commemoration stimulate recollection or oblivion? Conformity or controversy? Aggression or cooperation? Are the dead "already half forgotten" in 1923, as Richard Dalloway believes (112)? Even if a class cannot circle the London Cenotaph on foot, local monuments enable students to consider how the Great War inhabits their regional landscapes. The inscription on the Victory Square Cenotaph (erected in 1924) in Vancouver, for example, anticipates the neglect of motorists and pedestrians: "Is it nothing to you—all ye that pass by?" (Lam 1.12 [King James Vers.]). Although everyday habits often render neighborhood memorials invisible, the belated circling of ritual spaces recalls their origins dating from Woolf's time.

Propaganda, Gender, and the State

Students typically respond with fascination (undivided attention) and incredulity (loud guffaws) when I unroll large facsimiles of recruiting posters from the Imperial War Museum, London. One image appeals to men (*Britons [Kitchener] Wants You*), and another design targets unmarried women (*To the Young Women of London*).[5] The former depicts the confrontational gaze and accusing finger of Field Marshal Horatio Herbert Kitchener, while the latter exploits rhetorical rather than visual devices. Men, it seems, must act in concert with traditional values such as bravery and loyalty; women, on the other hand, must adapt to the national emergency by willfully relinquishing male companions. These complementary posters provide an ideal opportunity to simulate the gender segregation that distinguished home from front during the First World War. Accordingly, I request that men and women work in separate groups to study the form and content of each poster (color, font, image, layout, text, typography). General questions guide collaborative inquiry into past and present ideological scripts: Which attributes does each poster ascribe to men and women, respectively? Which tasks does the state assign to each sex? Would these tactics be effective today? Why or why not? After approximately twenty minutes, each group summarizes its observations. While the recruiting posters strike some as crude or antiquated, others counter that advertisements today shape desirable images of femininity and masculinity in comparable ways.

Propaganda serves as a provocative point of departure for discussions of gender and the state in *Mrs. Dalloway*. Why, students wonder, were thousands of British men eager to serve in 1914? Significantly, Septimus, "one of the first to volunteer," endorses the chivalry that informs Kitchener's summons when he enlists to protect Miss Isabel Pole (84). After Septimus's suicide, however, Dr. Holmes condemns the veteran as a "coward," a stigma reserved for those who shirked their patriotic duty (146). Long after demobilization, Dr. Holmes and Dr. Bradshaw reinforce Kitchener's martial conception of manhood. I situate Woolf's critique of medicine in context by relaying a short overview of British attitudes to shell shock. Alternatively, a segment from Gillies MacKinnon's film *Regeneration*, which dramatizes the distinct methods for treating shell shock of Lewis R. Yealland and W. H. R. Rivers, prompts extended dialogue.[6] Propaganda, an important locus of state power, sheds light on the arbitrary and insidious powers of "Proportion" and "Conversion" denounced by Woolf's narrator (97–98). Notably, the values allied with the sinister goddess of Conversion, "love, duty, self sacrifice," recapitulate recruiting rhetoric (98). Propaganda clarifies social norms that underpin both sanctioned and transgressive behaviors in *Mrs. Dalloway*.

To the Young Women of London also arouses mixed emotions in my classes— namely, condescension and indignation. Students bristle at the idea of pressuring friends and lovers to risk their lives in battle. Initially, they may discount the abiding impact of the Great War on women from nearly every age group and social class in *Mrs. Dalloway*. Yet I maintain that the enhanced presence of the state in private life warrants sustained analysis. Most prominently, Doris Kilman, who refuses to renounce her pro-German sympathies, mourns the loss of her brother and her professional station. Even wealthy Clarissa admonishes herself before a shopwindow: "one must economise" (5). Furthermore, she imagines how the bereaved mother Lady Bexborough "opened a bazaar . . . with the telegram in her hand, John, her favourite, killed" (4–5). Clarissa complies with the spoken and unspoken gender expectations that structure propaganda when she upholds the virtue of Bexborough's sacrifice. In contrast to private and public mantras extolling thrift and stoicism, Lucrezia Warren Smith rages against her fate: "Why should *she* suffer? . . . Why tortured? Why?" (64). Ironically, Mrs. Smith suffers precisely because her husband faithfully served king and country.

Locality and Advocacy

In 1921, Woolf posed a timely question in her diary: "Is it a proof of civilisation to envisage suffering at a distance . . . ?" (2:100). This ethical inquiry into spectatorship and suffering at home and abroad motivates my instruction. For instance, an excerpt from "Slaughter," an episode in the documentary series *The Great War and the Shaping of the Twentieth Century*, demonstrates how censorship polarized British civilians and combatants after the disastrous Battle of the Somme (1916).[7] Such divisions continue to influence postwar society in *Mrs. Dalloway*. Yet at the same time, the war exceeded regional boundaries and altered borders that formerly demarcated peoples, nations, and empires. I invite the class to enumerate Woolf's allusions to countries around the globe, including Burma, Canada, Germany, India, Italy, and Turkey. Despite international crises and corresponding appeals for aid (such as the Armenian crisis referenced by Woolf, during which the lord mayor of London sought "to reestablish the remnant of the homeless Armenian people" [Lord Mayor's Fund for Armenian Refugees]), Clarissa privileges her roses above the distant plights of others (117).[8] Students, too, can extrapolate from their own experiences with "suffering at a distance": they read about wars, watch disasters on television, and may even see violence and retaliation in real time on the Internet. Teaching *Mrs. Dalloway* as a novel about historical trauma both challenges and empowers students already inundated by sensational media coverage of complex geopolitical clashes around the world.[9]

Location inextricably shapes advocacy, the ability to imagine and to act on behalf of those suffering at a distance. Thus I read Clarissa's interior monologue on the veteran's suicide aloud in its entirety. By attending closely to rapid shifts of mood and emphasis, we chart her course from annoyance and anger to sorrow and affirmation (179–82). I conclude class work on *Mrs. Dalloway* with a handout composed of two pages of quotations from fourteen prominent Woolf scholars. On one side of the page I include brief citations from seven critics who judge Clarissa's perspective on the suicide sympathetically: Elizabeth Abel (*Virginia Woolf*), Gillian Beer, Jessica Berman, Allyson Booth, Allie Glenny, Emily Jensen, and Jean Wyatt ("Avoiding"). On the other side I present seven excerpts from critics who are suspicious of the connections that Clarissa makes between herself and Septimus: Tuzyline Jita Allan (*Womanist*), Karen DeMeester, John G. Hessler, Mark Spilka (*Virginia Woolf's Quarrel*), Susan Merrill Squier (*Virginia Woolf*), Trudi Tate (*Modernism*), and Caroline Webb. Students mull over dissenting approaches in small groups before sharing their opinions with the class. Does Clarissa bear responsible witness to Septimus's life or obscure the particular circumstances of his death?[10] The passionate arguments of academic commentators generate heated exchanges while familiarizing students with the scope and vitality of Woolf scholarship.

Who will remember the Great War in 2014–18 (Dyer 111)? At this critical historical transition, the documentary archive supplants the living memory of veterans. Thus, period artifacts play an increasingly important role in the cultural transmission of the First World War. Context-driven pedagogy on extreme events disrupts formulaic responses to the past, counteracting tacit norms and conservative practices that legitimate scapegoating and denial, issues subject to heightened scrutiny in *Mrs. Dalloway*. Why, as my students often ask, is Septimus shunned by the very society he served? Woolf grapples with problems in the aftermath of historical trauma that have by no means been solved and that necessarily compel the actions and concerns of subsequent generations.

NOTES

I dedicate this contribution to my students in the Twentieth-Century British and Irish Studies course at the University of British Columbia, especially the outstanding class of fall 2002, whose passion for learning inspired this essay.

[1] For influential formulations of trauma, testimony, and witnessing, see Caruth; Felman and Laub; and Herman. Notably, Herman informs scholarship on modernist literature by Henke ("Modernism") and Parsons ("Trauma"). LaCapra; Luckhurst; and Radstone develop critical approaches to trauma studies.

[2] See Weintraub on the 1918 armistice. Gregory; Mosse; and Winter (*Remembering*; *Sites*) consider postwar commemoration in Britain and elsewhere.

[3] Johnson mentions *Mrs. Dalloway* in his book on the influenza pandemic of 1918–19 (173–74).

[4] Black-and-white photographs from the Hulton Archive of Getty Images include *Whitehall Cenotaph* and *Peace Pageant*; other telling pictures are *Haig and Unknown Soldier* and *Armistice Day*, an image highlighting the ongoing social significance of the memorial ten years after the cease-fire.

[5] Instructors may purchase educational resources, including a facsimile poster of *Britons [Kitchener] Wants You*, through the Web site of the Imperial War Museum, London.

Potter analyzes recruiting posters as well as illustrations, pageants, pamphlets, postcards, and other modes of propaganda that "helped to codify the behaviour and actions of the wartime public" (70).

[6] On masculinity and shell shock in the First World War, see Bourke; Hipp; Hynes; Leed; Leese; and Showalter (*Female Malady*). The novelist Barker acknowledges her debt to Leed and to Showalter in *Regeneration*(251–52), the basis for MacKinnon's motion picture of the same name. On combat trauma in the Vietnam War, see Shay.

[7] This award-winning documentary series presents a comparative cultural history of the 1914–18 conflict. The segment on the Somme offers a compelling introduction to total war by addressing the conditions of men serving in combat, women working in hospitals, and British civilians encountering images of modern war in the cinema. See the companion book (Winter and Baggett); in addition, the updated Web site includes a section on the war's impact on the twenty-first century as well as numerous educational resources.

[8] On *Mrs. Dalloway* and the Armenian genocide, see Tate (*Modernism*). For approaches to teaching the Armenian genocide, see Hovannisian; Strom; on American responses to the crisis, see Balakian.

[9] For commentary on visual media and trauma, see Hartman; Kaplan; and Sontag (*Regarding*).

[10] Jayes contends that Lucrezia Warren Smith and Clarissa Dalloway dramatize the social dynamics of "failed witnessing" in postwar Britain (70).

Teaching *Mrs. Dalloway* as a World War I Novel

Margot Norris

Virginia Woolf began writing *Mrs. Dalloway* without the figure of the traumatized veteran, Septimus Smith, and with his suicide possibly displaced onto Clarissa Dalloway herself. In her introduction to the 1928 Modern Library edition of the novel, Woolf writes:

> Of *Mrs. Dalloway* then one can only bring to light at the moment a few scraps, of little importance or none perhaps; as that in the first version Septimus, who later is intended to be her double, had no existence; and that Mrs. Dalloway was originally to kill herself, or perhaps merely to die at the end of the party. (v)

This knowledge may have conditioned a tendency to treat the figure of Septimus more as a psychiatric casualty than as a war casualty and to shift the general focus of the novel away from World War I and toward postwar London social life. But World War I constitutes a deep structure for the novel, one arguably implicit in a curious metaphor Woolf deployed in discussing its construction as a tunneling process:

> I should say a good deal about The Hours, & my discovery; how I dig out beautiful caves behind my characters; I think that gives exactly what I want; humanity, humour, depth. The idea is that the caves shall connect, & each comes to daylight at the present moment. (*Diary* 2: 263)

Given that World War I has been described by Paul Fussell as a "troglodyte world" (36–74), a world of trenches and foxholes, we may configure the war as the psychic cave of memory and trauma behind the character of Septimus. But how does one teach the 1925 *Mrs. Dalloway* as a war novel to undergraduates whose earliest encounter with World War I may have been Charles Schulz's Snoopy trailing the Red Baron through the skies in his Sopwith Camel? World War II, with its clear moral issues of fascism and genocide, has a logic and a narrative contour that is readily accessible to students. World War I, in contrast, with its origins in an assassination resonant with obscure Central European ethnic conflicts, nondramatic imperialism, and assorted national alliances, remains historically and politically enigmatic. But Fussell titles a chapter of *The Great War and Modern Memory* "Oh What a Literary War" (155–90), demonstrating that the war's enormous poetic production proves an excellent resource for teaching *Mrs. Dalloway* as a World War I novel.

Mrs. Dalloway is readily included in courses on the literature of World War I, but it is probably taught more frequently as part of survey courses on Anglo-American modernism. Because modernism courses focus heavily on issues of poetic and aesthetic experimentalism, they face special challenges in bringing World War I into their discussion. My design for such a modernism course is to place Woolf's novel between two very different kinds of poetic texts: T. S. Eliot's *The Waste Land*, on the one hand, and trench poetry—poetry written by actual soldiers fighting in the trenches—on the other. As one of the great canonical works of high modernism, *The Waste Land* frequently acts as an ideological and aesthetic anchor for a modernism course. But although both Eliot's poem and Woolf's novel feature the World War I veteran as an important figure, Lil's demobilized Cockney husband and Rezia's disturbed spouse are accorded very different treatment. Woolf had an intimate relationship to Eliot's poem, even having worked on the typesetting for its 1923 publication by Hogarth Press. But beyond any question of influence, it is important to stress to students that both Woolf and Eliot were noncombatants with no experience of the front and that both represented England after, not during the war. Despite these similarities, though, each author treats the returning soldier differently in two respects: his sexuality and his class. Issues of sexuality are of ready interest to undergraduates, while issues of class in early twentieth-century Britain are elusive to them. The trench poetry will help address both.

Eliot's poem implicates the war and the returning soldier in a larger spiritual malaise—the severance of sexuality from the sacred, two things that were once connected in the ancient fertility rites the poet cites in his references to the Grail legend. Woolf implicates the war in the devastation of the returning soldier whose body is spared but whose mind and soul, including his ability to love, have been destroyed. Both works connect the veteran to a wife who functions as his transition back to the home front. But in Eliot's poem, the home-front understanding of veteran experience and expectations is heavily satirized. The veteran's wife, Lil, has a woman friend who urges her to "make yourself a bit smart" for Albert, her returning husband. "[T]hink of poor Albert, / He's been in the army four years, he wants a good time, / And if you don't give it him, there's others will, I said" (34). This small pub segment in *The Waste Land* conjures up working-class life as squalid and sordid—a wife left toothless by many pregnancies, her health impaired by an abortion, threatened with infidelity if she fails to satisfy the veteran's pent-up lust. It is not, of course, Eliot who represents the veteran as crazed for sex after the long abstinence of the war but the female speaker in the poem. But there is no reference to what the soldier might have experienced in his four years at the front or what sort of psychic damage he might be bringing back to his family. This lack of a psychic cave or background behind Eliot's veteran can be used to prepare students for the complexity of the soldier figure they will confront in *Mrs. Dalloway*.

In Septimus Smith, Woolf presents a casualty of the war in whom the libido— in its full sense as a lust for life—has been killed by the war. Indeed, Septimus marries his young Italian wife "when the panic was on him—that he could not feel" (85). The cave behind his mind is peopled with the ghosts of the dead, especially of his friend Evans. Because he could not allow himself to feel the loss of Evans, Septimus now feels nothing at all, including love or desire for his devoted wife. Eliot's Albert happily rejoins his family and friends at home—"Well, that Sunday Albert was home, they had a hot gammon, / And they asked me in to dinner, to get the beauty of it hot" (35). Septimus, on the other hand, returns from the war full of apprehension: "The world has raised its whip; where will it descend?" (14). Like Eliot's Albert, he survived the war physically, but mentally he has not: he is a figure of the living dead. Although his body is whole, he is psychologically damaged, and when he plunges to his death, he will join the war dead even though the war is over. Unlike the overly fertile Lil, Rezia will have no child, and as the widow of a suicide, she too will become an ancillary casualty of the war. *Mrs. Dalloway* shows that war does not end with an armistice but spreads its lethal effects through the civilian population even after the fighting is over. By reading the texts side by side, students can discern the war in Eliot's poem as a symptom of spiritual decay, while in Woolf's novel it is the cause of spiritual catastrophe.

One way to help students understand the British class system may be through the lens of sensitivity and its relation to culture. Though from a humbler background than Clarissa, Septimus is endowed with a keen love of literature—of Shakespeare and Keats, for example. In this way, Woolf counters a common perception of her time, that the war claimed chiefly miners from the Midlands and factory lads who presented no great loss to British culture. One can fairly point out that high modernists like Eliot and Pound turned against the war only when it began to kill their own—the sculptor Henri Gaudier-Brzeska and the poet Rupert Brooke, for example.

The British trench poets addressed the issue of class in two interesting ways. Wilfred Owen's "Dulce et Decorum Est" depicts the work of war not as heroic fighting but as brutal labor transforming the soldier into an oppressed working man or miner. "Bent double, like old beggars under sacks, / Knock-kneed, coughing like hags, we cursed through sludge" (182). Grimy and exhausting labor is here a trope for the deglamorized life in the trenches. Siegfried Sassoon's "A Working Party" aims to restore dignity to the actual working-class soldier— "a young man with a meagre wife / And two small children in a Midland town." Quiet and inexpressive—"[he] did his work and hadn't much to say"—Sassoon's soldier finishes his job with the working party when a flare lights up No Man's Land, and "the instant split / His startled life with lead, and all went out." But although now "[h]e must be carried back, a jolting lump / Beyond all need of tenderness and care," Sassoon's poem itself gives him tenderness and care, even in death. A small gesture of pride in his family—"He showed their photographs to all his mates"—takes the place of culture as a code for the man's sensitivity and feeling (124). The nameless soldier deserves reflection on and insight into the moment of his death, of the kind that Clarissa bestows on Septimus's suicide: "He had thrown himself from a window. Up had flashed the ground; through him, blundering, bruising, went the rusty spikes. There he lay with a thud, thud, thud in his brain, and then a suffocation of blackness" (179). It is as though Clarissa writes a postwar trench poem for Septimus.

Trench poetry is easily interpolated into a course on Anglo-American modernism because the poems tend to be short and can be dispersed as handouts. But a course on the literature of World War I opens far greater opportunity to dilate on the significance of the war in Woolf's novel. A stunningly effective resource has become available for addressing the specific psychic malady of Septimus. Pat Barker's trilogy of World War I novels, *Regeneration* (1991), *The Eye in the Door* (1993), and *The Ghost Road* (1995), explores the relationship between the poets Sassoon and Owen while both were treated at Craiglockhart Hospital in Scotland. The hospital was a major treatment site for soldiers and veterans suffering from shell shock and other posttraumatic effects. Barker's texts offer valuable insights into conditions like Septimus's madness and address the range of treatments—some horrifically brutal, some enlightened and humane—available at the time. Her work thus sheds light on the theme of insanity in *Mrs. Dalloway* and on the role the inadequacies of early psychiatry played in intensifying the psychic injuries of veterans. In addition, the Barker novels augment the topic of soldiers and sexuality by addressing homosexuality as an issue in the World War I combat experience and its literature.

The collective bulk of the three books presents a practical problem, however, unless the course is a small seminar. To solve this problem, each of the three books can be assigned to a panel of students. Each student can then summarize the plot and themes in a class report and direct the class to the most salient issues in the texts as they relate to both *Mrs. Dalloway* and to trench poetry. In this way, the work of reading the trilogy is shared and distributed among the members of the class. In a large lecture class, just one of the books—optimally *Regeneration*—can be assigned to productive effect. Including Barker's work in a course with *Mrs. Dalloway* has a number of virtues. In fictionalizing the experiences of two of the foremost British trench poets, Barker completes the poetic genre's rehabilitation begun by Fussell. It may be helpful to remind students of W. B. Yeats's rather brutal dismissal of trench poetry as work of inferior aesthetic merit in his 1936 edition of the *Oxford Book of Modern Verse*—"passive suffering is not a theme for poetry" (xxxiv). Yet subsequent wars in the twentieth century have made the expression of lived experience by soldiers and veterans more relevant than ever. In this respect it may be appropriate to point out that the 2003 United States invasion of Iraq had already produced over twenty-eight thousand injured American veterans by 2007. Given that the psychological conditions of these veterans has only slowly gained attention, Woolf's 1925 novel *Mrs. Dalloway* serves as a reminder of the psychic wounds soldiers cannot leave at the front.

Women and War in *Mrs. Dalloway*

Anne E. Fernald

The terrorist attacks on United States targets of September 11, 2001, caused many of the nation's students to understand in a new way that war's effects extend beyond the battlefield. Still, for traditional college-age students World War I is ancient history. In teaching *Mrs. Dalloway* as a novel about women and war, teachers face an audience at once ignorant and receptive—a pedagogical blessing. I supplement *Mrs. Dalloway* with both nonfictional and literary sources, taking my cue from Woolf's vision of war as a catastrophic human tragedy.

I have taught *Mrs. Dalloway* in a first-year seminar and in an upper-division elective. Both courses are called Woolf in Context, and in each, Woolf's texts constitute about half the readings. Mindful that Woolf is a difficult writer, that few undergraduates have read her, and that some may not like her, I have designed accessible assignments with many points of entry. I spend two weeks (four class sessions) on *Mrs. Dalloway*. The first week we spend on the novel, the second week on the contextual readings.

Students understand the novel's depiction of the uneven experience of grief. They live in a world in which some fall apart, while others struggle bravely to continue. The genuine, privileged innocence of Elizabeth Dalloway, untouched by war and on the threshold of benefiting from postwar social changes for women, resonates with many students. This focus has the added benefit of addressing students' frequent dislike of Clarissa Dalloway. In their eyes, she is old, rich, and snobby. Considering the effects of World War I helps students to see differences between Woolf and Clarissa and also to see the novel as an abundant and complex whole.

Mrs. Dalloway *Itself*

We begin with Clarissa. I ask students what she is like, if they like her, and if they think Woolf likes her. The class is often split on these questions, and our discussion helps show Clarissa as a sympathetic snob, ordinary and complex, likable and deeply flawed. We list the events of the opening pages. This exercise counters the impression that nothing happens and helps students learn the significance of every moment in the novel.

My third set of tasks regards the war and the novel's immediate context: June 1923. I show students the passages where Clarissa thinks, "For it was the middle of June. The War was over" (4); where Rezia thinks, "they had been married four, five years now" (15); and where Peter thinks, "Those five years—1918 to 1923—had been, he suspected, somehow very important" (70), so that they can learn how critics determine a text's chronology. Armistice was 11 November 1918; the Treaty of Versailles was signed on 28 June 1919. How can a novel set in 1923 be about the war? Where does the war come in? Students know Septimus is a veteran, but these questions have them flipping through the opening pages. Someone mentions the backfiring car as a representation of general postwar nervousness. We turn to Lady Bexborough, who opens a bazaar having just heard that her favorite son was killed (4). Such bazaars, in support of a village or a parish, offered rich women a symbolic avenue of activity. Some students find Lady Bexborough's behavior courageous; others find her heartless. Why, I ask, does Clarissa admire her (10, 75)? We talk about the name Bexborough, which alludes to Lady Bessborough (1761–1821), hostess, friend, and confidante of Lord Byron and mother to Byron's lover Caroline Lamb. In *A Room of One's Own*, Woolf uses Lady Bessborough's deference to Lord Gower to exemplify the waste of female talent (55; Hussey, *A to Z* 26). The linked names hint at Woolf's skepticism, and students see that a similar ironic distance may apply to Clarissa. Having laid out these early instances of the war's continuing impact, I ask, is this a war novel? Students generally feel that it is not, a judgment that leads to broader discussion of what makes a war novel, whether its author need be a soldier or journalist, and whether war novels need be set on battlefields or during wartime. We leave these questions open, returning to them often.

On the second day, we turn to Lady Bruton and Miss Kilman. Students may not at first understand the nature of Lady Bruton's project (encouraging working-class emigration to Canada [108]) but once they do, they see it as both classist and ridiculous. We talk again about Woolf's attitude toward her characters—an extension of our ongoing analysis of Clarissa—and her attitude toward women in politics more generally. We discuss Doris Kilman's overdetermined name—in terms of war, personality, and sexuality—and we discuss the novel's strong lesbian and homoerotic undercurrents (including Miss Kilman's attraction to Elizabeth Dalloway, Septimus's love for Evans, and Clarissa's friendship with Sally Seton). Students tend not to like Miss Kilman, but few understand how she came to be Elizabeth's tutor: she lost her teaching position for refusing to denounce Germany (12, 121). She pays for her honesty with lost wages, exemplifying the flimsy pretexts on which the war was fought and the vulnerability of working women.

Nonfiction Sources

For our third class session, we read nonfiction sources: David Thomson's "Britain at War, 1914–18," Paul Fussell's "A Satire of Circumstance" (the opening chapter of *The Great War and Modern Memory*), W. H. R. Rivers's "The Repression of War Experience," and Trudi Tate's "*Mrs. Dalloway* and the Armenian Question." These essays vary greatly, from the general overview of Thomson to the narrow focus of Tate. From Thomson, I want students to learn the flimsy cause of war, the shock of new technology, the diplomatic confusion, the devastation, and the unusual number of losses among educated men. Fussell's emphasis on irony, the gap between the ideals of recruitment literature and the brutalities of war, helps explain Septimus's decision to enlist "to save an England which consisted almost entirely of Shakespeare's plays and Miss Isabel Pole in a green dress" (84). Fussell describes the things that women like Lady Bexborough or Isabel Pole would know, believe, and teach. The work of Karen Levenback, David Bradshaw, and Vincent Sherry (*Great War*) would all provide engaging historical context for undergraduates.

We compare Rivers's groundbreaking identification and treatment of shell shock with the treatments offered by Dr. Holmes and Dr. Bradshaw. The only literary criticism I teach is Tate's. While I consult criticism in my preparation, I have found that students become paralyzed by published arguments, especially when they face a paper to write. Tate's historical argument is heavily researched; as such, it is unlike anything an undergraduate would attempt. They can read it without feeling overwhelmed. Tate demonstrates that Clarissa's confusion between Armenians and Albanians represents a shocking degree of willful ignorance. Just as Fussell and Rivers put Septimus into the larger context of World War I soldiers, so Thomson's overview and Tate's indictment of ruling-class politics after the war help students understand Clarissa's more oblique relation to the war's aftermath.

This is a lot of reading, especially for students still struggling to finish the book. To make the discussion worthwhile, I ask that students read every article but only master one. For that article, each student writes a discussion question to post online. To avoid the banal, I insist that the question be both interesting to them and tied to a passage in the article. I further stipulate that after the first student, all students must read the prior questions and tailor their questions accordingly (this eliminates duplication—innocent or not). Students complete these postings well before class time. I ask—and occasionally require—that they read and respond to one or two of their classmates' questions before class.

Thus my students do my preparation. Their questions show me where they have focused their attention, where they may have skimped or misunderstood. Students have asked such questions as, Does Rezia symbolize Italy? Does Woolf confirm or challenge Fussell's hypothesis that the war "reversed the Idea of Progress" (8)? How do the doctors' methods in *Mrs. Dalloway* compare with Rivers's methods? What role do ruling-class women play in the novel? What does the reference to the prime minister in the novel reveal about Woolf's political views? Throughout, I aim to use our forays outside *Mrs. Dalloway* to deepen our understanding of the novel.

Literary Contexts

The logistics are similar when we turn to literary sources, but the structure of the discussion can be looser, and my goal is slightly different. I seek to show students that the novel is one of many possible artistic responses to the war and that Clarissa's experience is individual rather than typical.

Among the abundant options for secondary literary reading, I choose four brief readings. To bring in the voice of a soldier, I teach two poems by Wilfred Owen, "Anthem for Doomed Youth" and "Dulce et Decorum Est." For a working-class home-front perspective, I teach D. H. Lawrence's "Tickets, Please"; students are amazed to read this revenge fantasy set in a workplace dominated by young women. Finally, Winifred Holtby's poignant "So Handy for the Fun Fair," about a woman veteran, provides a feminist counterdiscourse. Trudi Tate's anthology of war stories, which includes the Holtby story, offers many alternatives (*Women*).

Of all the secondary readings, Holtby's "So Handy for the Fun Fair" is the best for enriching students' understanding of the war's impact on women. Holtby (1898–1935) was a member of the Auxiliary Army Corps who later became a pacifist; she also wrote the first monograph on Woolf. In "So Handy for the Fun Fair," Clark, the protagonist, is on a family holiday in France. Shooing her children away, she reminisces about wartime in the French town where she is vacationing, the thrill of working and being promoted, and a love affair with a French veteran. Clark's voice is unpretentious, intelligent, vivacious, funny, and poetic. Still, the story is difficult; it challenges students' association between difficulty and bourgeois themes. Like Lawrence, Holtby emphasizes the war's opportunities for women, and as with Woolf, Holtby's pacifism must be inferred.

To understand Clark better, students work with pairs of quotations I provide for them. In small groups, they discuss what links their pair. For example, of her grown daughter, Clark says, "Few things are more broadening to the mind than being made love to in a foreign language" (53). But at the same time, she remembers thinking, years ago (and before she met François), "Fraternising with Froggies? With all those nice khaki lads about? Not likely!" (57).

Assignment and Conclusion

For their papers, I ask students to compare an aspect of the war and its aftermath in *Mrs. Dalloway* with one of the secondary sources. Students have written about the political involvement of women in 1920s Britain; how *Mrs. Dalloway* and "Tickets, Please" depict the way that World War I liberated women across the social spectrum; how Owen and Woolf draw our attention to society's mistreatment of soldiers; how Clarissa and Clark are linked by the intensity of their efforts to pretend that all's well; and how Lady Bruton is an allegory of postwar apathy.

Approaching *Mrs. Dalloway* as a war novel decenters some common assumptions: that war is mainly about battles, that women do not write on war, and that war is more important than its aftermath. I want students to think deeply about how war reverberates beyond the battlefield and to appreciate a novel even when it depicts a world alien to their own.

Mrs. Dalloway and Carpe Diem Conventions

David Leon Higdon

Only in retrospect can we identify those moments when the future entered our lives, shaping what we would teach and how we would teach it. I first read Virginia Woolf's *Mrs. Dalloway* one very rainy Halloween evening in 1969 during a South Central MLA convention in Houston. This was my first experience of Woolf's fiction, since my graduate courses in English literature (except for a seminar on Joseph Conrad and Ford Madox Ford) had stopped with the Victorians. But by the time the sentence "For Miss Helena Parry was not dead: Miss Parry was alive" (174) caused an electrifying shock to run up my spine—a reaction few novels before or since have ever evoked—I knew instantly that I must teach *Mrs. Dalloway*, despite the problems it would pose for a relatively inexperienced group of undergraduate students, typical of many universities.

The problems I saw in teaching this novel were located on three registers: the novel's modernist techniques, its cultural distance from students' lives, and the age discrepancy between the protagonist and students. One simply cannot get students to plunge immediately into *The Good Soldier* or *Ulysses* or *Mrs. Dalloway* the way they can into the more traditional *A Man of Property* or *A Room with a View* or *Sons and Lovers* because, even after a century, much of the general public has not acquired the reading techniques modernism demands. When one has read or taught a Charles Dickens novel, one can carry the same strategy over to a Charlotte Brontë or George Eliot work, but each modernist novel seems to demand a new strategy. A Conrad novel cannot be taught like a Woolf novel, and vice versa. Eugene Jolas's challenge, "Let the plain reader be damned" (qtd. in Ellmann 588), established early on that significant acts of mediation were essential if a broad reading audience was to be established for modernist fiction, and, indeed, modernist authors are responsible for some of the most important but most unread and untaught works: *Finnegans Wake, The Cantos, The Making of Americans, Pilgrimage, À la recherche du temps perdu, Berlin Alexanderplatz, La coscienza di Zeno,* and even the *Tractatus logio-philosophicus.* Despite a familiarity with modernist techniques in films and on television, readers still claim to have difficulty with novels that minimize plot and action, maximize character interiority, rearrange time sequences, valorize language, evade transitions, and suspend conclusions. Students immediately ask why the author is skipping around temporally, why the narrative voice is discontinuous, why causality has disappeared, and why there is so little action. Students also find the egotism of characters in the works of Conrad, D. H. Lawrence, Joyce, and Woolf off-putting and reject the pessimism of their novels, just as they often respond negatively to examples taken from the music of Stravinsky or the paintings of Picasso. Paul Morel's thought in Lawrence's *Sons and Lovers* that "[h]e was twenty four when he said his first confident thing to his mother" (345) evokes condescension from some students.

Even less bridgeable, it seems at times, is the vast gap separating contemporary casual American mores from the more formal customs of Clarissa Dalloway's social world. The etiquette of the Season of London society mystifies students who have little knowledge of servants and of the menus of formal breakfast parties, at-homes, musical evenings, and drawing-room receptions of the social leaders who made up the Ten Thousand in the early 1920s. Students ask why Clarissa would give a party on a Wednesday night, why her party starts so late, why the conversations are so shallow, and why Clarissa invites some but not all her guests to her dinner. They are staggered to learn that the duchess of Devonshire "entertained Her Majesty and thirty other guests [at dinner] in 1907 and afterwards received a thousand favoured friends" at her London house (Davidoff 5), that formal dinners could offer up to ten courses with two or three selections in each course, and that a woman might change clothing five times in one day in order to be thought properly fashionable. I have found it easier at times to explain human sacrifice in Greek tragedy than to explain the arcane practice of calling cards and their coded language of folded corners, in which Clarissa still participates. *Manners and Rules of Good Society,* a social guide of the period, stipulated:

> The etiquette of card-leaving is a privilege which society places in the hands of ladies to govern and determine their acquaintanceships and intimacies, to regulate and decide whom they will, and whom they will not visit, whom they will admit to their friendship, and whom they will keep on the most distant footing, whose acquaintance they wish further to cultivate and whose to discontinue.   (qtd. in Evans and Evans 43)

Confusion reigns even over facts, as one has to explain patiently that Evans is not Septimus's dog, that Septimus is more than merely upset, that well-to-do people in London actually walk on errands, that Elizabeth's dress is indeed red on one page (180) and pink on others (162, 165, 189), and that, no, Ellie Henderson is not the protagonist.

Finally, how could I interest eighteen- to twenty-year-olds in a fifty-one-year-old who is snobbish, petty, timid, ill, fearful, and a failure in many ways? All teachers know how much easier it is to engage students in *Romeo and Juliet* or *Hamlet* than in *King Lear*. Students share an interest in courtship, love, and sex with Romeo and Juliet, and their university life is akin to that of the young Hamlet, who is struggling with a parent's death, a troublesome love affair, suspect friends, and a meddlesome stepfather. They find little to relate to in Lear and may dismiss him as a senile old fool. There are, however, aspects of Clarissa's experience that students can immediately understand—for example, how disconcerting, even threatening, it is to have an old flame, especially one that proposed marriage, suddenly appear again in one's life (as Peter Walsh does), and the anxiety of planning and staging a successful party.

Teaching *Mrs. Dalloway* appeared to be an uphill battle, and I fought several skirmishes with myself, trying to find the magical *as if*, the appropriate analogy that would reveal the entirety of the novel to students, making it accessible and opening out its multiple facets while also giving them a sense of wholeness—a template for reading. With a work such as *Mrs. Dalloway*, the teacher must respond to the defamiliarizing aspects of the text by refamiliarizing much of it for the readers. I could have taught the novel as if it were a genteel imitation of Joyce's *Ulysses*, as if it were a modernist *Dr. Jekyll and Mr. Hyde*, as if it were a fictional manifestation of Henri Bergson's *durée*, as if it were a historically accurate depiction of the Conservatives in the Stanley Baldwin government—anything to help students bridge the gap between the known and the unknown. Each of these approaches would have been valid. The ties between Robert Louis Stevenson's and Woolf's novels, for instance, enable one to demonstrate how British culture was changing in its treatment of the id. Like Henry Jekyll, Clarissa attempts to reject the monster in her soul as she approaches the flower shop, but unlike Jekyll, she eventually discovers that she must embrace and accept it. The relation between *Ulysses* and *Mrs. Dalloway* remains an unsettled issue in criticism. *Mrs. Dalloway* certainly figures in the exciting discourse about time as a defining feature of the modernist movement, but this approach, as with the others above, can be too specialized to capture the overall meaning of the novel.

The *as if* that emerged through the details of the text was the possibility of teaching *Mrs. Dalloway* as a carpe diem poem. It may seem peculiar, even perverse, to link a key modernist work with a tradition shaped by the fourth-century Decimus Magnus Ausonius (whose Latin poem "De rosis nasentibus" ["On Budding Roses"] later inspired Robert Herrick's "Gather ye rosebuds while ye may, . . ." from "To the Virgins, to Make Much of Time," the best-known poem of the subgenre), but the kinship is strikingly evident. Of course, carpe diem poetry is far more ancient and extensive than just the works of Ausonius. Greek and Latin authors such as Alcaeus, Theognis, Aeschylus, Euripides, and especially Horace and Catullus turned the dialogue among the transience of life, the finality of death, and the uncertainty of the future into a recognized poetic type. During the Renaissance, carpe diem became a major poetic expression in the hands of Pierre de Ronsard, Edmund Spenser, William Shakespeare, Robert Herrick, Edmund Waller, Samuel Daniel, Thomas Carew, John Milton, and Andrew Marvell, and it survives as well in more recent manifestations, such as Edward Fitzgerald's translations; Carl Orff's *Carmina Burana*; and poems by A. E. Housman, William Butler Yeats, John Crowe Ransom, and others.

In her essay "The Strange Elizabethans," Woolf underlined the point that Elizabethan prose and poetry "could speak magnificently, of course, about the great themes—how life is short, and death certain; how spring is lovely, and winter horrid" (*Second Common Reader* 4)—the very essence of carpe diem. While in the midst of composing *Mrs. Dalloway*, she wrote to Gerald Brenan, "If I don't seize this moment, inauspicious as it is, I shan't write" (*Letters* 3: 36).

More to the point, my students already knew and understood this form: they saw and heard the phrase "carpe diem" on T-shirts, in songs, and in movies; struggled with an emerging sense of the unfair battle between their youth and their maturity; and practiced carpe diem, often with drunken ardor, each weekend.

Carpe diem poetry refers to the tight intertwining of several closely related conventions: a speaker who argues that the brevity and ephemerality of life demand that one embrace life joyously, fully, and quickly; a protagonist somewhat fearful of the fullness of human life and sexuality; an antagonist measuring the quickly passing moments, hours, and days; and the powerfully charged central symbol of the flower, traditionally a rose, whose transition from bud to blown petals captures the fleeting passage of human existence. Anyone who has seen this process of growth and decay in what are now called antique roses realizes just how appropriate, and perhaps frightening, the symbol is. Ausonius captured its essence in these lines:

> As long as is one day, so long is the life of the rose; her brief youth and age go hand in hand. . . . Then, maidens, gather roses, while blooms are fresh and youth is fresh, and be mindful that so your life-time hastes away.
> (279, 281)

The carpe diem protagonist wants to embrace life, but a timidity, a moral reticence, even a certain fear holds her back—and the protagonist is virtually always female, since most carpe diem poems are seduction arguments. This fear is seen quite well in both Clarissa Dalloway and her dark Other, Septimus Smith—perhaps even in Elizabeth, whose role in the novel often puzzles first-time readers. Clarissa and Septimus want to experience the joy of life, but there are barriers. Fear has already infected the eighteen-year-old Clarissa as she stands inside the house at Bourton, hesitating to step out onto the terrace because she feels that "something awful [is] about to happen" (3); similarly, as Septimus waits to cross the street, he feels "as if some horror had come almost to the surface and was about to burst into flames" (15). Both Clarissa and Septimus, however, sometimes manage to fight back the terror. As Septimus sits in Regent's Park, he experiences "this beauty, this exquisite beauty, and tears filled his eyes as he looked at the smoke words languishing and melting in the sky and bestowing upon him in their inexhaustible charity and laughing goodness one shape after another" (21), and Clarissa repeatedly reminds us how "with an absurd and faithful passion" she loves "this, here, now, in front of her" (5, 9). Her pressing fear is that she will die and "no one in the whole world would know how she had loved it all" (119).

As its opening paragraphs stitch, unravel, and then resuture the present and the past, the novel voices three carpe diem topics clearly for all students: time, love of life, and fear of extinction. Clarissa knows that Time is her enemy because she is in poor health, having had influenza, having entered her fifty-second year (making her fifty-one), and having been brushed by heart trouble.[1] She feels "unspeakably aged" (8). Although life-expectancy tables for 1921 predicted a woman of her age might reach seventy-three, her health says otherwise. Age, disease, and memories remind her that she has not much longer to live, and Time confronts her at every turn, as antagonist, as theme, and as novelistic technique.

Mrs. Dalloway is truly one of modernism's great time books, as important as *Ulysses* or *À la recherche du temps perdu*. Like *Ulysses*, *Mrs. Dalloway* is a circadian or one-day novel, a new genre in the 1920s, which had slowly evolved from only one example in the eighteenth century to six in the nineteenth century to the definitive shaping of the form by Woolf, Joyce, and Hermann Broch in the twentieth century as modernism wrestled with the demands of the new sciences and philosophies of Time. Can one day in a life be interesting enough to engage a reader's attention? The answer, yes, is a vindication of Dickens and Leo Tolstoy, who contemplated the form without achieving it. In "Modern Fiction," Woolf independently charged herself with "[e]xamin[ing] for a moment an ordinary mind on an ordinary day" (*Common Reader* [1953] 154). She soon extended the challenge further, writing in *Orlando*, "[A]n hour, once it lodges in the queer element of the human spirit, may be stretched to fifty or a hundred times its clock length" (98).

Time figures as Clarissa's most apparent enemy. As she walks across the park, she asks herself the rhetorical question, "[D]id it matter that she must inevitably cease completely; all this must go on without her; did she resent it; or did it not become consoling to believe that death ended absolutely?" (9). The obvious answer is that it matters immensely. Later in the morning, at home, she confesses even more tellingly:

> [S]he feared time itself, and read on Lady Bruton's face, as if it had been a dial cut in impassive stone, the dwindling of life; how year by year her share

was sliced; how little the margin that remained was capable any longer of stretching, of absorbing . . . the colours, salts, tones of existence.   (29)

Moreover, throughout the novel, the "irrevocable . . . leaden circles" (4) of Big Ben, the chimes of Saint Margaret, and the clocks of Harley Street remind the characters and the reader that darkness is coming: "death's enormous sickle had swept those tremendous hills" (79). We must never forget that the novel's working title was *The Hours*. Rather than follow a character's actions, I have my students collect as many of the statements about Time as they can, letting them see the spatial, thematic direction of Woolf's text.

Time's minions—death, age, and disease—do not fully account for Clarissa's fear of life. From childhood experiences, she has developed a pessimistic and fatalistic view of life. From the death of her sister, Sylvia, she evolves the analogy that people are "a doomed race, chained to a sinking ship" by the gods, "who never lost a chance of hurting, thwarting and spoiling human lives" (76). As a result, this glorious June day in 1923, she feels "that it was very, very dangerous to live even one day," that she is "a single figure against the appalling night," and that she has somehow become "timid; hard; something arrogant; unimaginative; prudish" (8, 30, 58). Clarissa has been tellingly wounded by Time and death; however, she has also been injured by the egotism of the people in her world, an egotism that transforms individuals into abstractions, threatens to break up family units, and strives to dominate. We see her hatred of this life-denying force in her attitude toward Doris Kilman, Peter Walsh, Millicent Bruton, Sir William Bradshaw, and others who are labeled by their quasi-allegorical names, all of whom become adjuncts to Time's war. Despite this, Clarissa still loves life and finds death unbelievable.

Clarissa's party is one way of responding to Time's threat. In addition, it has social and political agendas and is one small part of the Season's hundred-day party. As her guests wend their way to her home in Dean's Yard, passing through its imposing Victorian gates (and one can truly appreciate Clarissa's position in the establishment after standing in the courtyard of Dean's Yard),[2] they have had busy days at Lords, Ascot, Ranelagh, Hurlingham, the Westminster flower show, a garden party at Buckingham Palace, and gatherings at Hatfield House.

The formalities of the Season had been loosening since the 1890s, but its spirit remained strong in the 1920s. To Peter Walsh, it is "[a] splendid achievement in its own way, after all, London; the season; civilisation" (54), and even though Clarissa may dislike "that network of visiting, leaving cards, being kind to people; running about with bunches of flowers, little presents" (75) required by the etiquette of the day, she delights in her party as something quite apart from these trivialities. Stanley Baldwin, her guest of honor, has been prime minister only since May 1923. As a political hostess, she knows there may still be a place for Richard in the cabinet, and she also knows that it is her obligation to help advance her husband's career. Woolf's readers in 1925 would have known that Baldwin's government was voted out in January 1924, but they would not have known that he would serve eight more years as prime minister, from November 1924 to June 1929 and from June 1935 to May 1937. Clarissa's party is certainly not in the same league as those thrown at Marlborough House or Devonshire House, but Clarissa is every bit the political hostess whether or not she can distinguish between Armenians and Albanians or explain what and where the equator is.

Clarissa has at least three other refuges from Time and her fears. First, she has her role model, Lady Bexborough, opening the bazaar with one hand while holding notice of her favorite son's death in the other—an icon of English stoicism, privileging festivity over mourning. Lady Bexborough is sometimes devalued in the criticism, but she provides a clear foreshadowing of the intrusion of death into Clarissa's party. Second, Septimus Smith, whose despair and mania carry her tendencies to extremes, finally acts as a symbolic scapegoat or sacrifice for her. Third, present throughout the novel are the flowers: Moll Pratt with her roses; Maisie Johnson by the hyacinth beds; Sally Seton decorating the dining table with hollyhocks and dahlias; houses with their "swinging baskets of pale geraniums" (53); Aunt Helena's rare Burmese orchids; Rezia's artificial flowers; the beds of dahlias, hollyhocks, and pampas grass of Lady Bruton's childhood; Elizabeth Dalloway's impressing others as being "like a hyacinth" (120; perhaps an echo from T. S. Eliot's *The Waste Land*); Mrs. Morris and the Westminster flower show; and Lady Rosseter's vast beds of "hydrangeas, syringas, very, very rare hibiscus lilies that never grow north of the Suez Canal" (186).

But most of all there is Clarissa surrounded by flowers, perhaps most emphatically when she is walking along Bond Street, thinking how much she hates that "spectre" Doris Kilman.[3] The hatred "rasped her" like a "brutal monster" and "had power to make her feel scraped, hurt in her spine; gave her physical pain" (12). She brushes all this aside, however, denying it with the words "Nonsense, nonsense!" (12), establishing just how firmly the novel is built around a denial plot, and sweeps into the embrace of Miss Pym's flowers:

> delphiniums, sweet peas, bunches of lilac; and carnations, masses of carnations. There were roses; there were irises. Ah yes . . . turning her head from side to side among the irises and roses and nodding tufts of lilac with her eyes half closed, snuffing in, after the street uproar, the delicious scent, the exquisite coolness. (12–13)

Indeed, Woolf changed the entire direction and import of her novel when she decided to have Clarissa buy flowers instead of gloves. The gloves Clarissa goes to buy in "Mrs. Dalloway in Bond Street" signal Woolf's concern with the social context of manners, appearances, and etiquette—the static forms of society (19). The shift to flowers brings in nature and the life force, which Clarissa radiates in her best moments. With the flowers, the novel enjoins one to plunge into the enjoyment of life (seen especially in the vitality of the streets and parks, the excitement of the party, the invigorating revelation of Elizabeth's abduction by the omnibus) and recognizes that the "terror," "ecstasy," and "extraordinary excitement" of the novel's final page result from death's vitalizing life itself. "A whole lifetime," Clarissa thinks, "was too short to bring out, now that one had acquired the power, the full flavour; to extract every ounce of pleasure, every shade of meaning" (77).

With Time identified as the major protagonist, fear of extinction marked as one of Clarissa's chief worries, and flowers offered as escape, solace, and even denial, it is easy to see why I turn to carpe diem conventions when teaching this novel. There are two pointed carpe diem references in *Mrs. Dalloway*: the refrain of "Fear no more the heat of the sun," from Shakespeare's *Cymbeline* (4.2.258), and the more general reference to Lady Bruton's estate, where "[t]here was a vine, still bearing, which either Lovelace or Herrick . . . had sat under" (103).[4] Virginia Woolf certainly paid more attention to this vine than Lady Bruton ever did and in doing so gave her readers an extraordinary tool with which to understand the "incessant shower of innumerable atoms" that makes up *Mrs. Dalloway* ("Modern Fiction" 154). The carpe diem conventions establish characters, cluster symbols, and voice themes emphatically. Septimus virtually summarizes the conventions: "He did not want to die. Life was good. The sun hot. Only human beings—what did *they* want?" (146). Clarissa has an answer from both poetic subgenre and Woolf when she thinks, early in the novel, "how moments like this are buds on the tree of life . . . as if some lovely rose had blossomed for her eyes only" (28).

NOTES

[1] The influenza epidemic of 1918 killed 151,446 British citizens, some 5.2 per thousand in Clarissa's Westminster parish alone and over twenty million worldwide (Marwick 257).

[2] One wonders if Clarissa or her creator knew that Dean's Yard was once the site of a sacred spring (Ackroyd 13).

[3] Victorian books on the "language of flowers" provide no coherent symbolic scheme, instead associating most flowers with the Virgin Mary and assigning reputed healing qualities to some (see Lehner and Lehner 54, 63, 77–79). Dowling has counted nineteen types of flowers in *Mrs. Dalloway* (61), but his conclusion that "[f]lowers stand for the private life of emotion" (63) does not go far enough in assessing their significance. Woolf clearly associated flowers with certain types of women and particularly with their sexuality, fertility, emotionality, daring, and vitality. Her critics have provided interesting readings of the lesbian erotic in the floral imagery (see Roof, "Match"; Cramer, "Notes"; and Barrett, "Unmasking").

[4] Woolf's library and reading notes demonstrate a full knowledge of the carpe diem poets, especially Herrick. See Silver, *Virginia Woolf's Reading Notebooks* 122; Steele, app. B; and *Essays* 491–96. In *Essays*, Woolf quotes Herrick poems four times and Catullus once. Also, Clarissa confesses "to a passion for Donne on the strength of his portrait chiefly and some of the poems if you read them aloud" and claims "every woman is in love with Keats" ("Byron" 494). For a provocative but not finally persuasive discussion of the use of the Shakespeare quotation, see Henderson.

Mrs. *Dalloway* and the Long Nineteenth Century

Judith Scaboyer

I teach *Mrs. Dalloway* at a large state university in Australia at the conclusion of a thirteen-week undergraduate course called British Women Writers in the Long Nineteenth Century. *Mrs. Dalloway*'s centrality to the canon of high modernism may seem to make it an odd choice for the course, given that the other texts I assign are best classified as exemplary of nineteen-century domestic realism, but Woolf's text refocuses the course's aims. First, it expands students' political understanding of the systems that shaped the Romantic and Victorian texts we study. Second, throughout the course we attempt to read ethically and responsibly, which is to say that we try to recognize the irreducible otherness of our texts and their characters, resisting the comfortable integration of, say, Emma Woodhouse or Maggie Tulliver into versions of ourselves in Victorian guise. Clarissa, while no more assimilable, reminds us of the uncanny shadow of Victorianism that fell across the twentieth century and that remains perceptible in the twenty-first.

Within the framework of the Industrial Revolution and late-Victorian imperialism, our focus is the shaping of gendered subjectivities and fictional resistances to the entrenchment of a gendered division of labor supported by the false consciousness that came to be termed the doctrine of separate spheres: woman's natural sphere was private, domestic; man's public, political. Woman was the moral linchpin of the household and thence, through her influence on the male members of her family, a force for good in society. Paradoxically, that moral strength translated into a childlike innocence that meant she must remain sequestered, protected from the temptations of a corrupt world. The course grounds students in this complex ideology so that they are able to recognize its shadowy presence in Woolf's 1923 novel and even in their own lives.

The range of student preparedness for the course varies: most are literature majors in the second or third year of a three-year bachelor of arts degree. Some will have completed a course in Victorian literature, and some will have read *To the Lighthouse*. A small but significant number may have studied little or no literature. Of the eighty to one hundred students who enroll, very few are men. By the time we come to *Mrs. Dalloway*, students share an understanding of Victorian realism, and I introduce Woolf's novel as a paradigmatic modernist text that delineates a radical shift from the texts we have read so far. Nevertheless, I suggest, with its focus on psychologically believable protagonists functioning in a believable world, it remains within the tradition of realism. We address issues raised by Woolf's text that have been central to our discussions of Mary Shelley's *Matilda*, Jane Austen's *Emma*, Charlotte Brontë's *Villette*, Anne Brontë's *The Tenant of Wildfell Hall*, George Eliot's *The Mill on the Floss*, Elizabeth Gaskell's *North and South*, and Florence Nightingale's "Cassandra." To facilitate the journey back in time, and as an introduction to the course, in the first class meeting we read together projected images of nineteenth-century narrative paintings, as far as possible taking into account their context and the responses of their contemporaries. We consider, for example, the dutiful wives and daughters of George Elgar Hicks's triptych *Woman's Mission* and Jane Bowkett's *Preparing Tea*. We contrast the subtle gothicization of Richard Redgrave's saintly, isolated, impoverished, domestically contained *Seamstress* and *Governess* with the foregrounded community among the mill girls who spill out to occupy the sunlit public space outside the factory in Eyre Crowe's *Dinner Hour, Wigan*.

A course reader includes twentieth-century critical responses to the literature of nineteenth-century women in general and our texts in particular and a selection of Victorian essays on the woman question. Of those essays, we most often return in reading *Mrs. Dalloway* to Sarah Stickney Ellis's *The Women of England: Their Social Duties and Domestic Habits* and John Stuart Mill's *The Subjection of Women*. We also read literary criticism, beginning with extracts from three foundational twentieth-century feminist explorations of nineteenth-century women's writing (Moers; Showalter, *Literature*; Gilbert and Gubar, *Madwoman*), accompanied by a more recent critical response for each primary text. Trudi Tate's "*Mrs. Dalloway* and the Armenian Question," for example, supplies important historical and political background and deals with the issues of ethics and responsibility that I hope students will be ready to address as we conclude the course. Tate reads *Mrs. Dalloway* as "a novel about post-war complacency and collusion in British political circles" (469) and Clarissa as carelessly complicit (471).

We meet for three hours a week. We spend ninety minutes together for a lecture and discussion, and afterward I meet with five tutorial groups of fifteen to twenty students. Assessment consists of classroom participation, a short close-reading exercise, a research essay, and a brief examination—they write about four thousand words in total. I stress the importance of active participation and the necessity of preparedness for lectures and tutorials, convincing students that they will learn more from struggling with ideas as they read and then working them through with their peers than from passively absorbing (or not) my lecture.

I supply a weekly reading guide composed of questions as a way into what are, after all, complex texts. The questions draw attention to important concepts for the course and in each text, encourage active thinking, and ensure a shared focus. By the time students encounter Clarissa, they recognize her to be eminently Victorian, and I ask them to come to class ready to debate the political aspects of the novel based on two quotations. First, Quentin Bell, Woolf's nephew and biographer, said of her:

> [S]he belonged inescapably to the Victorian world of Empire, Class and Privilege. Her gift was the pursuit of shadows, for the ghostly whispers of the mind and for Pythian incomprehensibility, when what was needed was

the swift and lucid phrase that could reach the ears of unemployed working men or trades union officials.   (2:186)

Second, Woolf herself famously said of *Mrs. Dalloway* as she was writing, "I
want to criticize the social system, & to show it at work, at its most intense"
(*Diary* 2: 248).

Some accuse Bell of a failure to recognize the political potential of fiction,
and one student viewed his statement as symptomatic of a generation's denial
of its predecessors' wisdom—an oedipalized relation. Others are offended or
amused by so telling a use of gendered language and its assumptions about audience. Still others agree with Bell that Woolf's political message is simply too
diffuse to have been effective, her audience too narrowly her own intellectual
and social class. But whether readers ultimately lean toward Bell's or Woolf's
view, since Clarissa stands between us in the twenty-first century and them in
the nineteenth, she forms an interpretive bridge across time and space, drawing the earlier texts into perspective in productive ways. By now, students well
appreciate the alterity of the lives of nineteenth-century women, but Woolf's
modernist text enables the necessary doubled vision that reveals those lives to
be at the same time uncannily familiar. The alterity of the texts and their protagonists is maintained, but they are revealed to be "apt for the present and future" (Edmundson 73) and in ways that previously may not have been apparent.
And so *Mrs. Dalloway* leads students to ask new questions of the course as a
whole: "What can we do with [these works]? What aspects of our lives [do they]
illuminate? What action do they enjoin?" (73).

Students come to class ready to consider two propositions about Clarissa.
First, she is warm, generous, sensual, her pleasure in life infectious. She does
what she can to "decorate the dungeon with flowers" (76). The party is exemplary of the way she brings Londoners together, and her identification with
Septimus is just one example of her extraordinary powers of identification. Second, she is timid, snobbish, "[c]old, heartless, a prude" (8). Her passions only
extend to perfect shoes and gloves. She takes no interest in the world beyond
Westminster and so avoids responsibility for the situation following the war. She
is as rigid as England and as blind to a changing world. Discussion about these
propositions is lively, and the knowledge students have gained of women's lives
during the nineteenth century illuminates their understanding of Clarissa's life
and spills into discussions of Millicent Bruton, Milly Brush, Doris Kilman, Sally
Seton, and Elizabeth Dalloway.

Recalling Mill's insistence that the subordination of women was "one of the
chief hindrances to human improvement" (1), some are moved to ask how well
Woolf's characters use their new freedom. Girls may put on lipstick in public
and walk through London unaccompanied, and Elizabeth's difference from her
mother hints at new possibilities, but students hasten to point out that Clarissa too
was once "pure-hearted" (33, 187). She read William Morris, Plato, and Shelley,
and her love for Sally was passionate. In 1923, the doctrine of separate spheres,

they note, remains intact. Power remains in the hands of men like Richard Dalloway and his fellow parliamentarians and professional bullies like Sir William Bradshaw and Dr. Holmes. Women like Millicent Bruton continue to exert feminine influence through men like "the admirable Hugh" Whitbread (168) and over powerless women like Milly Brush, and Clarissa's failure to look beyond the domestic sphere begins to look like complicity. This realization offers an opportunity to revisit Ellis and the exercise of feminine moral influence, which might lead us back to Austen's Emma Woodhouse, Anne Brontë's Helen Huntingdon, or Eliot's Lucy Deane. The position of surplus women like Milly Brush or Doris Kilman returns us to the predicament of women like Austen's Miss Bates and Jane Fairfax or Charlotte Brontë's Lucy Snowe.

A comparison of Clarissa's late-Victorian education with that of, say, Maggie Tulliver is an opportunity to review women's education as an element of their infantilization. How well have "the few twigs of knowledge Fraülein Daniels" (8) passed on to Clarissa fitted her for responsible adulthood? Students are eager to discuss whether a feminine education and its effects are responsible for her ignorance or whether they are a convenient screen that allows her to ignore the sufferings of those whose interests go against her own or Britain's. The ghost of Ellis reappears, returning us to the "disinterested kindness" and selflessness of the angel in the house (85). Clarissa, students are relieved to note, is far from Ellis's self-abnegating ideal. She "loved success; hated discomfort; must be liked" (119). But her lack of ethical interest in Richard's political work leads some students to modify the scorn they heaped on Ellis's insistence on the moral influence of the "humble monitress" of the fireside (73)—fully aware as they are that they risk rallying behind the flag of Millicent Bruton. Before they take the easy route of damning Clarissa, however, I begin a discussion of our own engagement in the political sphere.

We discuss how Woolf's text situates Britain in a wider ethical context when it examines the intersecting lives of men and women living in London almost five years after the armistice. I provide a brief historical background to the British presence in India, Canada, and the Ottoman Empire, and we use Tate's essay to understand the relevance of the Armenian question. With this information students can see that in the context of the Allied victory, *Mrs. Dalloway* asks what responsibilities Britain and British citizens have to their imperial and postimperial colonies (symbolically represented by Peter's India and Lady Bruton's Canada) and to nations defeated in the Great War. We discuss the defeated nations in terms of the continuation of Britain's role in the imperialist Great Game that had been played out in central Asia and specifically in Afghanistan between the empires of Tsarist Russia and Britain from the early nineteenth century. Although it officially ended in 1907, many historians agree that its trace persisted in southwest Asia, symbolically represented by Richard's involvement in deciding the fate of the imperiled Armenians and Clarissa's careless confusion over just which national group and which territorial boundaries were at stake (117).

Tate explains that Britain's involvement was based on cynical geostrategic concerns, not human rights. In 1878, it suited British interests to overturn the Treaty of San Stefano because its removal of Armenia from the Ottoman Empire increased Russia's sphere of influence. In the years that followed, the Armenians suffered ongoing oppression at the hands of the Turks, culminating in the deaths in 1915 of 1,750,000 people. Tate quotes Lloyd George, who directly blamed Britain's "sinister intervention" for this "holocaust" (472–73). By the time Richard's committee was in place, Britain had the League of Nations's imprimatur for its control of a much more valuable chunk of the Ottoman Empire, just to the south of Armenia: the British-created oil-rich state of Iraq. Armenia had become all but irrelevant, but if part of it was to stay under Turkish rather than Russian control, it was surely all to the good for Britain's long-term strategic interests.

Arising from this critique of individual and national responsibilities, the text asks what Clarissa's particular responsibilities, and those of a woman of her privileged class, might be in such an environment. Given what our texts have shown of the limitations imposed on the lives of women in the nineteenth century, Clarissa, poised between their world and ours, jolts us into asking an additional ethical question: How should we, as privileged, enfranchised, educated women, live in the world we have inherited?

Reading at the Intersections:
Teaching *Mrs. Dalloway* in a Class on Retellings

Mary Beth Pringle

During a recent summer term at Wright State University in Dayton, Ohio, I taught *Mrs. Dalloway* in a course on literary retellings. Over five weeks, my students and I pondered Harold Bloom's theory of misprisioning: that all texts result from their authors' intentional misreadings of other texts. We also covered Annette Kolodny's thought-provoking response to Bloom, "A Map for Rereading: Gender and the Interpretation of Literary Texts." After briefly discussing James Joyce's misprisioning of the *Odyssey*, we examined key portions of *Ulysses* and read all of Woolf's *Mrs. Dalloway*, Michael Cunningham's *The Hours*, and Judith Kitchen's *The House on Eccles Road*. Applying Bloom's theory by reading at the intersections between *Mrs. Dalloway* and *Ulysses* and between *Mrs. Dalloway* and *The Hours* enriched students' understanding of all three texts. Although Kitchen's *The House on Eccles Road* misprisions *Ulysses* and not *Mrs. Dalloway*, it afforded students a contemporary and female revision of *Ulysses* related in intriguing ways to Woolf's great novel. Finally, reading *Mrs. Dalloway* in connection with these other works brought to life Bloom's theory of misprisioning and helped students look appreciatively at Kolodny's challenge to it.

In the first week of the steamy term, my class of twenty upper-level undergraduate and six graduate students acquainted themselves with Bloom's idea that undermines the stability of the printed word. First introduced in *The Anxiety of Influence* and developed in *A Map of Misreading* and *Kabbalah and Criticism*, Bloom's theory posits that "[r]eading a text is necessarily the reading of a whole system of texts, and meaning is always wandering around between texts" (*Kabbalah* 107–08). For Bloom, "a poem is a response to a poem, as a poet is a response to a poet, or a person to his parent." Thus "poems . . . are neither about 'subjects' nor about 'themselves.' They are necessarily about *other poems*" (*Map* 18). According to Bloom, readers don't seek to "'understand' any single poem as an entity in itself" (*Anxiety* 43). Instead, as Kolodny explains, they "attempt to map the psychodynamic relations by which the poet at hand has willfully misunderstood the work of some precursor (either single or composite) in order to correct, rewrite, or appropriate the prior poetic vision as his own" (46).

Once students grasped Bloom's key arguments, they turned to Kolodny's consideration of what happens when the carrying over of meaning from one text to the next "takes place among readers and writers [often women] who in fact have been, or at least have experienced themselves as, cut off and alien from that dominant tradition" (48). To illustrate, Kolodny directs readers to the first chapter of Woolf's *A Room of One's Own*, the memorable moment when the speaker reports "being barred entrance, because of her sex, to a 'famous library' in which was housed, among others, a Milton manuscript" (qtd. in Kolodny 48).

Reflecting on what happened, the speaker thinks "of the effect of tradition and of the lack of tradition upon the mind of a *writer*" (25–26; emphasis added). Kolodny takes Woolf's point one step further, saying that tradition and the lack of it affect "the mind of a *reader* as well . . . and, indeed, may respond to . . . readers' sense of exclusion from high (or highbrow) culture" (48; emphasis added).

My students grappled well with both arguments: Bloom's position that regardless of sex, writers and readers are coequal participants in a shared literary tradition and Kolodny's countering that their sex prevents them from being exactly that. When students had ingested both critics' ideas, we examined the various ways the novels for our course illustrated Bloom's views (they are all misprisions in different ways) and complicated Kolodny's (both male and female writers do the misprisioning, and, in my class, both men and women read the misprisioned texts). Discussion about each book increasingly involved the other three.

We finished week 1 by reviewing Homer's *Odyssey*, which Joyce retold in *Ulysses*. Woolf—her quirky education making her a special case among women in Great Britain in the early twentieth century—also knew the *Odyssey*, considered it part of her literary tradition, and misprisioned it in *Mrs. Dalloway*. While composing her novel, she noted elsewhere, "I shall write at *Mrs. Dalloway* till, next Monday, perhaps, bringing her into full talk . . . then do the Greek chapter, for which I shall have to read *Odyssey* (6 books)" (qtd. in Prose 2). Although my class did not linger on connections between the *Odyssey* and *Mrs. Dalloway*, instructors wishing to do so would benefit from reading Molly Hoff's thorough "The Pseudo-Homeric World of *Mrs. Dalloway*."

During week 2, the class read and discussed four chapters of Joyce's *Ulysses*: chapter 1, "Telemachus," which introduces Stephen Dedalus; chapter 4, "Calypso," which acquaints readers with Leopold Bloom; chapter 17, "Ithaca," which details Stephen and Leopold's late-night conversation over hot chocolate at 7 Eccles Street; and chapter 18, "Penelope," which reproduces Molly Bloom's early-morning thoughts on 17 June 1904. Although students would have benefited from reading all of *Ulysses*, the time constraints of summer term did not allow it.

Week 3 began with a bridge: an examination of Woolf's comments about *Ulysses* from letters and essays (Hussey, *Major Authors*). A bit overwhelmed by *Ulysses*, my students were delighted by Woolf's complicated but early negative take on Joyce's work: "Genius it has I think; but of the inferior water," she wrote. "The book is diffuse. It is brackish. It is pretentious. It is underbred, not only in the obvious sense, but in the literary sense" (*Diary* 2: 199). Although Woolf eventually tempers her views, she never wholly changes her mind, saying that *Ulysses* gives her a "sense of being in a bright yet narrow room" with a "self which, in spite of its tremor of susceptibility, never embraces or creates what is outside itself and beyond" ("Modern Fiction" 151).

With Woolf's critical remarks about *Ulysses* in mind, students plunged into *Mrs. Dalloway*. We started with the basics of comparison: the two novels' structural differences, the ways in which Clarissa's situation resembles and differs from Leopold's, the manner in which the Dalloways' marriage contrasts with the Blooms', and points of comparison between Septimus Smith and Stephen Dedalus. An excellent source of parallels is Harvena Richter's "The *Ulysses* Connection: Clarissa Dalloway's Bloomsday."

Week 4 focused on similarities, plentiful and sometimes playful, between Cunningham's 1998 novel *The Hours* and *Mrs. Dalloway*. One young man, a new English major, insisted that the corpse of Woolf snagged "against one of the pilings at Southease" at the beginning of *The Hours* is somehow narrating (through dream or flash forward) the entire plot of the novel (7). As evidence, he pointed to the text's pervasive water imagery, starting with the drowning. Given the self-reflexivity evident in that idea, the student's remark allowed us to undertake discussions of the postmodern, which provided a frame for the remainder of our work with *The Hours*. It also allowed us to contrast *The Hours's* postmodernism with the modernism of *Ulysses* and *Mrs. Dalloway*, building from Cunningham's assertion that "[t]o a greater extent than any novelist except Joyce, Woolf invented the modernist novel, . . . prismatic, ambiguous, at least slightly chaotic, amoral, poetic and concerned . . . primarily with outwardly unremarkable people" ("Virginia Woolf").

Week 5 concluded with an exploration of Kitchen's lyrical *The House on Eccles Road*. Students said they enjoyed reading a contemporary and local (set seventy miles away from us) misprisioning of *Ulysses* with Molly (now Bluhm), the wife of an English professor in Dublin, Ohio, as the protagonist. Kitchen's upended version of *Ulysses* helped the class appreciate Woolf's more subtle recasting of Ulyssean characters in *Mrs. Dalloway*.

During an extra class session one afternoon a week, I showed films of three of the four works: Joseph Strick's version of *Ulysses*, Marleen Gorris's interpretation of *Mrs. Dalloway*, and Stephen Daldry's adaptation of Cunningham's *The Hours*. The film versions of the novels helped students see relations and shades of misprisioning among the works that close reading and class discussion had missed.

What conclusions did my students reach about *Mrs. Dalloway* based on their study of Bloom's and Kolodny's theories? Reading at the intersections between *Ulysses* and *Mrs. Dalloway* helped them better appreciate Woolf's extraordinary art, especially its parodic elements. They delighted, for instance, in her play with flower imagery. A lively debate occurred between students who felt that her flower-strewn novel was an intentional mockery of Leopold Bloom and those who thought that the synchronicity of images was accidental. Without my guidance, they triumphantly located Peter Walsh mimicking Molly Bloom's affirmation, "Yes . . . Yes, yes, yes," a connection that Richter has noted (315). They were also interested in talking about Woolf's misprisioning of *Ulysses's* tripartite structure. Although each novel has three key protagonists, *Mrs. Dalloway*, they felt, all but discarded Leopold Bloom (Peter Walsh), reshaping Molly Bloom into Clarissa and Stephen into Septimus Smith. The result for them was that *Mrs. Dalloway* focuses more on relationships than, as happens in *Ulysses*, on three isolated individuals.

My students said they thought that Joyce crammed *Ulysses* with experience, tried to be encyclopedic. Woolf, on the other hand, wanted to transcend experience, to show that beyond experience lies happiness or despair. As a result, less happens in *Mrs. Dalloway* than in *Ulysses*, but what does happen is immensely rich: at her party, Clarissa thinks, "Nothing could be slow enough; nothing last too long. No pleasure could equal . . . straightening the chairs, pushing in one book on the shelf . . . lost . . . in the process of living" (181).

My students noticed, of course, that *Mrs. Dalloway* is far less sexually graphic than *Ulysses*. Did Woolf misprision Joyce's indecency? they asked. But while sex in *Mrs. Dalloway* is more covert, it is pervasive, they noted. To illustrate, they pointed to Woolf's erotic indirection: to Clarissa's empty attic bed; to Clarissa and Sally's long-ago, still-remembered kiss at Bourton; to Peter Walsh's name and pocketknife. I was delighted when someone proposed that for Woolf the point is not sex as it is conventionally depicted but a desire that is more spiritual, more ethereal: whatever impulses connect people profoundly to one another. Such connections, I suggested, are crucial for Woolf. For example, when Clarissa learns of Septimus's suicide, "her dress flamed, her body burnt" (179).

Once they warmed to the task of misprisioning, my students realized that Woolf and Joyce treat death differently. In *Ulysses*, characters stoically face death and then sadly get on with life. In *Mrs. Dalloway*, death is depicted in a far more positive light. My students pointed eagerly to numerous lines, such as "Death was defiance. Death was an attempt to communicate. . . . There was an embrace in death" (180).

Students also commented on the differences they saw in Joyce's and Woolf's uses of stream of consciousness. Joyce tries to capture identity through such a narrative perspective, while Woolf, misprisioning Joyce, uses stream of consciousness to underscore the impossibility of such a task. At Clarissa's party, Sally thinks, "[F]or what can one know even of the people one lives with everyday? . . . Are we not all prisoners? . . . Despairing of human relationships" (188).

Finally, students said they were struck by how political both novels are. Reading at the intersections helped them better appreciate the colonial politics implicit in *Ulysses* and the ways in which Woolf's novel, as well as the postmodern air we breathe, is dominated by war even during times of peace.

Considering *Mrs. Dalloway* and *The Hours* together—both works are, like *Ulysses*, quotidian, single-day novels—students analyzed Cunningham's sad prologue. Its first sentences, "She [Woolf] hurries from the house, wearing a coat too heavy for the weather. It is 1941," suggested, they said, that Woolf herself, time, and soon death are thematically important (3). The first sentence of Woolf's *Mrs. Dalloway*, however, keeps the focus squarely on Clarissa's art: "Mrs. Dalloway said she would buy the flowers herself" (3). The novels' party scenes subtly reinforce these thematic differences. Despite Septimus's suicide, Clarissa's party succeeds, affirming beauty and life. Clarissa Vaughan's party, on the other hand, nearly fails in that it is canceled after (or vastly altered by) Richard's suicide.

My students also considered why Cunningham misprisioned *Mrs. Dalloway* by making Richard Dalloway *The Hours*'s central character. One student offered that Cunningham must have wanted homosexuality to be a more prominent focus in his novel, compared with its muting in *Mrs. Dalloway*. Class discussion centered on today's interest in sexual identity, the recognition of its fluidity, and our greater freedom to explore sexual desire.

Several students said that reading between *Ulysses* and *The House on Eccles Road* made them aware that Joyce accords more sympathy to Leopold than to Molly Bloom. One student asked whether Joyce's lack of sympathy for Molly might help explain Woolf's recasting of characters in *Mrs. Dalloway*, in which Clarissa is assigned the central role. Seeing situations reversed in *The House on Eccles Road*—in Kitchen's novel, the nexus of power and respect shifts to Molly—caused students to rethink their opinions of all three works.

At the end of the term, students scolded Bloom—as Kolodny did—for using martial imagery (creation as "warfare," "psychic battles," "strong survivors" [47]) and for comparing the creative process to oedipal struggles (between the "ephebe" writer and "his poetic father/precursor" [Kolodny 47]). They agreed, however, that Bloom's theory of retelling gave them a keener, subtler understanding of all four novels. They stressed the pleasure of allowing an earlier novel to direct their responses to the one misprisioning it. Guiding them toward future reading, I mentioned other critics—John Barth, David Cowart, Sandra Gilbert and Susan Gubar (*Letters*), Nancy Walker—who have entered the critical conversation about literary retellings. I also referred them to other recent retellings of *Mrs. Dalloway*: *Mr. Dalloway*, by Robin Lippincott, and *Mr. Phillips*, by John Lanchester. Even Woolf acknowledged that "the creative mind . . . is prone to cannibalize other works of art" (Richter 305). We also discussed the implications of being female or male, gay or straight, for our reading process.

Because Woolf misprisioned two literary works by men (*Ulysses* and the *Odyssey*), students could have rejected Kolodny's argument. They did not. Agreeing that women have been excluded from the dominant literary tradition, they saw Woolf's misprisioning of *Ulysses* in *Mrs. Dalloway* as an anomaly, arguing that her family and special circumstances provided her with an education rare for her time. Kitchen's misprisioning of *Ulysses* in *The House on Eccles Road*, they concluded, indicates that conditions for women artists have improved, Woolf and Cunningham making possible Kitchen's misreading of *Ulysses*. That at least three male writers have recently misprisioned *Mrs. Dalloway* shows that this particular intertextual conversation continues to fascinate.

On the last day of class, I looked forward to seeing my students' final papers. Anticipating a remarkable essay by James Schiff that would be published later that summer, one student observed that misprisioning does not have to involve "struggle" and competition. Instead, another powerful emotion rules: "[T]he process of misprisioning requires, first and foremost, a fervent desire (so much time and work involved!) on the part of the writer to interact with a text. . . . I believe *The Hours* was written for *love*" (Mary Jo White; emphasis added). Cunningham provides plenty of support for this view. "The book just nailed me," he says of *Mrs. Dalloway* (Interview). He explains his efforts in *The Hours*: "I tried to take an existing work of great art and make another work of art out of it, the way a jazz musician might play improvisation on a great piece of music" (qtd. in Prose 107). As Schiff says of *The Hours*'s relation to *Mrs. Dalloway*, Cunningham has honored *Mrs. Dalloway* with an "homage" (363).

A few days after the quarter's end, an envelope appeared in my campus mailbox, put there by someone from the retellings class. Inside was a poem clipped from a recent *New Yorker*. I smiled as I read David Ferry's lines, so beautifully capturing the spirit of our class: "The page is blank until the mind that reads / Crosses the black river, seeking the Queen / Of the underworld" (56). The "mind that reads" was each of us in the class. During that hot summer term, a group of fine readers and I had clothed four novels "in the beautiful garment of our thousand / Misunderstandings of the sacred text" (Ferry 56).

NOTE

I am indebted to my retellings class, especially Mary Jo White and Crystal Owen, and to my colleagues Annette Oxindine and S. Lynette Jones for their several helpful suggestions when reviewing a draft of this essay.

Teaching *Mrs. Dalloway*(s) and Film

Leslie Kathleen Hankins

Teaching *Mrs. Dalloway* by the light of the cinema opens up rich possibilities for today's visually literate students, offering them innovative techniques for moving between written and visual texts. Whether we design such a course or take one, we learn that breaking through the scholarly divide between film studies and literary studies is rewarding and inspiring. I have taught *Mrs. Dalloway* and film in courses ranging from introductory first-year writing seminars to advanced undergraduate courses on Virginia Woolf. To enable students to develop the skills and knowledge base to approach Woolf and the cinema, these courses have evolved a step-by-step approach that includes attention to literary and cinematic aesthetics, close reading, film history, close viewing, adaptation theory, and creative projects. The course plan has two overlapping approaches: one studies *Mrs. Dalloway* in the context of films and film forums of her day; the other studies the novel in the context of adaptations of our day. By the end of their immersion in *Mrs. Dalloway* and the cinema, students have encountered a range of ways to read Woolf's novel and to consider the relations between film and literature, including adaptation.[1]

The first step is to invite students to engage fully with Woolf's novel as a literary experiment by reading her thoughts and theories about fiction and by doing close readings of short passages from the novel. We read Woolf's essay "Modern Fiction," the entries in her writing notebook that track her plans and discoveries about crafting the novel (Wussow 410–26), and entries about the process from her diaries. Mastery of one paragraph of Woolf's writing, through a close-reading paper, provides hands-on experience of the experimental structure of her writing.

Woolf's "The Cinema"

The next step is to connect Woolf's experimental writing to experimental film of her cultural moment.[2] We begin with her 1926 essay "The Cinema," which addresses both avant-garde cinema and film adaptation. Woolf harshly condemns film adaptations, effuses about film's potential, and finally offers abstract cinema a small role in art. The essay limits film's scope in order to make more room for literature: "all this, which is accessible to words and to words alone, the cinema must avoid" (594). Students recognize how "The Cinema" parallels her literary aesthetics in "Modern Fiction," written and revised from 1919 to 1925, and they discover that "The Cinema" demonstrates how the specter of film both challenges and inspires her.

The class then explores how "The Cinema" relates to actual films and writings about film in the period from 1922 to 1926. International avant-garde film culture was lively in the 1920s; the Film Society, inaugurated in 1925—the same year *Mrs. Dalloway* was published—transformed London's film culture over-night, bringing international film to the forefront of high fashion and highbrow life. To immerse ourselves in this cultural moment, we read essays by literary figures and cinéastes from that time period: an essay by Clive Bell in *Vanity Fair*; articles by Iris Barry, Bonamy Dobrée, Aldous Huxley, and others from the London *Vogue*; writings by Barry from the *Spectator*; and Gilbert Seldes's article in the *New Republic* that responds to Woolf's essay.[3] Because London was aware of Paris as a hotbed of avant-garde film, we also read essays by French film theo-rists, including the prolific theorist and director Germaine Dulac ("Aesthetics"; "Essence"; "Expressive Techniques"), and the painter and director Fernand Léger ("*Mechanical Ballet*"; "New Realism").[4] We also read poems and essays published in the film journal *Close Up* (which began publishing in 1927) and in other period sources by cinéastes such as HD, Bryher ("How"; "Sociologi-cal Film"), and Dorothy Richardson ("So"; "Continuous Performance"). These essays alert the students that Woolf was writing in a context that included other intellectuals and artists engaged with the new art of cinema.

Initiation into Avant-Garde Cinema: Screening Films

Accessible DVD compilations of experimental films initiate students into the compelling and bizarre world of avant-garde film of the 1920s. Because many of the films are brief, classes can experience a wide variety of works even in short class sessions. The following films are essential for understanding the genre:

The Cabinet of Dr. Caligari (about 50 minutes). Robert Wiene's 1919 German expressionist film was cited by Woolf in "The Cinema." Wiene's authoritarian psychologist, a doctor and a symbol of the warmongering state, abuses and manipulates the victim, Francis, and can be related to Woolf's Dr. Bradshaw and Dr. Holmes and their treatment of Septimus Smith in *Mrs. Dalloway*.[5]

Ballet mécanique (11–20 minutes). Léger and Dudley Murphy's highly influen-tial 1924 Cubist film features a technical choreography of modern objects, rhythms, and repetition, forming a new language for cinema. It is suggestive for Septimus's fragmented and intense experience of objects and rhythms.[6]

Entr'acte (about 15 minutes). René Clair's 1923–24 Dada film led Bell to riot at the Film Society. It plays with gender switching, antibourgeois cinematic tricks, and space and time, and it stages a mock suicide as a disappearing act. *Entr'acte*'s compelling challenges to logic, technical playfulness, and bizarre style bring to mind Septimus's hallucinations and quirky logic.[7]

J'accuse (166 minutes). Abel Gance's 1919 film, with its experimental camera work and moving antiwar critique, foregrounds a poet-soldier driven to a profound prophetic insanity by the war. This shell-shocked precursor of

Septimus Warren Smith has visions of the returning dead, and the film presents his poetic visions as visual poetry.[8]

Smiling Madame Beudet (*La souriante Mme Beudet*; 32 minutes). *Mrs. Dalloway*'s cinematic sister, Dulac's 1922 film uses the subjective camera and dazzling cinematic techniques to capture the tormented inner consciousness of a woman hallucinating in her drawing room.[9]

The Seashell and the Clergyman (*La coquille et le clergyman*; 40 minutes). Dulac's 1927 surrealist film with a scenario by Antonin Artaud includes hallucinations, sexual tension, antiauthoritarian rebellion against generals and priests, a deranged man, and cinematic pyrotechnics.

Because *The Cabinet of Dr. Caligari*, *Entr'acte*, and *Ballet mécanique* were discussed widely at the time, I print out facsimile programs for the Film Society performances 4 and 6 and schedule class screenings based on the programs; we screen *Entr'acte* from performance 4 and *The Cabinet of Dr. Caligari* and *Ballet mécanique* from performance 6.[10] We also screen Dulac's films and Gance's *J'accuse*. As the students watch the avant-garde films, they begin to make connections between their cinematic aesthetics and Woolf's literary aesthetics, such as the delight with spatial and temporal play, the break with the tyranny of plot, gender play, the celebration of the link between motion and emotion, and the fascination with rhythm, repetition, and the drama of objects. Students begin to draw links between Woolf and avant-garde directors, finding, for example, that Septimus's visions in the park seem to project avant-garde film clips as he murmurs bits of surreal scenarios and even calls out stage directions to the character, Evans, he conjures forth.[11]

I ask students to write papers responding to films we screen, papers in which they provide detailed close viewings akin to the close readings they did of the *Mrs. Dalloway* passages. They choose two to three minutes of film and analyze the cinematography, mise-en-scène, or editing choices in that fragment of film. To learn the appropriate film vocabulary and conceptual framework, they read relevant chapters in a standard film textbook. The project of film analysis leads us into a discussion of how one would adapt a novel for film. We read theoretical studies about adaptation and ask what is vital to adaptation and whether adaptation criteria for an experimental novel would be different from that for a traditional one.[12] The avant-garde films the students have watched help wean them from the assumption that film adaptations must be plot-driven, and so the discussions raise new questions.

Take 2: Mrs. Dalloway *and Adaptation*

Woolf's scathing indictment of some book-to-film adaptations of her day provides a humbling place to start our discussions of adaptations of *Mrs. Dalloway* in our day. After screening the 1920s films, reading film essays of the period, and writing about the films, students return to *Mrs. Dalloway* and choose a passage (the same one they chose for their close reading, if they wish) and, using Woolf's "The Cinema," brainstorm about how they would film that passage with an awareness of its aesthetics and ideology. We carefully consider the wild and exciting potential Woolf sees in cinema of the future—as well as her warnings about the ways adaptations fail—as we think about how we would craft her novel into a film that would fulfill her celebration of film's potential. We reread her notes about planning *Mrs. Dalloway*, paying close attention to her aesthetic choices and ideological goals. We discuss the challenges of keeping the aesthetics and ideology of *Mrs. Dalloway* in mind while putting our imaginations in play. Students delight in crafting these papers and are eager to share their imaginative visions in presentations to the class. Some write detailed scenarios, craft videos, or compose collages of their ideas. This project unleashes student creativity but contains that creativity in a historically specific frame that helps students probe parallels between experimental literature and film in this moment. The project provides a grounding critical context for the next step of the course, when we view actual adaptations of *Mrs. Dalloway*.

After they craft these often quite dazzling and innovative studies (say, of Septimus's watching a dog turning into a man or Septimus as a drowned sailor on a rock or with red flowers growing through his flesh), we screen film versions of *Mrs. Dalloway*, including a few scenes from the *Modern World: Ten Great Writers* program on Virginia Woolf (Evans)[13] and from the Marleen Gorris version. Because students have thought through the choices they would make to film *Mrs. Dalloway*, they are much more attentive to the choices that directors make. Enthusiastic about and invested in how the films present their chosen scenes, students generate lively discussions. In previous courses, when I had students just read *Mrs. Dalloway* and then view Gorris's film adaptation, they were much more passive in their acceptance of the adaptation. They tended to limit their discussion to plot changes and casting. But when they have seen the quirky and inspiring cinematic experiments of Dulac, Léger and Murphy, Gance, Wiene, Clair, and others, they come to realize that the usual techniques of mainstream film may not be the best choices for adapting experimental modernist fiction. They may be baffled and outraged about omissions of the dazzling hallucinations that are so essential to the novel, for example, and argue that conventional film is inadequate. Those who design innovative cinematic ways to capture the novel's depictions of reverie and hallucination are particularly disappointed by the failure of the films to adapt those passages with comparable levels of imagination.

Next I ask students to capture these insights by writing a research-informed review of Gorris's *Mrs. Dalloway* film based on their close study of "The Cinema" and their own imagined incarnations of the novel. We read the screenplay of *Mrs. Dalloway*, written by Eileen Atkins; Atkins's essay "Adapting *Mrs. Dalloway*," which discusses her decisions about the screenplay; and production releases from First Look Pictures. We explore popular and scholarly reviews of the film, using Web and library sources,[14] as well as interviews with Gorris and materials from the publicity packets from the film's release.

Finally, we screen John Fuegi and Jo Francis's award-winning 1992 documentary film, *The War Within: A Portrait of Virginia Woolf,* and read sections of Woolf's diary written from 1923 to 1925. These works provide a context for reading Michael Cunningham's *The Hours.* We read the novel and discuss and write about the ways Cunningham adapted/transposed/exploited/revived Woolf's life (and her diary) and her novel. We consider the relation between her diaries and his portrayal of her life, between her novel and his novel, and between Gorris's adaptation and Cunningham's. Then we screen the film *The Hours,* by Stephen Daldry. We debate the aesthetics and ideologies in play, asking questions about the relation between reading against the grain and appropriation and adaptation. Consulting the ongoing discussion of the film on the International Virginia Woolf Society e-mail discussion list and the many reviews and studies, our discussions range from Academy Awards to the fate of obscure films in archive vaults. By now, the class is quite aware of how our accumulated knowledge of *Mrs. Dalloway* and film enriches our critique.

This brief overview of a course projects only one possible montage of *Mrs. Dalloway* and film; the outtakes could fill many more courses.[15] Leaping from 1919 to 2009 and beyond, the course explores film history and aesthetics, adaptation and Woolf's novel. Bringing *Mrs. Dalloway* and films together in multimedia montages allows powerful new readings to emerge. Like Nancy Blow and Lord Gayton, the young aristocratic couple at Clarissa's party who talk about "cricket, cousins, the movies" (173), students who take such a course are able to move from Clarissa's party to the movies—and back—with ease. At the end of the course, they reread *Mrs. Dalloway,* but this time with the awareness that Clarissa's party was not the only chic gathering in London in 1925. They can envision a reader's purchasing a copy of *Mrs. Dalloway* at, say, Hatchards Bookshop and carrying the novel to the New Gallery Theatre on Regent's Street to watch the premier program of the Film Society—and they can imagine how that screening might shape the reading of the novel. And students have learned how to approach current film adaptations of novels by drawing on film history and theory and their own hypothetical creative adaptations.

NOTES

[1] As I developed the project of teaching *Mrs. Dalloway* by the light of the cinema, I presented my work on films and Bloomsbury figures each year at the Annual Virginia Woolf Conference and the Modernist Studies Association Conference, along with other scholars working in this new area. See Hotchkiss; Hankins, "Across," "*Cinéastes,*" "Colour," "Iris Barry," "Switching," "Tracking," "Abel Gance's *J'accuse,*" and "Complicating." The conference programs of the Woolf conferences and Modernist Studies Association conferences (available on the *International Virginia Woolf Society* Web site and the

Modernist Studies Association Web site, respectively) as well as the *Annual Woolf Studies Bibliography* compiled by the International Virginia Woolf Society are the best sources for locating original scholarship on cinema and modernism. In addition, several books have come out recently on the topic of cinema and modernism. See Trotter; L. Marcus, *Tenth Muse*; and Humm, *Modernist Women*.

[2] See my "Across" and "Virginia Woolf and Film" for studies of the cultural context for the essay and my "Virginia Woolf's 'The Cinema'" for a study of the archival drafts of that essay.

[3] Bonnie Kime Scott's anthology *Gender in Modernism* includes many of these film writings by Barry ("Cinema"; "Scope"), Woolf ("The Cinema"), Seldes, HD ("Projector I"), Bryher ("Sociological Film"), Richardson ("So"), and others. Donald, Friedberg, and Marcus's anthology *Close Up* reprints essays by HD ("Cinema"), Richardson, Bryher, and others from the late 1920s. The complete ten volumes of *Close Up* are available from Arno Press.

[4] Richard Abel's anthology contains valuable essays by Dulac ("Aesthetics"; "Expressive Techniques"), Léger ("Painting"; "*La Roue*"), Cendrars, Landry, and others.

[5] See essays about *The Cabinet of Dr. Caligari* by Landry; Cendrars; and C. Bell ("Art and the Cinema"); for more on the film, see Robinson; Budd; for connections between the film and Woolf, see my "Doctor."

[6] On *Ballet mécanique*, see Lawder; Turvey; and Freeman.

[7] On *Entr'acte*, see White; Latimer. See my "Across" and "Switching" for a discussion of Woolf and *Entr'acte*.

[8] At the 2008 Annual Virginia Woolf Conference in Denver, screening parts of Abel Gance's powerful 1919 antiwar poetic film, *J'accuse*, allowed participants to witness parallels between the poet-victims in *J'accuse* and in *Mrs. Dalloway*, the avant-garde visual poetry in both works, and their fierce antiwar ideologies. This film has been restored and was released on DVD by Flicker Alley in September 2008, with a booklet containing a brief article I wrote ("Abel Gance's *J'accuse*").

[9] See Flitterman-Lewis on Dulac. She connects Dulac and Woolf (325–29).

[10] Additional films may be drawn from records of the Film Society screenings: Walter Ruttmann's *Absolute Films*, Paul Leni's *Waxworks*, and many more. Amberg's *Film Society Programmes* is an invaluable guide. Though some of the films are lost or difficult to locate, reading the programs allows students to envision the context.

[11] See Desnos; Goudal. Also, see C. Bell ("Cinema Aesthetics") for a discussion of surrealist film.

[12] See Andrew; Bluestone; Corrigan; Stam; Tibbetts.

[13] See Gillespie, who first introduced scholars to this idea.

[14] See, for starters, Cuddy-Keane, "*Mrs. Dalloway*"; Groen; H. Harper.

[15] World War I films can also be rich sources of insight for teaching *Mrs. Dalloway*. See L. Marcus, "Great War." At the 2007 Annual Virginia Woolf Conference at Miami University, I screened King Vidor's 1925 *The Big Parade* and gave a paper about the antiwar lesson plans a reader of *Mrs. Dalloway* and watcher of *The Big Parade* would find in those works.

Mrs. *Dalloway* and the Ideology of Death: A Cultural Studies Approach

Madelyn Detloff

In *A Room of One's Own*, Virginia Woolf suggests that "fiction is like a spider's web, attached ever so lightly perhaps, but still attached to life at all four corners" (41). It is appropriate to begin a discussion of teaching *Mrs. Dalloway* with Woolf's analogy because it acknowledges the material scaffolding of any cultural production without dismissing the work's intricacy—its deliberate and deliberately beautiful construction as an aesthetic object. Precisely because *Mrs. Dalloway* is a text of perambulations—a collection of characters who walk the streets and pathways of London without knowing how intricately their lives are connected with other lives—it lends itself to mapping not just the perambulations of characters in the text but also the migration of discourses (about pleasure, death, and social duty, for example) between and among other cultural texts and contexts. These weavings are important to understand not simply because we can locate them but also because they partake in the process of "articulation"—responding to and reshaping the cultural forces that influence our everyday lives and possibilities (Felski).[1]

Mrs. Dalloway is a promising text for demonstrating how articulation works, especially because threads of the narrative have been taken up by contemporary filmmakers and novelists in such provocative ways (e.g., Morrison, *Sula*; Gorris, *Mrs. Dalloway*; Lippincott). Reading the novel together with Hanif Kureishi's film *Sammy and Rosie Get Laid* and David Hare's film adaptation of Michael Cunningham's novel *The Hours*, for example, can help students better understand the cultural stakes of each representation and how these stakes change when the temporalities of representation—time of action, time of composition, time of reception—shift. In addition to introducing students to cultural studies of gender, sexuality, class, and imperialism, this approach encourages them to read intertextuality as more than a literary device and to understand the complexities and consequences of what Brenda Silver calls "versioning"—the telling and retelling of variants of a story (*Virginia Woolf: Icon* 13).

To take up Woolf's spiderweb metaphor once more:

> [O]ne remembers that these webs are not spun in mid-air by incorporeal creatures, but are the work of suffering human beings, and are attached to grossly material things, like health and money and the houses we live in.
>
> (*Room* 42)

Woolf's metaphor about fiction certainly applies to teaching as well. Demographics matter, but not always in the ways that we think they do. I have taught Woolf in a wide variety of courses (from general education surveys to graduate seminars) in very different universities. Before coming to Miami University (a medium-sized, state-supported, liberal arts university with a student body that is overwhelmingly white and upper-middle-class), I taught *Mrs. Dalloway* regularly at an underfunded, urban, state university with a student population that was largely made up of multilingual, working-class students of color, often the first in their families to attend college. From the outside, one might imagine that the students at the urban university would have more trouble engaging with the work of a British high modernist than students from the dominant class and culture in the Midwest. This was not the case. London of 1925 is as far away from Southwest Ohio as it is from East Los Angeles. To make assumptions about what students will or will not bring to a reading of a text invariably gets in the way of actually listening to what they can and will contribute to the classroom discussion—if they are given space to do so in a setting that is free from what Paulo Freire calls "narration sickness."[2]

That said, one of the demographic realities of working at a state university is that classes tend to be larger than would be ideal for an engaged discussion. The temptation in these classes is to fall into the talk-show-host trap: the teacher-host discourses for a while on the topic of the day, then fields questions from the gallery until the hour is up. Students rarely get to engage one another directly in conversation. From a cultural studies standpoint, facilitating direct engagement with others is necessary, for not only is culture ordinary, to paraphrase Raymond Williams, but it is also "made and remade in every individual mind" in a dual process of recognition and refinement. "A culture," for Williams, "has two aspects: the known meanings and directions, which its members are trained to; the new observations and meanings, which are offered and tested" (6). To practice cultural studies as pedagogy, the instructor must balance the students' need for scaffolding—"the known meanings and directions"—with their need for enough autonomy to begin formulating and testing "new observations and meanings." One technique I have developed to help cultivate this balance is a scaffolding-and-space approach. It entails presenting a minilecture on the first day of teaching a novel and devoting the next class meeting to structured small-group discussions of student questions, which I have collected by e-mail the night before the class.

To illustrate how this works, I will sketch out what might happen in a modern British fiction course that meets twice a week. We will just have finished discussing Rebecca West's *Return of the Soldier* after covering James Joyce's *The Dead* the week before. We will therefore have discussed issues such as intimacy and secrets in convention-bound marriages; cultural imperialism and hospitality in colonized space; psychological concepts such as the uncanny, mourning, and melancholia in connection to scenes of being haunted by ghosts from the past; the violence of the Great War; and the emergence of shell shock as a culturally intelligible way to understand the effects of trauma. On the first day of teaching *Mrs. Dalloway*, I present a minilecture on frameworks for understanding the novel. Bonnie Kime Scott has provided a wonderful contextualization of the novel in her introduction to the Harcourt annotated edition, and so in lieu of providing a general background to the text, I might begin by asking students to comment on one of the connections they found most compelling in Scott's introduction.

I then talk more specifically about Woolf's mental illness, discussing the cultural baggage that often attaches to depictions of madness—ideas about gender, creativity, guilt, shame, social protest, traumatic victimization, normality, control. I introduce Susan Sontag's analysis of "illness as metaphor" (a critique that will resurface when we consider the representation of illness in *The Hours*) and then ask students to contemplate how the idea of mental illness might operate as a metaphor in cultural productions (*"Illness"* 3–11). I ask them to compare the mechanical function of Chris Baldry's shell shock in *Return of the Soldier* with Septimus Smith's struggle with the same disorder in *Mrs. Dalloway*. Because Septimus is a complex character, whereas Chris is relatively flat, we are better able to see in Septimus how normative forces such as the school, the military, the family, the office, and the medical establishment make Septimus into a "good subject" and then destroy him when he no longer fits their definitions of "normal."

At this point I introduce a passage from Herbert Marcuse's essay "The Ideology of Death." Marcuse describes the state's usurpation of the power over life and death and argues that "[m]an is not free as long as death has not become really 'his own,' that is, as long as it had not been brought under his autonomy" (74). Has Septimus made his life "his own" through his suicide? How does this choice connect to Clarissa's decision to live at the end of the novel? This issue comes up again when we discuss Woolf's suicide (the biographical fact as well as the representation of it in *The Hours*), the suicide of Rafi in *Sammy and Rosie Get Laid*, and the suicide of Richard Brown in *The Hours*. The point is not to get into a debate ("Suicide: For or Against?") but to give students the language to be able to discuss the political and cultural meanings attached to taking one's life in each of these situations.

On the second day of teaching the novel, I come to class with the students' questions compiled and grouped into thematic clusters that tend to emerge organically. I ask students to freewrite for five to ten minutes in response to a question they find especially compelling (usually their own) and to pick one passage from the text that they can analyze in their response. They then break into groups according to theme. Each group is charged with coming to some consensus based on their discussion of their questions and with sketching out a provisional thesis statement that a group spokesperson will articulate to the whole class when we reconvene after thirty minutes.

This format becomes especially helpful when we examine the effects of versioning in the films *Sammy and Rosie Get Laid* and *The Hours*. I begin by suggesting that Kureishi invites us to read his London against the London of *Mrs. Dalloway*. In *Mrs. Dalloway*, Peter Walsh returns from India to find a sense of home in his shared nostalgia with Clarissa. In *Sammy and Rosie Get Laid*, Rafi receives no such welcome on his return from South Asia. This permutation may inspire us to take a second look at the racial homogeneity of the London that Woolf depicts. In class discussion we compare the upper-crust friends of the Dalloways with the heterogeneous mix of people invited to Sammy and Rosie's party. The new eclectic community of Kureishi's London must confront the untenable violence of Rafi's position, because his suicide takes place in the home rather than safely on the other side of town. We may read this difference temporally—look how much London has changed in sixty years!—but to do so exclusively is to turn a blind eye to the colonial violence (e.g., the Amritsar Massacre of 1919) that undergirds the Dalloways' way of life (Phillips, *Virginia Woolf* 10).[3]

Cunningham and Hare's film *The Hours* presents a much more overt version of the *Mrs. Dalloway* story. It is illuminating to analyze the effects of exchanging the role of the shell-shocked soldier with that of a gay man dying from AIDS. Noting the parallel, students might point out that both Septimus and Richard Brown struggle in cultures that display willful ignorance about the continued suffering of World War I combatants and persons with AIDS, respectively. Lady Bruton's callous scheme to encourage young men like Septimus, "the super-fluous youth of our ever-increasing population," to emigrate to Canada is one symptom of a larger wish to banish the effects of war from public consciousness in post–World War I Britain (107).

Because the portion of *The Hours* set in the twenty-first century is in many ways remarkably faithful to the *Mrs. Dalloway* story, it is helpful to discuss where the parallels break down and the version takes on a different cultural resonance. Woolf's overt critique of death-producing sites of cultural power (the medical and psychiatric institutions, the parliament, the peerage, the military) is absent from the film. Nor is Richard's social standing symmetrical with Septimus's. If we buy Marcuse's argument, we can suggest that the British society of *Mrs. Dalloway*, in order to maintain its fantasy of a just and useful war, requires Sep-timus to live, and so Woolf has him choose to die as a means of protest. On the other hand, in its cultural context of the twenty-first century, *The Hours* seems to collude with lethal public fantasies of a postgay and post-AIDS world, sup-ported on the phobic side by a distorted view of AIDS as the manifestation of a gay male death wish, but also in a more complicated way by gay intellectuals such as Andrew Sullivan, who sees protease inhibitors as ushering in the "end" of the "plague" (3–10). This fantasy is, as Douglas Crimp (9–11) and Philip Brian Harper (93–94) argue, disturbingly ethnocentric and unconscious of the inequities of class, race, and nation that limit the benefits of life-prolonging drugs to those who are privileged enough to have access to them.

The Hours, through its depiction of Richard as someone whom the liberal les-bian character must let die so that she can live her own life, participates in the fantasy that AIDS is a thing of the past. The implicit message of the film, if read from within its cultural moment, is that we should "fear no more" the indignity of the diseased body, which Richard has wiped out with his sacrifice (*Mrs. Dal-*

loway 9). A cultural studies approach helps us trace the ideological formations that make such sacrifices seem necessary, even beautiful. Fortunately, as we are participants and not just observers of the process of articulation, our responses to such messages have a part to play in shaping the culture we inhabit. My goal as a teacher is to show students just how important that part is.

NOTES

Many thanks to my students, who have taught me much over the years; to my colleague Mary Jean Corbett and her students, who allowed me to infiltrate their course for a day on *The Hours*; and to Robyn Wiegman, for her suggestions on a draft of this essay.

[1] As Rita Felski explains, "At the heart of cultural studies lies the idea of articulation, best described as a theory of social correspondences, non-correspondences, and contradictions or alternatively as a theory of how contexts are made, unmade, and remade" (510–11).

[2] Freire uses the phrase "narration sickness" to describe a one-way dynamic between teacher and student, where the teacher has all the knowledge and fills the passive, inert students with the "contents of his narration" (52).

[3] For a discussion of the colonial violence taking place in the background of *Mrs. Dalloway*, see Phillips, "Devouring."

Wading into the Narrative Stream: Techniques for Two-Year College Readers

Karen McLeer

The first time I taught *Mrs. Dalloway* was a disaster. After assigning about one-fourth of the novel as homework, I began the next class session with a lecture on modernism, Freud, and stream-of-consciousness narration. At the end, a student remarked, "I'm in the stream all right—way over my head!" That launched a string of other complaints: "This book is confusing." "I gave up after ten pages." "I don't know what is going on!" In my desire to have them dive into Woolf's novel, to experience the sights and sounds and smells of postwar London and the musings of her fascinating characters, I had missed an important preparation step. By shoving them into this novel without any prereading activities, I was telling them to wade into a stream in their jeans and sneakers and then wondering why they complained of getting wet. If I wanted them to enjoy the experience of standing in the narrative stream, I had to give them hip waders.

I teach *Mrs. Dalloway* to nonmajors as part of the course Women in Literature at a two-year liberal arts college in the Midwest. Some of my students love to read, others recoil at the sight of a book, and only the occasional prospective English major has prior knowledge of Virginia Woolf. Even among my most eager readers, none has encountered anything like the narrative style presented in this novel. Therefore my quest to improve my teaching of *Mrs. Dalloway* began by putting myself in their shoes. How did this novel look to them? Foreign. Intimidating. What analogous experience would help them understand Woolf's narrative philosophy? A writing assignment, in a familiar setting using their own thoughts to mimic Woolf's style. How might I get them reading and thinking analytically in two weeks, with only five hours of class time for discussion? Prereading activities and directed note taking would be essential. I had found my hip waders.

In the session before I assign any reading, I conduct an in-class exercise on the narrative stream. I tell students to take out their journals and prepare to write for eight minutes. "Any questions?" I ask. One of the outspoken class leaders will ask, "What are we supposed to write about?" "Write about whatever is in your head," I respond, "and simply be aware of your environment." They are no less perplexed, but since I am looking at the clock and pointing at their pens, they begin to write. After two to three minutes, I drop a book on the floor. Everyone pauses, looks up, and then resumes writing. After another couple of minutes, I turn off the lights. They continue writing in the dark, and then I turn the lights back on. The distractions vary from semester to semester. My intent is to illustrate how a story line, in a narrative of their own creation, can move between interior thoughts and exterior events.

At the end of the writing task, I ask a student to read her narrative aloud. When she mentions the book dropping, I stop her and ask a second reader to begin reading his narrative from the point where the book dropped. The student starts with a similar sentence about dropping books and continues. When he arrives at the lights-out moment, I ask for another student to pick up the thread. This communal narrative prepares students to read carefully for the shared exterior events Woolf uses to mark a shift in narrative perspective. Look for the common sights and sounds, I tell them, and then you will know that you are leaving one character's interior thoughts and entering another's.

I share this excerpt from Woolf's essay "Modern Fiction":

> Examine for a moment an ordinary mind on an ordinary day. The mind receives a myriad impressions—trivial, fantastic, evanescent, or engraved with the sharpness of steel. From all sides they come, an incessant shower of innumerable atoms, and as they fall . . . they shape themselves into the life of Monday or Tuesday. . . . Let us [modern novelists] record the atoms as they fall upon the mind in the order in which they fall, let us trace the pattern, however disconnected and incoherent in appearance, which each sight or incident scores upon the consciousness.   (149–50)

I ask my students to pull apart this quotation and restate Woolf's ideas in their own words. "How do our minds work?" I ask. "What are you thinking about right now?" Through a close analysis of the passage, students make connections between our activity and Woolf's description of how our minds work. Once it is established how Woolf distinguishes between external events and internal thoughts, I shift to a discussion of Woolf's representation of those interior thoughts with a focus on memory. I ask students to think about what triggers memory. They can easily come up with smells, sounds, people, and places. Reminding them again of the narrative-stream writing exercise, I emphasize that memory triggers can also be used to show shifts between the present moment and past experiences of a character. The smell of a flower, a particular song, the dropping of a book are all atoms of life that can be put together, not in the order in which they occurred but in the order in which a character recalls or experiences them. Woolf shows us that these memories and present moments intertwine to become a narrative—a day in the life of Clarissa Dalloway.

My goal for the prereading exercise is to dispel the initial frustrations that arise when students encounter a narrative style that is different from what they are used to. In our first class discussion after they read the novel, they are ready to talk about the motorcar on Bond Street, the skywriting airplane, and the tolling of the bells. I have found that this prereading technique helps the class move into analytic discussions. Instead of going over who said what and when, we can delve into questions like, Who was the person in the car?, What was the message the plane was trying to write?, and, of course, my favorite, Why does Woolf leave those questions unanswered? Prereading exercises alone cannot guarantee high-quality analytic discussions, but I have found them effective when combined with directed note taking.

I assign daily writing of one to two pages. I always give students a note-taking activity or an interpretive prompt so that we have a strong starting point for class discussion. My writing assignments for *Mrs. Dalloway* emphasize narrative, which helps their comprehension and ties in nicely with our prereading exercise. I have used the following note-taking activity with success:

> Read carefully to explore Woolf's use of clocks and time. Using a two-column format, begin on the left and make a list of every reference to the time of day or the striking of clocks in today's reading. In the right-hand column, note the tone of the passage, the characters in the scene, and the function of the reference (for example, a transition, establishment of setting, reflection of plot or character).

With this activity, I want them to read actively (with pen and paper ready) and also purposefully. Their search for the clock and time references allows them to seek out specific narrative signposts. When they find them, they can pause and briefly reflect on their meaning. A typical student notes page includes the conversation between Rezia and Septimus in the park as she asks him the time: "'I will tell you the time,' said Septimus. . . . As he sat smiling at the dead man in the grey suit the quarter struck—the quarter to twelve" (69). In their individual reading, students easily recognize this passage as a transition from the consciousness of one character to another as Peter walks past Septimus, both hear the clock, and the narrative then follows Peter as he walks and thinks about Clarissa. Had a student not been actively looking for the clock striking, the shift in narrator might have been missed.

Another student notes page focuses on the description that announces half past one (the time of Lady Bruton's lunch): "Shredding and slicing, dividing and subdividing, the clocks of Harley Street nibbled at the June day" (100). The language in this passage alludes to commerce, society, and the fraternal community, which transitions to Hugh and anticipates his and Richard's competitive lunch. Class discussion that begins with an analysis of Woolf's language in this passage can quickly move to Clarissa's jealousy of Lady Bruton and Richard's struggle to tell Clarissa he loves her. Focused reading outside class allows students to begin the close reading on their own. They engage in the narrative instead of simply letting the words wash over them, devoid of meaning. I have used note taking that focuses on flowers, vehicles, and streets. All these writing assignments help students navigate through the story and orient themselves to the characters and their experiences.

I also challenge my students with interpretive prompts. The questions, interpretive or analytic, require them to use textual examples to support their responses. Some of my favorites are, What is significant about Mrs. Peters's hat? Why does Miss Kilman believe she has "a perfect right to anything that the Dalloways did for her" (121)? What does she want from Elizabeth? Do you think Clarissa's party is a success? Why or why not? Students respond to the prompts as homework, and I use their responses to open class discussion. They gain confidence in their ability to read analytically because they are prepared to debate significant interpretive questions, and they use the text to defend and explain the subtleties of Woolf's narrative.

Through examination of the narrative, we continue to explore Woolf's reflection of our interior and exterior experiences. Another directed note-taking assignment asks students to examine conversations between characters, recording only what is said out loud and omitting the memories that interrupt the dialogue. This assignment works especially well for Clarissa and Peter. My students' previous reading experiences dictate that Clarissa and Peter should connect, and yet the note taking reveals that these characters cannot really talk to each other. Their interior thoughts are blocking and clouding their external speech when they are together. "Do you remember a time," I ask my students, "when you were so focused on memories that you were unable to concentrate on the moment before you?" Many can recognize Clarissa and Peter's reunion as a profoundly emotional experience, and they begin to empathize with the characters' verbal paralysis. Reading for the present dialogue and separating it from the memories of the characters' pasts help students sort out Peter and Clarissa's history and relationship—a task that would be difficult without the directed note taking.

Teaching *Mrs. Dalloway* is a joyous challenge. While I guide my students as much as I can in their individual reading, I tend to let class discussions move in many directions at once. I am continually delighted by my students' discoveries, and I see something new in this novel each time I teach it. On our final discussion day, when we begin to ask the question "What does this novel mean?," I like to share this quotation with my class: "Life is a luminous halo, a semi-transparent envelope surrounding us from the beginning of consciousness to the end"

("Modern Fiction" 150). Woolf's observation about life—and fiction—reminds us that narrative can be a swirling, eddying movement of past and present, interior and exterior, private and universal experiences. My task is to help my students experience and appreciate *Mrs. Dalloway* as fully as possible, but now I give them prereading exercises and specific writing activities—hip waders—before they plunge into its narrative stream.

Drawing *Mrs. Dalloway* in a Literary Masterworks Course

Ruth Hoberman

Literary Masterworks, a general education course, is filled with students who are not English majors and who tend to bring little enthusiasm for literature to the class. As a result, my main concern in teaching the class is to give students a reason to care about what they read. The course's title is useful here: if a book is famous, students think, those difficult sentences must be worth untangling. But I also want students to see that the difficulty is itself part of what the books are about. Each writer asks us to see the world through a different lens, one formed by unique syntactic, structural, and thematic choices. By learning to see through those lenses, students complicate and deepen their understanding of themselves and their relation to others.

My aim in teaching *Mrs. Dalloway*, then, is to leave students with a sense of why Woolf had to tell the story as she did. I want them to see that she forces us to read in a particular way: tentatively, tactfully, with a pervasive sense of our interpretive uncertainties. I want them to see that reading *Mrs. Dalloway* offers not just an intellectual challenge but also an ethical one: it asks us to recognize the complex interiority of other people and the web of relationships that links us to them and to our environment. I find drawing a useful way of getting students who are insecure about their interpretive abilities to participate in this challenge.

First we agree on some general guidelines for interpreting the novel. I begin by dividing the novel into surface plot, psychological plot, and metaphysical plot. By surface plot I mean the physical actions that happen during the course of the day (Fleishman [*Virginia Woolf*] provides a useful timetable, which I sometimes distribute to the class). I take notes on the board as students contribute actions they have noticed: Clarissa goes to buy flowers; she runs into Hugh Whitbread; an airplane skywrites.

Then we look at hinges: places where the surface plot flips the novel's focus into the past or into the mind of other characters. The first such hinge is literal, as the door opens "with a little squeak of the hinges" (3), and we move from the lovely June day in London to one at Bourton many years earlier. Since this shift exemplifies Woolf's "tunnelling process" (*Diary* 2: 272), I hand out excerpts from her "Modern Fiction" on perception and from her diary on the "beautiful caves" she digs behind her characters (*Diary* 2: 263), and we collectively sort out London from Bourton, talking about why these past events might still haunt Clarissa. This focus on individual characters' memories and concerns—Septimus's guilt and visions, as well as Clarissa's thoughts of Bourton—is what I call the novel's psychological plot.

One focus of this psychological plot is Clarissa's choice of Richard Dalloway over Peter Walsh. There is always a lively discussion when I ask whether she made the right choice. When someone suggests that the right choice might have been Sally, I hand out excerpts from Adrienne Rich's "Compulsory Heterosexuality and Lesbian Existence." As for the two men, I point out the implied contrast between Richard's considerate detachment and Peter's intrusive sexuality, as exemplified by his following a woman in the street as well as by his pocket-knife and his romantic entanglements.

The hinges connect people in space as well as in time. The prime minister's car, for example, interlaces Clarissa, Miss Pym, Edgar J. Watkiss, Septimus, and Lucrezia, as well as miscellaneous strangers in shops and clubs and pubs (16–18), much as the skywriting links Mrs. Coates, Mrs. Bletchley, Mr. Bowley, the Smiths, Mrs. Dempster, Mr. Bentley, and Clarissa (19–28). As we follow these shifts, we talk about the textual clues that let us know we are entering another character's viewpoint. These clues are often subtle, as when the collective comments of the "poor people" at Buckingham Palace merge seamlessly into the thoughts of Sarah Bletchley (18–29). Students often ask at this point why Woolf chose to write in so confusing a way. I suggest that this insistence on the interiority of multiple characters—including those who never turn up in the novel again—is a crucial aspect of her writing. Throughout her work, Woolf connects the relatively crude character drawing of Victorians and Edwardians to their overly external view of the world. In her *Diary*, she writes that war would be impossible if we had access to the inner lives of those we sought to kill (1: 182). Male modernists' work, she complains in *A Room of One's Own*, is too ego-bound, with its phallic "straight dark bar," that authorial "I" overshadowing its pages (103).

This interconnectedness of characters' consciousnesses is also one aspect of what I call the novel's metaphysical plot: its dramatization of the "meaning of life," as Woolf calls it in *To the Lighthouse* ([1981] 161), and the nature of selfhood. Her sentence structure, narrative method, use of recurring motifs ("Fear no more the heat o' the sun," for example [see 9, 29, 39, 136, 182]), and imagery (particularly water and wave) evoke the building up of disparate materials into tentative, temporary interrelatedness; the interconnectedness of multiple consciousnesses; and a porous, labile sense of self. In addition, characters occasionally articulate these notions explicitly, as when Clarissa thinks about her parties, which bring people together, or when Peter remembers Clarissa's "transcendental theory" that

> since our apparitions, the part of us which appears, are so momentary compared with the other, the unseen part of us, which spreads wide, the unseen might survive, be recovered somehow attached to this person or that, or even haunting certain places after death . . . perhaps—perhaps. (149)

At this point the students understand the reading process well enough to make their own decisions about key moments in the novel. I ask them to bring to the next class session diagrams of such moments: they are to draw what is happening both on the surface and psychologically on a particular page or two of the novel, supplying speech bubbles to show conversation and thought bubbles to show thoughts. They may have to draw whole scenes within those thought bubbles, as characters remember earlier interactions. Reassuring them that no particular drawing ability is required, I demonstrate on the board with my own awkward stick figures.

Although such an exercise may seem to flatten out the novel's interiority by making it visible, its effect is just the opposite. As students make their drawings, they must distinguish between surface and psychological plots, paying close attention to subtle clues about whether a scene is enacted or remembered or imagined. They must think carefully about time and space, noticing simultaneities and juxtapositions that may relate to the metaphysical issues raised by the novel. What might otherwise seem an impenetrable blur gets sorted out into disparate impressions that are, in turn, assembled into a single picture. Drawing in this sense, then, is just a careful kind of reading, but one particularly appropriate to a writer who was herself—through both her sister and her friends—immersed in the visual arts.

The next class session is spent looking at the pictures. As students explain what they drew and why, important themes emerge. For example, one student's picture depicted Clarissa as she looks in the window of Hatchards' bookstore. In a thought bubble (connected to a character's head by a dotted line, as in comic books) were the words, "somehow in the streets of London, on the ebb and flow of things, here, there, she survived, Peter survived, lived in each other, she being part, she was positive, of the trees at home. . . ." A speech bubble (connected by a solid line) emerged from one of the books on display—"Fear no more the heat o' the sun"—and above it was a second thought bubble extending from the first, in which appeared Lady Bexborough (9). The thought bubble contained, of course, Clarissa's "transcendental theory," and the speech bubble allowed us to talk about the recurring line from *Cymbeline*, the novel's obsession with death and World War I, and its depiction of shopping and urban life as sources of both connectedness and separation. Another drawing depicted Septimus, Lucrezia, and Peter in Regent's Park. In Septimus's first thought bubble, Septimus was pictured drowned, under the sea; in his second, Evans stood behind a tree. In between, Lucrezia's speech bubble read, "It is time." On the far right, Peter Walsh looked on, thinking, "And that is being young" (67–69). The drawing led to a discussion of Septimus's sacrificial role in the novel, speculation about his relationship to Evans, and the contrast between clock time and experienced time in the novel (I mentioned Henri Bergson's concept of *durée* at this point [see Gillies 109]). It also dramatized the different wavelengths on which these three characters are operating, even as they are momentarily interrelated.

The drawings thus allow students to articulate aspects of the novel they might not otherwise notice and to explore the novel's themes and characters while experiencing at a visceral level the complex perceptions and emotional lives

Woolf grants her characters. Oversimplified ways of perceiving others, the over-valuation of deed over thought, and the overestimation of one's autonomy and importance were to blame, according to her, for militarism, imperialism, and patriarchy. The drawing of scenes from *Mrs. Dalloway* forces students to avoid these mistakes as they recognize the complexity, interiority, and porousness of the characters they draw. When we are faced with a few moments when the text is undrawable, we talk about the complexity of Woolf's language and narrative method, her resistance to traditional realism, and her insistence that her readers recognize the instability underlying both language and identity.

As we approach the final class session on the novel, I ask students to do something even stranger: to draw their own selves in relation to the world. Although I give them five minutes at most and refuse to elaborate on this vague instruction, they inevitably produce useful images that open up discussion of Woolf's—and their own—vision of the self. Some depict a clearly delineated self facing off against a landscape of people; others place themselves on a map or amid a crowd, their selves designated by an arrow. No matter what, the drawings tend to suggest an autonomous, bounded, and unique self. At this point I may hand out the passage from "A Sketch of the Past" in which Woolf talks about her theory that "behind the cotton wool is hidden a pattern" to which we are all connected (72). We collectively construct a new drawing, based on Woolf's notion of the self as expressed in this passage and, implicitly, in *Mrs. Dalloway*. Such a drawing might consist of dotted lines with multiple points of attachment to the external world.

I then ask students to categorize the novel's characters in terms of their relationships with others. I put a line on the board, one end labeled "most intrusive" and the other "least intrusive." I ask them to think about which characters seem to thrust themselves into the private space of others and which characters concentrate on providing themselves with privacy and protection from this kind of penetration. It does not take long to get Dr. Holmes and Dr. Bradshaw at one extreme of the spectrum and Clarissa at the other. That Peter Walsh and Miss Kilman generally turn up toward the more-intrusive end leads to a discussion of Woolf's linking of love, proportion, and conversion as threats to the autonomy of the soul, an autonomy exemplified by the woman in the room opposite Clarissa's window. That Septimus generally turns up next to Clarissa among the least intrusive prompts a discussion of the many ways in which they are linked.

This exercise also points to the different layers of the self. Both Clarissa and Peter seem to have access to a surface self that coheres and "kindles" and a deeper self that dives and dissolves. "For this is the truth about our soul," Peter thinks on his way to Clarissa's party:

> our self, who fish-like inhabits deep seas and plies among obscurities threading her way between the boles of giant weeds, over sun-flickered spaces and on and on into gloom, cold, deep, inscrutable; suddenly she

shoots to the surface and sports on the wind-wrinkled waves; that is, has a
positive need to brush, scrape, kindle herself, gossiping.   (157)

The passage suggests why the novel as a whole is saturated with water and wave
imagery. It suggests why the conscious pulling together of the self (e.g., Clarissa's
composing herself before the mirror earlier in the novel [36]) and the cultiva-
tion of social contacts (as exemplified by her party) are so important. While sub-
mersion in those deep seas allows the soul to merge with its surroundings, it also
threatens dissolution and death. "Kindling"—a word also used to describe Richard's effect on Clarissa—offers the opposite: a social interaction that involves
individuation, artifice, and life. Each of these sides to the self has its drawbacks,
of course, and the novel, far from endorsing one or the other, seems to enact a
flipping back and forth between them.

Finally, I hope students come away feeling that they have internalized a new
way of reading both book and world, a way that asks them to tunnel, along with
Woolf, into the often conflicting perceptions of others—perceptions that are
themselves a complex conglomeration of memory, abstract thought, and sensory
experience. Asking students to draw thought and speech bubbles for characters is one way of deepening their understanding of how the novel's narrative
method creates, on many different levels, what one student called a "web of
community."

"They Have Loved Reading":
Mrs. *Dalloway* and Lifelong Common Readers

Beth Rigel Daugherty

I teach at Otterbein College, a small, comprehensive liberal arts college in Ohio, where my specialty is twentieth-century English literature, particularly Virginia Woolf. But much of my annual teaching in our quarter system, five courses out of seven, is in Integrative Studies, our general education liberal arts core. Integrative Studies courses are not distribution requirements or discipline introductions but are created to view human nature through various disciplinary lenses. Those faculty members charged with helping all students master academic writing skills must also help them discern what literature says about humanity's age-old issues.

I used Woolf's novel in the sophomore-level Integrative Studies composition and literature course, Relationships and Dialogues, a course I revised and tested for a Scholarship of Teaching and Learning project. I had become uneasy about the disconnect between what I believed and how I was teaching. My real goal in Integrative Studies courses was to develop lifelong readers, but student assessments told me that many students were either not doing the reading or not enjoying it. Was I encouraging lifelong *non*readers?

Woolf's essay "How Should One Read a Book?" nagged at me. If the developmental process she outlines there fits most readers—gluttonous reading, comparing books, seeing patterns, and then analyzing and asking questions that lead to criticism and theory—my assumption that nonmajors (and nonreaders) could analyze literature from the moment they stepped into an Integrative Studies course was not only erroneous but also counterproductive. How could my students take the fourth step, analysis, if they had never taken the first, gluttony?

These questions ultimately fueled my project: What could Woolf teach my students about reading? How could I help students, many of whom do not love to read, get involved in reading? How could I replicate, in a classroom, in ten weeks, what Woolf suggests and what my own experience and observation confirm about developing a love of reading?

To construct and teach a course focused on the development of lifelong common readers, I foregrounded reading in course goals, discussion, and assessment; structured the course around a book club format; and put Woolf and her ideas about reading front and center. In that context, *Mrs. Dalloway* became a test case and a touchstone.

Encouraging lifelong reading meant nurturing a lively, student-centered, risk-taking classroom for them and me. Building the course around two main reading goals—read lots of books and have good conversations about them[1]—I shared with students my research into college reading. Reading itself was the subject of surveys, discussion (both in-class and online), and focus groups. Students' final writing assignment was an autobiographical essay about their reading lives, and their last assessment prompt was, Has your attitude toward reading changed in this class? If so, from what to what? How? Why? If not, why not?

My first survey revealed a typical class. Three reported they groaned when assigned to read something in a class, nineteen sighed and resigned themselves, and three thought they might enjoy it. When asked to read literature, two reacted with excitement, two with anticipation, eight with acceptance, seven with resignation, two with indifference, and four with fear. Four never read in their free time, five rarely did so, eight occasionally, six often, and two frequently. When asked to choose statements that most nearly described their attitude about reading, two said they hated it, five said they did not mind it but would rather do almost anything else, one was neutral, eleven said they enjoyed reading on their own but did not enjoy reading required material, and six enjoyed reading on their own and did not mind required material. When asked to pick one word that described reading or themselves as readers, seven used positive words such as *enthusiastic, avid, imaginative, dedicated,* or *curious*; five used neutral words such as *necessary, persistent, visual,* or *precise*; and thirteen used negative words such as *hate, unenthusiastic, slow, distracted, hurried,* or *difficult*.

Three texts, *Mrs. Dalloway*, Oliver Goldsmith's *She Stoops to Conquer*, and Deborah Tannen's *That's Not What I Meant!*, were required for everyone. To encourage self-directed learning,[2] I asked students to choose which book they wanted to read in each of five categories: Greek drama, ancient tales, nineteenth- and twentieth-century fiction, contemporary short stories, and contemporary nonfiction. Given a list of six books in each of the categories, students did a bit of research before selecting their top two and providing a rationale. They self-selected fairly evenly, and all got their first or second choice. Each student then had an individualized course reading list, and thirty books had at least three readers each.

To stimulate good conversations, I strove to create a book club atmosphere. For our thrice-weekly meetings, I used a jigsaw-like activity with two group discussion pieces. In the first, students discuss what they have in common, talking about what they know and asking about what they do not, as in a book club in which everyone reads the same book. In the second, students discuss what they do not have in common, instructing and learning from others, like two friends talking about books read in different book clubs.

Here is how it worked in practice. Each week, everyone read a book from the same category, such as Greek drama. The students who had read *Antigone*, say, talked about the play in an online conversation and met to discuss it in class on Mondays and Wednesdays, whereas the students who had read *The Trojan Women* discussed that. Because I said on the syllabus and repeatedly in class, "Weekends are for reading entire books," I urged them to read fast to get big ideas, mark passages that struck them, and note questions as they read. When students arrived in class, they found an overall outline of the day's work on the board and general discussion questions and tasks on their book club tables (along with signs indicating book titles and member names). Each table might have a literary reference work such as *Benét's Reader's Encyclopedia* (Murphy), and book club members might be charged with looking up their book's author, title, important characters, or even a literary term. Early in the quarter, questions were general: Who are the characters? What's going on? What does the book seem to be about? How would you describe the men and women in it? Underneath the surface, what deep human issue does the book explore? Questions became more specific as students gained confidence. After they had talked, I called on clubs, putting each club's discoveries about its book on the board.

On Fridays, representatives from each book club met in four groups of six and discussed the category of the books (e.g., Greek drama) by telling each other about the six different books they had read. Then the groups reported, and the class as a whole tried to find patterns, answering questions like, What did all the Greek dramas have? How did these Greek dramas relate to the theme of the course? The students compiled those patterns from the board for the class wisdom on the category. As the quarter progressed, we looked back at what we had learned in previous weeks and began to compare specific books and genres. By the end of the course, each student had read three common books and five books of his or her choice and had learned about twenty-five more.

Since book club membership changed every week, students saw their responsibility to one another ("I read all the books . . .'cause if I didn't, I felt left out in the conversation the next day in class"), and the atmosphere of the class became communal. Students came early, consulted their books, and talked and talked. All I did was structure activities and discussion, ask questions, use the board to pull together what they came up with, supplement their findings a bit, encourage them to compare and synthesize, and bring food on Fridays.

Starting in the third week, we proceeded chronologically, from Greek drama to contemporary short stories and nonfiction. Woolf, though, began, threaded through, and ended the course.

Students left class the first day with questions to answer about Woolf's essay "How Should One Read a Book?" "What is Woolf's advice," I asked, "and what surprises or interests you about it?" They liked most her suggestion that no one can tell you what to read or what to like. Many were also intrigued by her suggestion that you must first read as an author's "fellow-worker and accomplice" (259). One student was relieved that he did not have to be critical immediately, and another realized that she tended to quit on books too soon without trying to "banish all . . . preconceptions" or "open [her] mind as widely as possible" (259). As discussion continued, students brought forward phrases they liked, such as, "The poet is always our contemporary" (265), noted other insights (many had never considered reading different books in different ways), teased out the two-part reading strategy Woolf recommends (first friend, then judge), and talked about why we read and how the "end" of reading gets further and further removed from pleasure as school progresses (270).

Knowing that students needed to put Woolf's reading strategies into practice, trust my counsel to read quickly over weekends, and experience the kinds of conversations they could have after quick reading, I began with *Mrs. Dalloway*. "I'm asking you to read a lot," I acknowledged, "and *Mrs. Dalloway* will be the most difficult book you read all quarter—isn't it better to read it now, when you're fresh?" I reminded them to try to read with Woolf, not against her, urged them not to stop and go back when they got confused, and said it was normal to get confused the first time through *Mrs. Dalloway*. I reassured them repeatedly that it was all right to read quickly or not to get everything. Just keep going, I told them. Admitting that the novel would seem "all over the place," I divided the class into groups based on five characters. Each student was to focus on a character while reading, mark three important passages related to that character, and write down two questions about him or her. Students first discussed their characters in character groups and then represented them at *Mrs. Dalloway* tables later.

By having students focus on what they knew about their characters, read their chosen passages out loud, and ask and answer their own questions in the larger class discussion, I could weave apt quotations from "How Should One Read a Book?" into their comments about being frustrated and remind them that Woolf was fully aware of the demands she puts on readers. They were achieving something difficult and important; they were practicing an art; they had Woolf's (and my) respect. *Mrs. Dalloway* thus gave them a chance to use the skills and attitudes they needed not only for the course but also for the world beyond campus. Woolf's novel allowed us to focus on relationships and dialogues; humanity's inner life; and large concepts about love and war, proportion and conversion, society and the individual. Every Friday's compare-and-contrast session referred to *Mrs. Dalloway* (when we read Greek drama, for example, points of comparison included Greece and England, external and internal, suicide, and drama and fiction), and student perceptions of the novel kept changing as we turned the kaleidoscope to another category.

In the tenth week, I noted Woolf's belief that "the book as a whole is different from the book received currently in separate phrases" ("How" 267) and asked students to reread both "How Should One Read a Book?" and five key passages from *Mrs. Dalloway*: pages 3 to 13 ("Mrs. Dalloway said" through "all *her* fault"), pages 21 to 27 ("Lucrezia Warren Smith" through "the hyacinth beds"), pages 96 to 100 ("To his patients" through "did not like that man"), pages 179 to 182 ("Sinking her voice" through "'Where's Clarissa?'"), and pages 189 to 190 ("When one was young" through to the end). Now that they had read lots of books and had had conversations about them, now that they had discussed *Mrs. Dalloway* in several contexts, what did they see? They wrote about the still difficult language, the more clear connections, and the much more vivid detail. Even the students who did not like the novel picked up on more when they reread—noting its somber mood, for example, or discovering that it had "more underlying meaning than I first thought." Almost all concluded that the novel now made sense, one noticed "more flowing togetherness," and several saw the value of rereading.

When I asked students to reflect on the three most important things about literature and reading they had learned, some answers revealed how great the gap between literature and life had been for them before. Some said that literature tells you about people in general; others, literature reflects a time period. It is easy to forget that such ideas are new to students, are discoveries for non-readers: "The more you read, the better you read," "I can like books even if I don't agree with what the author is saying," "Reading is a conversation between yourself and the author," "Reading helps me be a better writer/thinker."

Twenty-two of the twenty-five students responded to the last assessment prompt. Twenty said their attitudes toward reading had changed; two reported no change, but one said his or her attitude had always been positive, and the other reported he or she still did not like to read but added, "[What] might have changed is how I look at books. They are all connected. . . . I never thought of books as being connected [before]." Twenty-one responses exhibited attitude changes, eighteen of those indicated significant change, and nine of those recognized the significance themselves. Significant changes fell into these categories, many students noting more than one: improved overall attitude toward reading ("I copied down the title and author of a book one of my group mates had read. I liked how it sounded during the discussion and figured that I might want to read it someday. This was a big change for me. I actually *wanted* to read a book"), increased confidence in reading ("Before this class I hated reading and would never read a book unless required. Through this course I was able to understand each and every book"), increased confidence in discussing reading ("I am now inspired to possibly join a reading group at a local bookstore. . . . After the elaborate conversations we had in class, I know I could hold up my own end in another one"), increased skills in reading ("My goal was to work on comprehension of text and I have accomplished that. I also learned how to communicate book summaries and meaning better"), difference in perception of own skill level ("I will be more courageous [and] read . . . harder lit"), and difference in the way one reads ("I feel . . . able to read books more wholly").

David Pace and Joan Middendorf suggest that students benefit from discussing the kind of reading expected of them and the idea that different disciplines demand different kinds of reading ("Decoding"). Being transparent about my interest in college students' reading and using Woolf's "How Should One Read a Book?" helped me launch those discussions and approach *Mrs. Dalloway* in a more creative way. My Scholarship of Teaching and Learning project taught me that yes, gluttony is important; yes, the more students read and talk about books, the more they can compare and see patterns; and yes, students tackle analysis more readily if they get to wallow first. Students improved their attitudes about reading and about discussing, comparing, and analyzing literature; they learned they could enter and enjoy literary conversation, even about *Mrs. Dalloway*. Woolf ends "How Should One Read a Book?" with a joke about readers who approach heaven's gate, books in hand. The Almighty comments to Peter, "Look, these need no reward. We have nothing to give them here. They have loved reading" (270). Book clubs, choice, and Woolf's reading strategies helped my students experience at least a taste of that heaven on earth, a taste that maybe, just maybe, will motivate them to become lifelong common readers.

NOTES

I am grateful to the Center for Teaching and Learning for creating a three-year professional learning community, Scholarship of Teaching and Learning; the McGregor Fund, for supporting that community; and my Scholarship of Teaching and Learning colleagues, Tammy Birk, Regina Kengla, Marlene Deringer, Duane Buck, Doris Ebbert, S. A. Smith, Pat Keane, and Amy Jessen-Marshall. I would also like to thank John Ludlum, for coding my qualitative data, and my students, for providing it. My research project had the approval of Otterbein's Institutional Review Board. The project followed standard protocols for the gathering of data from students, and students gave me permission to use the results.

[1] I did not forgo other Integrative Studies goals—students attended cultural events, wrote traditional essays, and analyzed literature—but I did privilege reading and reading goals. I am happy to share my list of texts with interested instructors who contact me.

[2] Maryellen Weimer asserts that shifting the responsibility for learning to students creates "dramatic effects on student motivation and engagement" (10). On course evaluations, ninety-one percent of the students agreed or strongly agreed that being able to choose some of the books they read contributed to their learning, and eighty-one percent said that learning about books other than the ones they read was valuable.

Overcoming Resistance to
Lesbian Readings of *Mrs. Dalloway*

Christine W. Sizemore

Although one critic called *Mrs. Dalloway* "the most lesbian specific piece of writing Woolf ever published" (qtd. in Barrett, "Unmasking" 151), some students resist a lesbian reading of the novel both because it conflicts with their own backgrounds and because, as Patricia Cramer notes, "Woolf deliberately hid her lesbian themes from hostile readers" (Introduction 122).[1] At Spelman, a historically black, women's college, a number of students come from conservative religious families in which homosexuality is often framed as "deviant" and a "white disease." Furthermore, some students' parents come from a tradition of black cultural nationalism grounded in black essentialism. For black homosexuals, this essentialism creates problems, because "the structural demands of race discourse [result in] the erasure of subtlety and black difference" (McBride 271). Investigating lesbian readings of a text thus makes some of my students uncomfortable, given their exposure to religious fundamentalism, coupled in some cases with the continuing effects of mid-twentieth-century race discourse in the United States.

To counteract this discomfort and to open discussion in my seminar Twentieth-Century British Women Writers, we first read a contemporary lesbian novella, *The Threshing Floor*, by the Jamaican-British writer Barbara Burford. *The Threshing Floor* creates sympathy for the black lesbian protagonist because the story opens with the loss of her white partner to cancer and tells the story of her grief and the regaining of her artistic powers as a glassblower. Although there are historical differences between the 1987 novella and Woolf's 1925 novel and there is the additional element of racial difference in Burford's novella, the two works share a number of themes, including the concept of multiple subject positions, the fluidity of sexual identity, the achievement and charisma of an artist figure, and negative as well as sympathetic lesbian characters.

Before reading the novels, the class reads several short theoretical pieces to set the context: Woolf's essay "Professions for Women," Audre Lorde's "Uses of the Erotic," Heidi Mirza's introduction to *Black British Feminism*, and the first chapter of Susan Stanford Friedman's *Mappings*. Friedman offers various ways of conceptualizing feminisms, in particular the ideas of "multiple oppression, multiple subject positions [where Woolf is her example, and] contradictory subject positions" (20). Burford, whose father was white and who herself is one of the program directors of the British National Health Service Executive, likewise occupies multiple subject positions. In Burford's *The Threshing Floor*, Hannah Claremont's white mother left her in an orphanage at birth, but Hannah is a successful artist and a founding partner of a glassblowing cooperative. Hannah's class position, however, does not always protect her from uncomfortable situations because, as Mirza points out, black women's "eroti-cized, exoticized bodies have become objects of desire. They preoccupy and obsess the white gaze" (17). Because this view of black women is a feature of both lesbian and heterosexual sexuality for black women, it provides a point of identification for students. Although as readers we must be careful not to erase the potential power differentials in cross-race relationships, Burford con-centrates on the class parallels and artistic commitment of Hannah and her partner, Jenny. Burford acknowledges the racial dynamic when Hannah tells one of her black artist friends about Jenny, but overall Hannah and Jenny are happy in their cross-race relationship. Jenny also makes it clear that she is not a mother figure for Hannah: "I love you. I will *not* be a mother to you" (112). In this way Burford raises both the issues of cross-race relationships and disman-tles the simplistic idea that lesbianism is just the search for an absent mother figure.

In connection with the discussion of potential power differentials, I introduce a concept from Teresa de Lauretis's *The Practice of Love*, in which the author argues that "the figure of the lesbian in contemporary feminist discourse rep-resents the possibility of female subject *and* desire: she can seduce and be se-duced, but without losing her status as subject" (156). Burford presents not only the lesbian woman as a desiring subject but also the dangers a black woman faces as the object of desire. *The Threshing Floor* opens with a lyrical portrayal of the desiring subject, stricken now by grief. Burford's novella draws in a number of potential readers, even those uncomfortable with lesbian themes, because most readers can sympathize with the grief that Hannah feels as she awakens from sleep and reaches out for her lover of twelve years, only to remember that Jenny is gone. Passages from the funeral service and phrases from Jenny's poems echo through Hannah's mind as she experiences the rawness of her loss. In the elegiac opening chapter, which describes Hannah's memory of her relationship with Jenny, Hannah is in a subject position, capable of desiring and responding to desire. That tone gives way to realistic chronological narration in the second chapter, in which Hannah must cope with the social complexities of being made the exotic object of desire.

Burford portrays the black lesbian as an object of white desire when a friend, Heather Hartley, who is white, married, forty years old, and pregnant, starts talking about how jealous she has been of Jenny's relationship with Hannah. Hannah listens to Heather with surprise and confronts her: "Come off it. . . . You enjoy flirting with me. Especially when there are people around that you wanted to scandalize. I was the moral outrage status symbol to end all status symbols" (96). Burford commented in an interview that in the 1970s, a lot of women "were really getting into women's issues and feminism. They had links with families and husbands, but there was an awful fascination" with black les-bians ("When Everything Else" 30).

With Jenny, Hannah had a mutual relationship, one between two subjects. Although Hannah briefly feels attracted to Heather, she will not allow herself to be made into an object by her. Heather's attempt to seduce Hannah shocks students because it illustrates the fluidity of sexual desire and provokes discussion on how a woman can be married and pregnant and yet be interested in a lesbian affair. This discussion sets a precedent for students' analysis of Clarissa Dalloway, who is married to Richard but remembers her youthful erotic experience of kissing Sally Seton.

A comparison of Heather in *The Threshing Floor* and Miss Kilman in *Mrs. Dalloway* offers an opportunity to explain how different historical periods have created different negative frames around lesbians. Heather is a character drawn from the 1970s at a time when black women's sexuality was viewed as exotic by both white men and women. Linda Bellos notes:

> [B]eing viewed as sexually more interesting by white women . . . is, profoundly racist. . . . The myths and stereotypes about Black sexuality in the predominantly heterosexual world were alive and well . . . within the lesbian community.   (56)

Heather's seductive approach portrays a racist attempt to use a black woman to create scandal and thus achieve status. In contrast, the portrait of Miss Kilman, as Barrett explains, is based on the early-twentieth-century sexologists' "'trapped soul theory' of sexual inversion" ("Unmasking" 149). Miss Kilman's attempts to control Elizabeth end up making Miss Kilman seem pathetic: "[S]he's the predator who fails; one can't get more abject than that" (Wachman, "Pink Icing " 345). Heather and Miss Kilman, however, remain minor characters, historically significant but not the primary focus of the novels.

As Burford narrates Hannah's recovery from grief and her return to her art, she uses Lorde's linking of artistic achievement with erotic feelings. When Hannah returns to the glassblowing workshop, both erotic and spiritual feelings begin to surface. As she "listened to the croon of the furnace . . . [she felt] something loosen and begin to flow within her, much like the molten glass in the tank furnace, pregnant with wild possibilities" (116–17). She had feared that after her loss of Jenny, "she would not be able to tap the deep grief-silted wellspring of her creativity" (142), but she is able finally to heal and again create masterpieces in glass.[2]

When we read *Mrs. Dalloway*, the first issue that my students raise is not Clarissa's sexuality but her race and class. Initially my students tended to see her as only white, wealthy, privileged, and perhaps frivolous in her preoccupation with her party. As we refer back to Hannah Claremont and the concept of multiple subject positions, students realize that although Clarissa is privileged by race and class, she feels inadequate in her education and ability to operate in the public and political world. She feels inferior to Lady Bexborough in both looks and status, she is hurt that Lady Bruton thinks her too insignificant to ask to luncheon, and she is intimidated by both Miss Kilman's intellect and her relationship with her daughter. Once Clarissa's class position has been mitigated by these other more vulnerable subject positions, students are ready to think about her sexuality.

In survey classes in which I have not first taught *The Threshing Floor*, students often dismiss Clarissa's relationship with Sally Seton as a youthful crush. They think of sexuality as "hardwired" and presume that, because Clarissa is married and thinks back to Peter as well as to Sally, she must be exclusively heterosexual. In my seminar, however, since we have already worked through the idea of sexual fluidity in *The Threshing Floor*, students are open to accepting Jesse Wolfe's argument:

> Feminine and masculine traits circulate in and out of both male and female characters . . . carrying widely divergent moral connotations, depending on circumstances: such is the essence of the novel's sexual antiessentialism.   (41)

Having understood "sexual antiessentialism," students can then analyze Clarissa's thoughts about her marriage and her memories of Sally Seton.

As Clarissa reviews her life decisions, she reaffirms that she had been "right . . . not to marry [Peter Walsh]. . . . For in marriage [there must be] a little license, a little independence" (7). Although she sometimes feels that she has lost herself in the social role of "being Mrs. Richard Dalloway" (10), she nonetheless recognizes that in her marriage she has the independence that she values, and part of that independence, as Cramer argues, "is the sanctity of her sexual and emotional preference for women" ("Notes" 180). Clarissa has not lost or outgrown her love for Sally Seton; she retains an active memory of it and uses that memory to heal herself of depression and potential despair. When Lady Bruton does not include her in the luncheon invitation, Clarissa retreats to her attic room and thinks back to Sally's kiss, "the most exquisite moment of her whole life . . . a diamond, something infinitely precious" (35). She is aware that she did "undoubtedly then feel what men felt" (31). Her startling imagery provides a healing memory: "some pressure of rapture, which . . . gushed and poured with an extraordinary alleviation . . . an illumination; a match burning in a crocus" (31). Unlike Septimus, whose loss of Evans, combined with shell shock, has driven him into psychosis and suicide, Clarissa uses a cherished memory of love to pull herself out of depression and return to the ordinary task of mending her dress for the party. She also differs here from Miss Kilman in that she can cherish the memory of Sally's kiss, whereas Miss Kilman remains mired in bitterness and anger.

Having used her memory of lesbian love to chase away despair, Clarissa is able to tap into her artistic and intuitive nature to host her party. As Cramer notes, "Because Clarissa's parties are her artwork, Woolf equates lesbian sexuality and female creativity" ("Notes" 183). Since we discussed this equation in relation to Hannah, students can easily apply Lorde's words to Clarissa: "When I speak of the erotic, then, I speak of it as an assertion of the lifeforce of women;

of that creative energy empowered" (55). It is this life force that Peter Walsh recognizes in Clarissa at the end of the novel: "[W]hat is this ecstasy? . . . What is it that fills me with extraordinary excitement? It is Clarissa" (190). Because Clarissa, like Hannah, has been able to access the erotic, the life force within herself, she has been able to heal herself and create not just a party but art.

In evaluating Hannah and Clarissa as artists who have tapped into a life force within themselves that is connected to their lesbian sexuality, students begin to see conceptualizations of lesbians different from those they previously encountered in their experience of black cultural nationalism and religious fundamentalism. Reading about Hannah as a black character and a lesbian, students begin to dismantle the structures of black essentialism. Burford notes in her interview: "We make assumptions about black sexuality . . . which makes it very hard for a black woman [to reconcile her various identities]. For a black woman who happens to be lesbian, it's even harder because it's 'a white woman's disease'" ("When Everything Else" 30). Once we have had these discussions about a black lesbian character and the fluidity of sexual identity in *The Threshing Floor*, students are more open to similar discussions in their reading of *Mrs. Dalloway*.

NOTES

[1] In her essay "Professions for Women," Woolf explains that she succeeded in killing the always subservient "Angel in the House," but "the second, telling the truth about my own experiences as a body, I do not think I solved" (153).

[2] See my book *Negotiating Identities in Women's Lives: English Postcolonial and Contemporary British Novels* for a fuller analysis of the novella.

Mrs. Dalloway Goes to Prison

Martha Greene Eads

In *The Theatre of the Absurd*, Martin Esslin describes *Waiting for Godot*'s remarkable impact on an audience of 1,400 San Quentin penitentiary inmates in 1957. Esslin speculates that the men's appreciation for the play rose from its "confront[ing] them with a situation in some way analogous to their own" and from their having

> come to the theatre without any preconceived notions and ready-made
> expectations, so that they avoided the mistake that trapped so many estab-
> lished critics who condemned the play for its lack of plot, development,
> characterization, suspense, or plain common sense.   (3)

Thirty-four years later, Sidney Homan recounted similar experiences with *Godot* in the Florida prison system, describing inmates' discussions of Samuel Beckett's play as "informed and eloquent beyond anything I had ever known in the classroom" (157). The power of Esslin's and Homan's accounts helped persuade me to include an equally challenging work, *Mrs. Dalloway*, on the syllabus for my introductory fiction theme course What Do Women Want? at the North Carolina Correctional Institution for Women. Would women inmates' complicated personal histories and relative lack of scholarly experience, I wondered, enable them to respond to Woolf's novel as perceptively as male prisoners had to *Godot*?

Although inmates of a medium- to maximum-security prison might first appear to have even less in common with *Mrs. Dalloway*'s pampered protagonist than with Beckett's hapless antiheroes, their longings are, after all, much like Clarissa's. "What do *you* want in life?" I asked my new students on the first night of class, recording their answers on the board as they called them out: "Privacy!" "Respect!" "Love!" "Freedom!" "Identity!" Clarissa meditates on what she calls "privacy of the soul," even from the haven of her upstairs bedroom (124), and Woolf's account of Clarissa's attempts to claim that privacy, along with respect, love, freedom, and identity, offers readers a model for their own life quests. Furthermore, the novel provides student-inmates not only with a literary treatment of some of their most pressing concerns but also with a means of cultivating the respect many of them crave—from an instructor, from peers, and from themselves. Learning to interpret a text that they at first find impenetrable and that they learn is notoriously difficult gives them a sense of accomplishment, even mastery. Such an experience is, for some, transformative.

In the prison summer school course, as in my semester-long fiction courses for traditional university students, *Mrs. Dalloway* serves as the case study in modernism alongside five other texts: Doris Betts's "The Ugliest Pilgrim," Charlotte

Brontë's *Jane Eyre*, Mary Webb's *Precious Bane*, Gloria Naylor's *The Women of Brewster Place*, and Betts's *The Sharp Teeth of Love*. In discussing different literary periods and narrative styles, we also look for thematic links among all the works. Such themes include love, loss, and longing—concepts nearly every reader finds compelling. Student-inmates quickly recognize those themes in *Mrs. Dalloway* as they overcome the difficulties of the narrative. Moreover, adult women prisoners typically bring to *Mrs. Dalloway* insights that few college sophomores possess. Like Woolf herself, many have suffered abuse and depression. They understand, among other things, the novel's subtle exploration of the tension between autonomy and relationship.

To uncover such themes, however, we first consider the nature of Woolf's project. Near the end of our final class on our third text, before starting *Mrs. Dalloway*, we consider the way writers present their material. Since the works we have read previously all feature first-person narrators, I provide students with the opening paragraphs of Arnold Bennett's *Hilda Lessways* to introduce them to both third-person omniscient narration and literary realism. A student reads Bennett's prose aloud, and we compare his narrative style with Webb's in *Precious Bane*. I then ask students to read the first page of *Mrs. Dalloway* to themselves, marking points in the passage where the narration surprises them. "Where does the speaker change?" I ask. When they finish, another student reads the passage aloud. I ask the rest of the class to stop her in places where they have marked narrative shifts. We then discuss those shifts and the way they imitate the ebbs and flows of our reveries. We ask, "Why might Woolf want to write this way?" and "What can her style do that Bennett's doesn't?"

With this discussion as preparation, students plunge on their own into *Mrs. Dalloway* before our next class. When we meet again, we compare our reactions to the novel. Then we read and discuss "Modern Fiction," an essay in which Woolf describes realism's shortcomings. Looking at examples of realist and modernist visual art helps illustrate Woolf's argument. We also explore the political and intellectual currents that informed modernism's development, adding to the literary time line we are building throughout the course.

Some students still find *Mrs. Dalloway* frustrating, wanting to find and follow a conventional plot. Often, they are impatient with Clarissa, declaring her dull and indecisive and questioning her choice of Richard Dalloway over Peter Walsh. Watching scenes from the 1997 film by Marleen Gorris, however, helps most of them appreciate the novel more. When I showed the film during my first summer course, I was surprised to hear the delightfully opinionated Tina sniffle toward the end.[1] When I flicked on the lights, she wiped her eyes and exclaimed, "So Richard really *did* love her!" While watching the video afforded us all an occasion to evaluate one filmmaker's rendering of a novel, Tina and I were also able to discuss the dramatization's effect on her perception of Woolf's characters.

Another student from the first summer whose reaction to *Mrs. Dalloway* surprised me was Joanie, one of the two weakest readers in the class. When students shared their initial impressions of the novel, well before we had watched any of the film, I was amazed by the vigor with which Joanie defended it. Although she was still working on her General Educational Development tests and had struggled to complete *Jane Eyre*, Joanie understood *Mrs. Dalloway*. Perhaps she was so used to having texts wash over her that she was more willing than most to entrust herself to Woolf, to see where the literary voyage would take her. Joining her in appreciating Woolf from the start was Lisa, a classmate whose academic ability far exceeded Joanie's. A high school honors student who had developed a taste for Toni Morrison and Gabriel García Márquez in college before her arrest, Lisa chose to write her course research paper on Septimus Warren Smith and posttraumatic stress disorder.

Joanie's and Lisa's equivalent enthusiasm for Woolf's work demonstrated that an individual's academic background does not determine her receptivity to a text—a good thing, since the Bureau of Justice Statistics reports that only fifty-six percent of women in state prisons have graduated from high school and only thirty to forty percent of those have any postsecondary education (Greenfield and Snell 7). Most of the women in Joanie and Lisa's class had, however, finished high school, and one, Anna, had already completed her bachelor's degree by extension since being sentenced to life in prison. Clearly, my students' skills varied as widely as their life experiences.

One experience many inmates share, despite their diverse backgrounds, is that of abuse. Bureau of Justice Statistics surveys show that nearly sixty percent of women in state prisons are, like Woolf, survivors of physical or sexual abuse; over twenty-five percent report that their abusers were family members (United States 1). Many inmates can also identify with Woolf's history of mental illness. The bureau reports that twenty-nine percent of white women, twenty-two percent of Latinas, and twenty percent of black women in state prisons are mentally ill. Rates of mental illness among the incarcerated are at least double the rates among Americans overall (United States 1). The inmates who read *Mrs. Dalloway* in my courses, like my traditional students, find Woolf's biography troubling, but some of them express a sense of kinship with the novelist as her life story takes shape. Becoming aware of the context in which Woolf wrote seems particularly meaningful to the student-inmates who spend the class canteen break at the prison clinic, waiting for antipsychotic and antidepressant medications. I wait to discuss Woolf's biography until our final class on *Mrs. Dalloway*, hoping that they will refrain from reading the novel as autobiography. In any case, we move forward to our next novel, having seen rich possibilities for art's emergence from suffering.

Although a wide range of personal problems—and occasionally happier circumstances, such as institutional transfer or parole—can prevent students from completing the prison fiction course, those who finish earn solid grades and college credit. While they generally demonstrate a good grasp of *Mrs. Dalloway* during discussions and on papers and tests, their overall development as readers and writers is even more impressive. In response to a recent questionnaire

about student-inmates' memories of the course and of *Mrs. Dalloway* in particular, Anna reports that she followed up on our work together by reading on her
own a biography of Woolf. She goes on to describe her intellectual pursuits:

> Unfortunately, I have not been able to continue with formal education
> partly because I now work second shift and have had some heart-related
> problems. I do read daily and have become quite diverse in my selec-
> tion of books. I continue to like authors such as Josh McDowell, John
> Grisham, and Nora Roberts. However, since completing your class, I have
> also begun to read authors such as Tolkien, Yeats, Homer, and many oth-
> ers. I generally read 200–400 pages daily, so you can imagine the books
> I go through. Thank you for awakening the desire to read many authors,
> instead of a limited few.

Three years after earning an A– in What Do Women Want?, she observes that
"the student who takes these [prison] classes truly wants to learn and will go the
extra mile to help achieve a needed feeling of self-accomplishment." Undoubtedly, Anna describes herself.

While Anna used the survey to reflect on *Mrs. Dalloway* and noted that responding made her want to reread the book, her classmate Stacey confessed
on the questionnaire that she remembers little about Woolf's novel. She has,
however, reread *Jane Eyre* and has earned both a cosmetology diploma and
an associate's degree in business in the past three years. Perhaps her greatest
achievement, however, has been surviving cancer. She was undergoing chemo-
therapy when she took the course, and I feared that she might not survive the
summer. She did, happily for us all, earning a C+ and my lifelong respect for
her persistence. Remembering the course as "therapy of a sort where we could
openly express our opinions with others for discussion," Stacey asserts that "it's
so important for inmates to have an opportunity to study while they are incarcerated. There is so much negativity and bad that we experience here. It means
a lot to know you can turn something bad into something good."

Leigh, a respondent from my second summer school course, also wrote to
share her recent academic accomplishments. In addition to earning a diploma in
computer information systems, she has completed twenty-four extension credit
hours at the University of North Carolina, Chapel Hill, and has received an invitation to join the National Society of Collegiate Scholars. Like Anna, Leigh has
learned more about Woolf since completing the course, listing *A Room of One's
Own* among the books she has read by authors on our syllabus. She explains that
What Do Women Want? helped her "realize how different circumstances can
change people, altering their life in a number of ways. It also made me realize
that a person's outlook on life can have an enormous effect on the end result."
Although she at first "had difficulty understanding the meanings behind some
of the passages," Leigh ultimately found *Mrs. Dalloway* to be

a story about different people and their reflections on life. It seemed that the characters were each in a prison of their own, questioning their significance and purpose in the world. Septimus endured mental anguish due to the war. Mrs. Dalloway suffered from her own fears and uncertainties. These two people were linked through their thoughts and feelings, in a way.

Being able to recognize links among characters in *Mrs. Dalloway* gave Leigh not only a new confidence in her interpretative abilities but also a reason to reflect on her links to others.

For the student-inmate, a heightened awareness of such links fosters both self-esteem and empathy—qualities most correctional institutions do little to nurture. Introducing prisoners to Woolf, like acquainting them with Beckett, helps them recognize "the truth about their own human relationships" (Esslin 48). *Mrs. Dalloway*'s capacity to cultivate such recognition, as well as its sensitive treatment of our universal longings for privacy, respect, love, freedom, and identity, make it rich teaching material for the prison classroom.

NOTE

[1] All students' names have been changed.

Practically Speaking:
Mrs. Dalloway and Life in the Professions
Marcia Day Childress

At first glance, Virginia Woolf's *Mrs. Dalloway* hardly seems a book to engage physicians in reflecting on their lives. The opening words—"Mrs. Dalloway said she would buy the flowers herself" (3)—suggest a world quite apart from, even irrelevant to, the concerns of medicine. Yet they chart a step into a world just recovering from World War I, which like a deep trench divides 1923 London from innocent Victorian Bourton. For the shell-shocked veteran Septimus Warren Smith, the war killed possibilities, leaving only a survivor's guilt and a mental-health specialist's terrifying prescription for proportion. For the society hostess Clarissa Dalloway, at midlife, the war, her recent illness, and the late-day news of Septimus's suicide—all intimations of mortality—darken and deepen this day of her party. Loss and death may lie at its heart, but Woolf's novel is also a fierce celebration of survival and creativity, attesting that life is all the more precious by virtue of its precariousness. This impassioned engagement with death and life makes *Mrs. Dalloway* a rich text to share with medical professionals.

Being a physician has a strong moral component, and moral imagination and self-reflection contribute to medical practitioners' attentiveness, effectiveness, and well-being.[1] But the demands of training and practice can allow doctors too little time to consider just what it means to forge a professional identity and to serve the troubled, sick, and dying among us. While students of medicine can learn basic rules of conduct in classroom and clinic, a more open, conversational forum, like a book discussion, may provide a better venue for developing empathy and ethical awareness, along with the sort of measured engagement that protects against burnout.

At many medical schools in the United States and abroad, medical humanities programs create moral space in which physicians in training can inquire into the values of medicine and reflect on their professional formation.[2] The Center for Biomedical Ethics and Humanities at the University of Virginia School of Medicine offers seminar courses in humanities disciplines (e.g., literature, history, religious studies) as part of the elective curriculum for fourth-year medical students. Faculty members also teach literature courses with clinical faculty members and community practitioners and, for students of medicine and law, seminars in ethical values organized around literary works.

The field of literature and medicine brings materials and methods of literary study to medicine.[3] Like books, patients and their bodies require interpretation: the same critical-reading skills apply. Reading literature provides a vocabulary for moral discourse that physicians may discover nowhere else in their training and helps them acquire narrative competence or "the ability to acknowledge, absorb, interpret, and act on the stories and plights of others," arguably a proficiency at the heart of doctoring (Charon, "Narrative Medicine" 1897). Literary works—especially texts lacking obvious connections to modern medical practice—spark physicians' inquiry into the ethical challenges, responsibilities, and rewards of professional life. And even as reading literature attunes doctors to varieties of voice and experience encountered in practice, it also prompts their self-examination and, frequently, their own storytelling.

I taught *Mrs. Dalloway* in two medical school courses. One was a reading retreat for alumni physicians and their spouses or partners, the other a seminar for medical and law students. Each course sought to foster self-reflection through literary study and to personalize professionalism as participants connected texts with their life's work and their profession's values.

Woundedness was the theme of our weekend-long Literature and Medicine Reading Retreat. Twenty physicians and their spouses or partners enrolled; all forty were classroom equals in our three sessions, though only physicians received continuing-medical-education credit. Each two-hour session addressed a single book. Facilitators included an internist on the medical faculty, an English professor, and me, a literature scholar in the medical school. Two months before the retreat, participants received brief reading guides prepared by the facilitators. Besides *Mrs. Dalloway*, we assigned two other works in which war is a powerful backdrop: Sophocles's *Philoctetes* and Ernest Hemingway's *In Our Time*. We met in a windowed classroom in the medical school, with tables configured in a horseshoe and facilitators in the center.

We began the retreat with *Mrs. Dalloway*. I introduced Woolf's life and work, then spoke about her likely bipolar illness, her prolonged breakdown of 1913 to 1915, and the doctors who treated her.[4] With this explicitly medical avenue into discussion, the physicians could engage, if critically, with psychiatric and neurological medicine of the early twentieth century; assess which of her own psychiatric symptoms Woolf assigned to Septimus; and critique her Harley Street specialists George Savage, Henry Head, and Maurice Craig, who were models for Dr. Holmes and Dr. Bradshaw. I then discussed World War I as the setting in which Septimus is traumatized, inviting participants to consider *Mrs. Dalloway* as Woolf's direct response to the war and, not incidentally, to her desperate battle with mental illness during the war years. How might her book be an act not only of surviving, remembering, and commemorating but also of healing? I invoked contemporary medicine's fondness for war imagery when characterizing disease and doctors' work—how might this association sometimes be at odds with healing? Since the norm for medical presentations is a slide show, I organized my twenty-minute introduction around slides, mostly photographs obtained from books and freely available Web sites, including images of Woolf, her family, and her doctors; World War I battlefield scenes; and views of 1920s London.[5]

We then had a freewheeling discussion about what they, the readers, had discovered in the book. Discussion went where they took it; their queries were my cues. To my surprise, our conversation did not dwell inordinately on either Woolf's mental illness or her portrayal of Septimus and his doctors, although participants noted the vivid, sympathetic rendering of Septimus's paranoia and Woolf's derisive descriptions of Holmes, Bradshaw, and their versions of Silas Weir Mitchell's rest cures. When we considered Woolf's displacement of her own symptoms onto Septimus, we discussed how the British psychiatrists Charles Myers and W. H. R. Rivers, diagnosing hysteria in the shell-shocked doughboys of World War I, redefined what was then a predominantly female illness as a serious neurosis also affecting men traumatized in combat.[6] Participants grasped Woolf's view that whether the afflicted is male or female, this condition is highly stigmatized—and feminized—socially, its supposed lack of proportion deeply feared. They then recognized that Evelyn Whitbread, marginalized in the book and confined to a nursing home in the country with what her doctors deem (for her) female complaints and (for them) a lucrative hypochondria, joins Septimus as yet another foil for Clarissa, whose own recent grave illness and its sequelae (it was perhaps the Spanish influenza of 1918–19 that left her pale, white-haired, and with a heart murmur) required sequestration and long convalescence.

The physicians and their partners alike found Woolf's treatment of time compelling and spoke passionately, if ruefully, of their own—and the health-care system's—preoccupation with time. The average age of participants being in the midfifties, they were drawn especially to the midlife status and characteristically midlife ruminations of Clarissa and Peter Walsh. One female participant, who had last read *Mrs. Dalloway* in college (until the mid-1960s the novel was taught chiefly for its experimental form), confessed that she had had to age to appreciate its content; now, at sixty-something, she joyously proclaimed Clarissa her soul mate. Characters' interior monologues gave everyone insights not only into patients whose serious illnesses prompt significant life review but also into themselves. They mused on how memories and desires of years past enriched and complicated the present, how they too had made concessions and compromises in order to live with choices made long ago, how we come to know ourselves more deeply over time in all our self-presentations, public and private. Two couples who had become acquainted three decades earlier during medical school related to the Bourton experiences shared by Clarissa and Richard, Peter, Hugh, and Sally when the friends reunite at Clarissa's party. Speaking very personally, all participants sympathized with Clarissa's meditations on mortality in the wake of war, illness, and suicide. And they sympathized deeply with her impulse to craft, in the face of life's impermanence and fragility, something beautiful, good, worthy, and memorable—the splendidly orchestrated, glittering offering of her party.

The second course, the year-long Interprofessional Seminar in Ethical Values and Professional Life, enrolled twelve senior students from medicine and law, professionals much younger and at a much earlier developmental stage, personally and professionally, than the reading-retreat participants. Sponsored by the University of Virginia's Institute for Practical Ethics and Public Life and offered for credit in the medical and law schools,[7] this class met in my home five evenings over the school year for dinner followed by two hours of discussion inspired by literary works. A law professor and I team-taught the seminars. I took the lead with *Mrs. Dalloway*.

Mrs. Dalloway was assigned twice. The earlier seminar (2001–02) examined crucial ethical choices, and companion books included Ernest Gaines's *A Lesson before Dying* and Bernhard Schlink's *The Reader*. The more recent course (2005–06) addressed public/private lives, especially professional and personal tensions. Supplementary texts were *Philoctetes*, Edward Albee's *Who's Afraid of Virginia Woolf?* (the play and Mike Nichols's film), Margaret Mohrmann's nonfiction *Attending Children: A Doctor's Education*, and Ian McEwan's novel *Saturday*, which owes significant debts to *Mrs. Dalloway*. The first seminar discussed *Mrs. Dalloway* only months after the deadly terrorist attacks in the United States on 11 September 2001; the second convened early in the Iraq War and not long after terrorists bombed Woolf's beloved London, including her own Tavistock Square, on 7 July 2005. Just as the Great War figures in the novel's recent past, so twenty-first-century war and terrorism proved a dark, painful backdrop to our conversations, as to our lives. *Mrs. Dalloway* became an exemplum for how one survives cataclysmic harm and heals from collective or individual trauma, how one lives in a wounded world.

With just a dozen students gathered in my living room, sessions were informal and intensely interactive. Study questions I had circulated earlier served as scaffolding for our conversation, but the students steered discussion. Here and there, I found opportunities to comment on Woolf, her illnesses and doctors, the war, and British social institutions in the 1920s.

For all its stylistic challenges, *Mrs. Dalloway* deeply engaged the students. At the start of one class, a future psychiatrist exclaimed, "Woolf writes like I think!," then described her own highly associative interior monologue, which confers continuity, pattern, and meaning on events and emotions. A lawyer in training, married and with children, spoke of recognizing in Clarissa's stream of consciousness his own musings about self in society and obligations to others. Medical and law students alike identified with Clarissa's manifold self-presentations and wondered aloud about their own disparate, more or less authentic selves: Who am I in class, in court, in clinic, versus who I am with my spouse, my friends, or when I'm alone? Some were surprised that, deep down, Clarissa seems incompletely confident of who she is; perhaps they expected more of someone their mothers' age. They reveled in Woolf's caustic portraits of arrogant, paternalistic doctors and her arch take on the career civil servants Richard and Hugh. Medical students especially grasped Septimus's plight, which matched what they had encountered on psychiatry rotations, and praised Woolf's compelling, even personally disturbing rendering of his paranoia.

Women students, in the majority in both seminars, focused on women in professional life, then and now. They inquired into Lady Bruton's behind-the-scenes politicking, Doris Kilman's hungry resentments, Rezia Warren Smith's millinery skills, Sally Seton's domestication into Lady Rosseter, Evelyn Whitbread's invalidism, Clarissa's career as consummate hostess, and daughter Elizabeth's expanded educational and professional prospects after the war's wholesale slaughter of young men. For all students—idealistic women and men in their twenties making major life decisions (the medical students were interviewing for residencies, the law students for jobs and clerkships, and several students were newly wed or engaged to be married)—Clarissa's flashbacks to that momentous summer at Bourton stood out: What is love? How do I find my life's mate? Will my passionate attachments endure? Will disappointment in love compromise my other choices? How do two people make a life together, and what if this life is not altogether satisfying? How do I choose to live, as does Clarissa, when death may sometimes seem irresistible?

I closed both seminars by speaking of the artist's response to trauma and proposing that the lyrical language of *Mrs. Dalloway* simultaneously recalls and repairs a broken world (Orr 4), telling dark truths of loss and death but also knitting up "orts, scraps, and fragments" into a shimmering whole, all with a beauty at once faithful to and healing for our woundedness (Woolf, *Between the Acts* 188). It is this "whole made of shivering fragments" (Woolf, *Passionate Apprentice* 393) that arrests eye and heart and, in effect, demands (to borrow Mrs. Ramsay's words from *To the Lighthouse*), "Life stand still here" ([1981] 161). Life stands still, I suggested to the students, at Clarissa's creation—her party—and triumphantly so at the novel's close, when we, with Peter, glance expectantly about the crowded room in search of what fills us with terror, ecstasy, excitement—and hope: "It is Clarissa, he said. For there she was" (190).

NOTES

[1] See, for example, Novack, Suchman, et al.; Charon and Montello; Coulehan; and Charon, *Narrative Medicine*.

[2] Medical humanities as a discipline is examined in Kirklin and Richardson; and Evans and Finlay. For an overview of medical humanities education in medical schools, see Dittrich and Farmakidis.

[3] Charon, Banks, Connelly, et al.; and Greenhalgh and Hurwitz.

[4] See Trombley; Caramagno; and Banks.

[5] For images of Woolf, her family, and friends, see Lehmann; Spater and Parsons; and Humm, *Snapshots*. Photographs of Woolf and her family can be found at *Leslie Stephen's Photograph Album*. Pictures of Woolf's doctors appear in Banks. World War I combat images may be found on the Web or in books such as the one by Martin Gilbert.

[6] See, for example, Rivers; Showalter, *The Female Malady*, esp. ch. 7.

[7] Seminar funding was provided to the Institute for Practical Ethics and Public Life by the Donchian Foundation, a private family foundation.

NOTES ON CONTRIBUTORS

Meg Albrinck is associate professor of literature and writing, chair of the humanities division, and honors program coordinator at Lakeland College. She has contributed articles on Woolf to *Virginia Woolf Miscellany* and *Woolf and the Art of Exploration* (ed. Helen Southworth and Elsa Kay Sparks). Her research and teaching interests include twentieth-century British literature, modernism, women's writing, feminist theory, and cultural studies. She is working on a book focused on gender, genre, and the First World War.

Eileen Barrett is professor of English and director of the Faculty Center for Excellence in Teaching at California State University, East Bay. Her publications include an award-winning article on *Between the Acts*, a contribution to the *Approaches to Teaching Woolf's* To the Lighthouse volume, and essays on *Mrs. Dalloway*. She is coeditor of *American Women Writers: Diverse Voices in Prose*, three volumes of *Selected Papers* for the Annual Conference on Virginia Woolf, and *Virginia Woolf: Lesbian Readings*.

Marlene A. Briggs is assistant professor of English at the University of British Columbia. She has contributed to *Virginia Woolf and Communities* (ed. Jeanette McVicker and Laura Davis) and *Modernism and Mourning* (ed. Patricia Rae). Her research and teaching interests include questions of memory, mourning, and trauma in modern and contemporary literature. She is writing a book that charts the complex aftermath of the First World War in three generations of British writers.

Marcia Day Childress is associate professor of medical education and director of programs in humanities in the Center for Biomedical Ethics and Humanities at the University of Virginia School of Medicine. She is author of an essay in the volume *Stories Matter: The Role of Narrative in Medical Ethics* (ed. Rita Charon and Martha Montello). Her teaching and research interests include narrative in medicine and the use of literature in medical education. She is writing a book on Woolf's relation to language in her autobiographical writings.

Beth Rigel Daugherty is professor of English at Otterbein College. She is coeditor of *Approaches to Teaching Woolf's* To the Lighthouse and has published several articles on Woolf. Her research and teaching interests include pedagogy, the essay, twentieth-century English literature, Appalachian literature, and magical realism. In 2002, she received the Distinguished Teacher Award at Otterbein College. She is writing a book about how Virginia Stephen's apprenticeship affected Virginia Woolf's essays.

Madelyn Detloff is associate professor of English and director of women's studies at Miami University, Ohio. She is author of *The Persistence of Modernism: Loss and Mourning in the Twentieth Century*. Her research and teaching interests include queer theory, modernism, trauma studies, cultural studies, and women's studies.

Martha Greene Eads is professor of English in the language and literature department at Eastern Mennonite University. Her research and teaching interests include twentieth-century drama, English modernism, and contemporary southern fiction, and her articles on those topics have appeared in the *Carolina Quarterly*, *Christianity and Literature*, the *Cresset*, *Modern Drama*, and *Theology*.

Anne E. Fernald is associate professor of English and the director of writing and composition at Fordham University. She has published articles on Woolf as well as a book titled *Virginia Woolf: Feminism and the Reader*. Her research and teaching interests include modernism, women's literature, African literature, feminist theory, rhetoric and composition, and the history of the essay. She is editing the Cambridge University Press edition of *Mrs. Dalloway*.

Leslie Kathleen Hankins is professor of English at Cornell College, where she teaches twentieth-century literature and film courses, including a variety of experimental courses on Virginia Woolf and the cinema. Her scholarship on Woolf and film includes an essay in Diane Gillespie's *The Multiple Muses of Virginia Woolf* and *"Cinéastes* and Modernists: Writing on Film in 1920s London" in *Gender in Modernism*, edited by Bonnie Kime Scott. She has presented on Woolf and cinema, the London Film Society, Iris Barry, and film forums of the 1920s at the annual Virginia Woolf conferences, Modernist Studies Association conferences, and MLA conventions.

David Leon Higdon is Paul Whitfield Horn Professor Emeritus at Texas Tech University. He is the author of *Time and English Fiction* as well as essays on contemporary British authors. His research and teaching interests include nineteenth- and twentieth-century British fiction, bibliographical studies, and the theory of fiction. He is writing a textbook on teaching introductory fiction classes.

Ruth Hoberman is professor of English at Eastern Illinois University. She is author of *Modernizing Lives: Experiments in English Biography, 1918–1939* and coeditor of *Trespassing Boundaries: Virginia Woolf's Short Fiction* (with Kathryn N. Benzel). Her research and teaching interests focus on twentieth-century British literature. She is writing a book titled "Museum Trouble: Narratives of Conflict in the Edwardian Museum."

James F. Knapp is professor of English and senior associate dean of arts and sciences at the University of Pittsburgh. He is the author of books on modernism including *Literary Modernism and the Transformation of Work*. His research and teaching interests include British and American modernism as well as Irish literature. He is working on a study of the arts and crafts movement.

Antonia Losano is associate professor of English and American literature at Middlebury College. She has published articles on British authors including Jane Austen, Henry James, and the Brontë sisters. Her research and teaching interests include Victorian literature, women's studies, and literary theory. She is writing a book on the literary, artistic, and cultural representations of solitude.

Karen McLeer is associate professor of English and associate dean at the University of Wisconsin, Richland. In addition to her work on Woolf, she is author of "Keep It Wild(e): Reclaiming Reader Expectation in 'Reading Gaol'" (*European Studies Journal*). In 2003, she received the University of Wisconsin's Underkofler Excellence in Teaching Award. She is working on a study of clergy and their wives in the novels of Barbara Pym.

Margot Norris is Chancellor's Professor of English and Comparative Literature at the University of California, Irvine. Her book *Writing War in the Twentieth Century* includes chapters on World War I poetry and fiction, the Manhattan Project, the book and film of *Schindler's List*, writings on Hiroshima, Francis Ford Coppola's film *Apocalypse*

Now, and military censorship during the Persian Gulf War of 1991. She has published four books on the work of James Joyce.

Mary Beth Pringle is professor of English at Wright State University. She is coeditor of *Approaches to Teaching Woolf's* To the Lighthouse. She has published articles on James Joyce and Virginia Woolf as well as on Charlotte Perkins Gilman and Toni Morrison. Her research and teaching interests include women's world literature, creative memoir, and nonfiction writing.

Lecia Rosenthal is assistant professor of English at Tufts University. Her research and teaching interests include modernism, psychoanalysis, and feminist and postcolonial theory. She is author of the forthcoming *Mourning Modernism: Literature, Catastrophe, and the Politics of Consolation.*

Victoria Rosner is associate professor of English at Texas A&M University. She is the author of *Modernism and the Architecture of Private Life*, winner of the Modernist Studies Association Book Prize. She is working on a book tentatively titled "Machines for Living: Modernism, Literature, Domesticity" and editing (with Geraldine Pratt) a collection of essays, "The Global and the Intimate: Toward a Twenty-First-Century Transnational Feminism."

Ruth O. Saxton is professor of English and cofounder of the women's studies program at Mills College, where she has been recognized for exemplary teaching. She coedited *Woolf and Lessing: Breaking the Mold* (with Jean Tobin), edited *The Girl: Constructions of the Girl in Contemporary Fiction by Women*, and is working on a collection of essays about the aging female protagonist in contemporary fiction.

Judith Seaboyer is lecturer in the School of English, Media Studies, and Art History at the University of Queensland. She has published essays on authors such as Robert Coover, Ian McEwan, and Jeanette Winterson. Her research and teaching interests include contemporary British and American fiction as well as Victorian fiction. She is writing a book on contemporary fiction set in Venice.

Christine W. Sizemore is professor of English at Spelman College. She is author of *A Female Vision of the City: London in the Novels of Five British Women* and *Negotiating Identities in Women's Lives: English Postcolonial and Contemporary British Novels.* She has written articles on Woolf, Doris Lessing, and Zadie Smith. Her research and teaching interests include postcolonial women writers, twentieth-century British women writers, and urban novelists.

Nick Smart is associate professor of English and department chair at the College of New Rochelle. His work includes "The Family Business: Folklore as Psychobiography in Helen Papanikolas's *An Amulet of Greek Earth*" in *Charioteer*, "I, Bernard: Notes from the Feminist Classroom" in the *Virginia Woolf Miscellany*, and "Nothing but Affections for All Those Who've Sailed with Me: Bob Dylan from Place to Place" in *Popular Music and Society.* He is at work on a book about literature and emotional healing.

SURVEY PARTICIPANTS

Marilyn R. Abildskov, *Saint Mary's College*
Andrea Adolph, *Kent State University*
Meg Albrinck, *Lakeland College*
George Bahlke, *Hamilton College*
Steven Barfield, *University of Westminster*
Eric L. Berlatsky, *University of Maryland*
°Harriet Blodgett, *California State University, Stanislaus*
Rita Bode, *Trent University*
Allyson Booth, *U.S. Naval Academy*
Brad Bowers, *Barry University*
Marlene A. Briggs, *University of British Columbia*
Judith Caesar, *American University of Sharjah*
Brycchan Carey, *Kingston University*
Rebecca L. Carpenter, *McDaniel College*
Marcia Childress, *University of Virginia School of Medicine*
Myunghee Chung, *Kookmin University*
Robert Courtright, *Catholic University of America*
Beth Rigel Daugherty, *Otterbein College*
Cynthia Davis, *University of Maryland, University College*
Madelyn Detloff, *Miami University of Ohio*
Jeanne DuBino, *Plymouth State College*
Martha Greene Eads, *Eastern Mennonite University*
Patricia M. Feito, *Barry University*
Maryanne Felter, *Cayuga Community College*
Anne E. Fernald, *Fordham University*
Ariela Freedman, *Concordia University*
Cayo Gamber, *George Washington University*
Jeannie Goodwin, *Marshall High School*
Michael Groden, *University of Western Ontario*
Jay L. Halio, *University of Delaware*
°Leslie Kathleen Hankins, *Cornell College*
Susan Harrington, *University of South Florida, Sarasota/Manatee*
Suzette Henke, *University of Louisville*
David Leon Higdon, *Texas Tech University*
Katherine Hill-Miller, *Long Island University*
Ruth Hoberman, *Eastern Illinois University*
Chris Hopkins, *Sheffield Hallam University*
°Mark Hussey, *Pace University*
Sally A. Jacobsen, *Northern Kentucky University*
Suzanne Keen, *Washington and Lee University*
Katerina Kitsi-Mitakou, *Aristotle University of Thessaloniki*
James Knapp, *University of Pittsburgh*
Andrew Kunka, *University of South Carolina, Sumter*

Antonia Losano, *Middlebury College*
Karen McLeer, *University of Wisconsin, Richland*
John Mepham, *Kingston University*
Jill Mowbray, *Marshall High School*
Margot Norris, *University of California, Irvine*
Ann V. Norton, *Saint Anselm College*
Patricia Garcias Ocanas, *Our Lady of the Lake University*
Paula Osborn, *Madeira School*
Jo Alyson Parker, *Saint Joseph's University*
*Mary Pinkerton, *University of Wisconsin*
Louise A Poresky, *Rockland Community College*
Mary Beth Pringle, *Wright State University*
Lecia Rosenthal, *Tufts University*
Victoria Rosner, *Texas A&M University*
Diana Royer, *Miami University of Ohio*
Richard Russell, *Baylor University*
Margaret Scanlan, *Indiana University, South Bend*
Andrew Schopp, *University of Tennessee, Martin*
Marilyn R. Schuster, *Smith College*
*Bonnie Kime Scott, *San Diego State University*
Judith Seaboyer, *University of Queensland*
Christine W. Sizemore, *Spelman College*
Nick Smart, *College of New Rochelle*
Sue Sorenson, *University of Winnipeg*
Elisa Kay Sparks, *Clemson University*
Hilde Staels, *Catholic University of Leuven*
Wendy Weber, *University of North Carolina, Chapel Hill*
Lisa Williams, *Ramapo College of New Jersey*
Natalie Wilson, *Alliant International University*
Nancy Workman, *Lewis University*
Christa Zorn, *Indiana University, Southeast*

* Provided student survey responses

WORKS CITED

All essays in the volume cite the 2005 Harcourt edition of *Mrs. Dalloway*, annotated and with an introduction by Bonnie Kime Scott.

Writings of Virginia Woolf

Between the Acts. New York: Harcourt, 1941. Print.

"Byron and Mr. Briggs." *Essays* 3: 474–99.

"The Cinema." *Nation and Athenaeum* 3 July 1926: 381–83. Rpt. in *Essays* 4: 348–54.

Collected Essays. 4 vols. New York: Harcourt, 1967. Print.

The Common Reader. 1925. New York: Harcourt, 1953. Print.

The Common Reader. 1925. Ed. Andrew McNeillie. Annotated ed. New York: Harcourt, 1984. Print.

The Diary of Virginia Woolf. Ed. Anne Olivier Bell. 5 vols. New York: Harcourt, 1977–84. Print.

The Essays of Virginia Woolf. Ed. Andrew McNeillie. Vols. 1–3. New York: Harcourt, 1986–88. Vol. 4. London: Hogarth, 1994. Print.

"How Should One Read a Book?" *Second Common Reader* 258–70.

Introduction. *Mrs. Dalloway*. New York: Modern Lib., 1928. V–ix. Rpt. in Mrs. Dalloway *Reader* 10–12.

The Letters of Virginia Woolf. Ed. Nigel Nicolson and Joanne Trautmann. 6 vols. New York: Harcourt, 1975–80. Print.

"Modern Fiction." *Common Reader* (1984) 146–54.

"Mr. Bennett and Mrs. Brown." *"The Captain's Death Bed" and Other Essays*. San Diego: Harcourt, 1978. 94–119. Print.

"Mr. Bennett and Mrs. Brown." *Collected Essays* 1: 319–37.

Mrs. Dalloway. 1925. Fwd. Maureen Howard. Orlando: Harcourt, 1981. Print.

Mrs. Dalloway. 1925. Ed. G. Patton Wright. Introd. Angelica Garnett. London: Hogarth, 1990. Print.

Mrs. Dalloway. Narr. Eileen Atkins. Abr. ed. Penguin Audio, 1996. Audiocassette.

Mrs. Dalloway. 1925. Ed. Morris Beja. Oxford: Blackwell, 1996. Print. Shakespeare Head Press ed.

Mrs. Dalloway. 1925. *The Longman Anthology of British Literature: The Twentieth Century*. Ed. Kevin Dettmar and Jennifer Wicke. New York: Addison, 2003. 2386–485. Print.

Mrs. Dalloway. Narr. Virginia Leishman. Unabridged ed. Recorded Books, 2003. Audiocassette.

Mrs. Dalloway. Mrs. Dalloway *Reader* 196–371.

Mrs. Dalloway. 1925. Annotated and introd. Bonnie Kime Scott. Pref. Mark Hussey. Orlando: Harcourt, 2005. Print.

"Mrs. Dalloway in Bond Street." *Mrs. Dalloway's Party*. Ed. Stella McNichol. New York: Harcourt, 1978. 19–28. Print.

The Mrs. Dalloway *Reader*. Ed. Francine Prose. Fwd. Mark Hussey. Orlando: Harcourt, 2004. Print.

"On Not Knowing Greek." *Common Reader* (1984) 23–38.

Orlando. 1928. New York: Harcourt, 1956. Print.

A Passionate Apprentice: The Early Journals, 1897–1909. Ed. Mitchell A. Leaska. San Diego: Harcourt, 1990. Print.

"Professions for Women." *"The Death of the Moth" and Other Essays*. London: Hogarth, 1942. 149–54. Print.

A Room of One's Own. 1929. New York: Harcourt, 1989. Print.

The Second Common Reader. 1932. Ed. Andrew McNeillie. Annotated ed. San Diego: Harcourt, 1986. Print.

"A Sketch of the Past." *Moments of Being*. Ed. Jeanne Schulkind. 2nd ed. San Diego: Harvest, 1985. 64–159. Print.

"Street Haunting: A London Adventure." *Collected Essays* 4: 155–66.

Three Guineas. 1938. New York: Harcourt, 1966. Print.

To the Lighthouse. 1927. Foreword by Eudora Welty. New York: Harcourt, 1981. Print.

To the Lighthouse. 1927. New York: Harcourt, 1989. Print.

Virginia Woolf The Hours: *The British Museum Manuscript of* Mrs. Dalloway. Transcribed and ed. Helen M. Wussow. New York: Pace UP, 1996. Print.

A Writer's Diary. Ed. Leonard Woolf. New York: Harcourt, 1981. Print.

Other Sources

Abbott, Reginald. "What Miss Kilman's Petticoat Means: Virginia Woolf, Shopping, and Spectacle." *Modern Fiction Studies* 38.1 (1992): 193–216. Print.

Abel, Elizabeth. "Between the Acts of Mrs. Dalloway." Abel, *Virginia Woolf* 30–44.

———. "Narrative Structure(s) and Female Development: The Case of *Mrs. Dalloway*." *The Voyage In: Fictions of Female Development*. Ed. Abel, Marianne Hirsch, and Elizabeth Langland. Hanover: UP of New England, 1983. 161–85. Print.

———. *Virginia Woolf and the Fictions of Psychoanalysis*. Chicago: U of Chicago P, 1989. Print.

Abel, Richard. *French Film Theory and Criticism: A History/Anthology, 1907–1939*. Vol. 1. Princeton: Princeton UP, 1988. Print.

Abraham, Julie. *Are Girls Necessary? Lesbian Writing and Modern Histories*. New York: Routledge, 1996. Print.

Ackroyd, Peter. *London: The Biography*. New York: Anchor, 2000. Print.

Adams, David. *Colonial Odysseys: Empire and Epic in the Modernist Novel*. Ithaca: Cornell UP, 2003. Print.

Adorno, Theodor W. "The Position of the Narrator in the Contemporary Novel." *Notes to Literature*. Trans. Shierry Weber Nicholsen. Vol. 1. New York: Columbia UP, 1991. 30–36. Print.

Albee, Edward. *Who's Afraid of Virginia Woolf?* 1962. New York: Signet, 1983. Print.

Allan, Tuzyline Jita. "The Death of Sex and the Soul in *Mrs. Dalloway* and Nella Larsen's *Passing*." Barrett and Cramer, *Virginia Woolf* 95–113.

———. *Womanist and Feminist Aesthetics: A Comparative Review*. Athens: Ohio UP, 1995. Print.

Alley, Henry. "*Mrs. Dalloway* and Three of Its Contemporary Children." *Papers on Language and Literature* 42.4 (2006): 401–19. Print.

Alter, Robert. *Imagined Cities: Urban Experience and the Language of the Novel*. New Haven: Yale UP, 2005. Print.

Amberg, George. *The Film Society Programmes, 1925–1939*. New York: Arno, 1972. Print.

Ames, Kenneth J. "Elements of Mock-Heroic in Virginia Woolf's *Mrs. Dalloway*." *Modern Fiction Studies* 18.3 (1972): 363–74. Print.

Andrew, J. Dudley. "Adaptation." *Concepts in Film Theory*. Oxford: Oxford UP, 1984. 96–106. Print.

Annual Bibliography of Woolf Studies. *International Virginia Woolf Society*. Univ. of Toronto, 1996–2007. Web. 1 Mar. 2008.

Ardis, Ann, and Bonnie Kime Scott, eds. *Virginia Woolf: Turning the Centuries: Selected Papers from the Ninth Annual Conference on Virginia Woolf*. New York: Pace UP, 2000. Print.

Armistice Day. 1928. *Getty Images*. Web. 22 Feb. 2008. Image no. 3097526.

Ashley Adams Trio. *Flowers for Mrs. Dalloway*. Evander Music, 1997. CD.

Atkins, Eileen. "Adapting *Mrs. Dalloway*: A Talk with Eileen Atkins." *Scenario* 5.1 (1999): 159–63, 190–91. Print.

———. *Mrs. Dalloway*. *Scenario* 5.1 (1999): 124–58. Print.

Auerbach, Eric. "The Brown Stocking." *Mimesis: The Representation of Reality in Western Literature*. Trans. Willard R. Trask. Princeton: Princeton UP, 1953. 525–53. Print.

Ausonius, Decimus Magnus. *Works*. Trans. Hugh G. Evelyn White. Cambridge: Harvard UP, 1985. Print.

Backus, Margot Gayle. "Exploring the Ethical Implications of Narrative in a Sophomore-Level Course on Same-Sex Love: *Mrs. Dalloway* and *The Last September*." Barrett and Cramer, *Re: Reading* 102–05.

Balakian, Peter. "From Ezra Pound to Theodore Roosevelt: American Intellectual and Cultural Responses to the Armenian Genocide." *America and the Armenian Genocide of 1915*. Ed. Jay Winter. West Nyack: Cambridge UP, 2004. 240–53. Print.

Baldwin, Dean R. *Virginia Woolf: A Study of the Short Fiction*. Boston: Twayne, 1989. Print.

Banks, Joanne Trautmann. "Mrs. Woolf in Harley Street." *Lancet* 351.9109 (1998): 1124–26. Print.

Barker, Pat. *The Eye in the Door*. New York: Viking, 1993. Print.

———. *The Ghost Road*. London: Penguin, 1995. Print.

———. *Regeneration*.1991. New York: Penguin, 1993. Print.

Barrett, Eileen. "Septimus and Shadrack: Woolf and Morrison Envision the Madness of War." Hussey and Neverow 26–32.

——— "Unmasking Lesbian Passion: The Inverted World of *Mrs. Dalloway*." Barrett and Cramer, *Virginia Woolf* 146–64.

Barrett, Eileen, and Patricia Cramer, eds. *Re: Reading, Re: Writing, Re: Teaching: Virginia Woolf: Selected Papers from the Fourth Annual Conference on Virginia Woolf*. New York: Pace UP, 1995. Print.

———, eds. *Virginia Woolf: Lesbian Readings*. New York: New York UP, 1997. Print.

Barry, Iris. "The Cinema: A Comparison of the Arts." *Spectator* 3 May 1924: 707. Rpt. in Scott, *Gender* 824–26.

———. "The Scope of Cinema." *Vogue* [London] late Aug. 1924: 65+. Rpt. in Scott, *Gender* 826–28.

Barth, John. "The Literature of Exhaustion." *Atlantic* Aug. 1967: 29–34. Rpt. in *The American Novel since World War II*. Ed. Marcus Klein. Greenwich: Fawcett, 1969. 267–79. Print.

Beebe, Maurice. "Criticism of Virginia Woolf: A Selected Checklist with an Index to the Studies of Separate Works." *Modern Fiction Studies* 2.1 (1956): 36–45. Print.

Beer, Gillian. *Virginia Woolf: The Common Ground*. Ann Arbor: U of Michigan P, 1996. Print.

Beja, Morris. "The London of *Mrs. Dalloway*." Map. *Virginia Woolf Miscellany* 7 (1977): 4. Print.

———. "Text and Counter-text: Trying to Recover Mrs. Dalloway." *Editing Virginia Woolf: Interpreting the Modernist Text*. Ed. James M. Haule and J. H. Stape. Houndmills: Palgrave, 2002. 127–38. Print.

Beker, Mirslav. "London as a Principle of Structure in *Mrs. Dalloway*." *Modern Fiction Studies* 18.3 (1972): 375–85. Print.

Bell, Clive. "Art and the Cinema: A Prophecy That the Motion Pictures, in Exploiting Imitation Art, Will Leave Real Art to the Artists." *Vanity Fair* Nov. 1922: 39–40. Print.

———. "Cinema Aesthetics: A Critic of the Arts Assesses the Movies." *Theatre Guild* Oct. 1929: 39+. Print.

Bell, Michael. "The Metaphysics of Modernism." Levenson 9–32.

Bell, Quentin. *Virginia Woolf: A Biography*. 2 vols. London: Hogarth, 1972. Print.

Bellos, Linda. "A Vision Back and Forth." *Talking Black: Lesbians of African and Asian Descent Speak Out*. Ed. Valerie Mason-John. London: Cassell, 1995. 52–71. Print.

Benzel, Kathryn N., and Ruth Hoberman. *Trespassing Boundaries: Virginia Woolf's Short Fiction*. New York: Palgrave, 2004. Print.

Berman, Jessica. "Ethical Folds: Ethics, Aesthetics, Woolf." *Modern Fiction Studies* 50.1 (2004): 151–72. Print.

Berman, Marshall. *All That Is Solid Melts into Air: The Experience of Modernity*. New York: Simon, 1982. Print.

Bishop, Edward. "*Mrs. Dalloway*: Writing, Speech, and Silence." *Virginia Woolf*. By Bishop. New York: St. Martin's, 1991. 49–66. Print.

————. *A Virginia Woolf Chronology*. Boston: Hall, 1989. Print.

Bloom, Harold. *The Anxiety of Influence: A Theory of Poetry*. New York: Oxford UP, 1973. Print.

————, ed. *Clarissa Dalloway*. New York: Chelsea, 1990. Print.

————. *Kabbalah and Criticism*. 1975. New York: Continuum, 1993. Print.

————. *A Map of Misreading*. New York: Oxford UP, 1975. Print.

Bluestone, George. *Novels into Film*. Berkeley: U of California P, 1966. Print.

Booth, Alison. *Greatness Engendered: George Eliot and Virginia Woolf*. Ithaca: Cornell UP, 1992. Print.

Booth, Allyson. *Postcards from the Trenches: Negotiating the Space between Modernism and the First World War*. New York: Oxford UP, 1996. Print.

Bourke, Joanna. *Dismembering the Male: Men's Bodies, Britain, and the Great War*. London: Reaktion, 1996. Print.

Bovril. Advertisement. *Times* [London] 25 Nov. 1918: 6. Print.

Bowlby, Rachel. *Carried Away: The Invention of Modern Shopping*. New York: Columbia UP, 2002. Print.

————. *Feminist Destinations and Further Essays on Virginia Woolf*. Edinburgh: Edinburgh UP, 1997. Print.

————. *Shopping with Freud*. London: Routledge, 1993. Print.

————. "Thinking Forward through Mrs. Dalloway's Daughter." Bowlby, *Feminist Destinations* 69–84.

————. "Walking, Women, and Writing: Virginia Woolf as Flâneuse." Bowlby, *Feminist Destinations* 191–219.

Bradshaw, David. "'Vanished, Like Leaves': The Military, Elegy and Italy in *Mrs. Dalloway*." *Woolf Studies Annual* 8 (2002): 107–25. Print.

Briggs, Julia. *Virginia Woolf: An Inner Life*. Orlando: Harcourt, 2005. Print.

Briggs, Marlene A. "Veterans and Civilians: The Mediation of Traumatic Knowledge in *Mrs. Dalloway*." *Virginia Woolf and Communities: Selected Papers from the Eighth Annual Conference on Virginia Woolf*. Ed. Jeanette McVicker and Laura Davis. New York: Pace UP, 1999. 43–49. Print.

Britons [Kitchener] Wants You. 1914–16. Poster. Imperial War Museum, London.

Brower, Ruben Arthur. "Something Central Which Permeated: Virginia Woolf and *Mrs. Dalloway*." *The Fields of Light: An Experiment in Critical Reading*. By Brower. New York: Oxford UP, 1951. 123–37. Print.

Bryher. "How I Would Start a Film Club." Donald, Friedberg, and Marcus 290–92.

————. "The Sociological Film, I." *Film Problems of Soviet Russia*. Territet: Pool, 1929. 84–91. Rpt. in Scott, *Gender* 853–58.

Budd, Mike, ed. The Cabinet of Dr. Caligari: *Texts, Contexts, Histories*. New Brunswick: Rutgers UP 1990. Print.

Burford, Barbara. *The Threshing Floor*. New York: Firebrand, 1987. Print.

————. "'When Everything Else Is Done and Dusted': An Interview with Barbara Burford, Scientist and Writer." Interview by Christine W. Sizemore. *Macomère* 2 (1999): 23–35. Print.

Burns, Christy L. "Powerful Differences: Critique and Eros in Jeanette Winterson and Virginia Woolf." *Modern Fiction Studies* 44.2 (1998): 364–92. Print.

Butler, Judith. "Values of Difficulty." *Just Being Difficult? Academic Writing in the Public Arena*. Ed. Jonathan Culler and Kevin Lamb. Stanford: Stanford UP, 2003. 199–215. Print.

Caramagno, Thomas C. *The Flight of the Mind: Virginia Woolf's Art and Manic-Depressive Illness*. Berkeley: U of California P, 1992. Print.

Caruth, Cathy, ed. *Trauma: Explorations in Memory*. Baltimore: Johns Hopkins UP, 1995. Print.

Cather, Willa. *A Lost Lady*. New York: Vintage, 1990. Print.

Caughie, Pamela L. *Virginia Woolf and Postmodernism: Literature in Quest and Question of Itself*. Chicago: U of Chicago P, 1991. Print.

Caws, Mary Ann. *Virginia Woolf*. New York: Overlook, 2001. Print.

Cendrars, Blaise. "On *The Cabinet of Doctor Caligari*." *Broom* 2 (1922): 351. Rpt. in R. Abel 271.

Certeau, Michel de. *The Practice of Everyday Life*. Trans. Steven Rendall. Berkeley: U of California P, 1984. Print.

Chaplin, Charles, dir. *Modern Times*. Perf. Chaplin and Paulette Goddard. United Artists, 1936. Film.

Charon, Rita. "Narrative Medicine: A Model for Empathy, Reflection, Profession, and Trust." *Journal of the American Medical Association* 286.15 (2001): 1897–903. Print.

———. *Narrative Medicine: Honoring the Stories of Illness*. New York: Oxford UP, 2006. Print.

Charon, Rita, Joanne Trautmann Banks, Julia E. Connelly, et al. "Literature and Medicine: Contributions to Clinical Practice." *Annals of Internal Medicine* 122.8 (1995): 599–606. Print.

Charon, Rita, and Martha Montello, eds. *Stories Matter: The Role of Narrative in Medical Ethics*. New York: Routledge, 2002. Print.

Childs, Donald. "Boers, Whores, and Mongols in *Mrs. Dalloway*." *Modernism and Eugenics: Woolf, Eliot, Yeats, and the Culture of Degeneration*. Cambridge: Cambridge UP, 2001. 38–57. Print.

Christian, Barbara. "Layered Rhythms: Virginia Woolf and Toni Morrison." Hussey and Neverow 164–77.

Cisneros, Sandra. *The House on Mango Street*. New York: Vintage, 1984. Print.

Clair, René, dir. *Entr'acte*. 1924. *A nous la liberté*. Criterion, 2002. DVD.

Clarke, Stuart N. "A *Mrs. Dalloway* Walk in London." *Virginia Woolf Society of Great Britain*. Virginia Woolf Soc. of Great Britain, June 2000. Web. 4 Mar. 2008.

———. "Recommended UK Paperback Editions of Virginia Woolf's Works." *VirginiaWoolfSociety.co.uk*. Virginia Woolf Soc. of Great Britain, Sept. 1999. Web. 30 Oct. 2008.

Close Up: *A Magazine Devoted to the Art of Films*. Ed. Kenneth Macpherson and Bryher. 1927–33. New York: Arno, 1971. Print. Arno Ser. of Contemporary Art.

Cohen, Scott. "The Empire from the Street: Virginia Woolf, Wembley, and Imperial Monuments." *Modern Fiction Studies* 50.1 (2004): 85–109. Print.

Corrigan, Timothy. *Film and Literature: An Introduction and Reader*. Upper Saddle River: Prentice, 1998. Print.

Coulehan, Jack. "Today's Professionalism: Engaging the Mind but Not the Heart." *Academic Medicine* 80.10 (2005): 892–98. Print.

Courington, Chella. "From *Clarissa* to *Mrs. Dalloway*: Woolf's (Re)Vision of Richardson." Barrett and Cramer, *Re: Reading* 95–101.

Cowart, David. *Literary Symbiosis: The Reconfigured Text in Twentieth-Century Writing*. Athens: U of Georgia P, 1993. Print.

Cramer, Patricia. Introduction. Barrett and Cramer, *Virginia Woolf* 117–27.

——. "Notes from the Underground: Lesbian Ritual in the Writings of Virginia Woolf." Hussey and Neverow-Turk 177–88.

——. "Response." Ardis and Scott 116–26.

Crary, Jonathan. *Suspensions of Perception: Attention, Spectacle, and Modern Culture*. Cambridge: MIT P, 2001. Print.

Crater, Theresa. "Septimus and Charles Watkins: The Phallic Suppression of Masculine Subjectivity." *Journal of Evolutionary Psychology* 21.3-4 (2000): 191–202. Print.

Crimp, Douglas. *Melancholia and Moralism: Essays on AIDS and Queer Politics*. Cambridge: MIT P, 2002. Print.

Cuddy-Keane, Melba. "*Mrs. Dalloway*: Film, Time, and Trauma." Davis and McVicker 171–75.

——. *Virginia Woolf, the Intellectual, and the Public Sphere*. Cambridge: Cambridge UP, 2003. Print.

Cunningham, Michael. *The Hours*. New York: Picador, 1998. Print.

——. Interview. *Publishers Weekly*. Reed Business Info., 2 Nov. 1998. Web. 16 Dec. 2008.

——. "Virginia Woolf: The Quiet Revolutionary." *Salon*. 22 June 2000. Web. 1 Mar. 2008.

Daiches, David, and John Flower. "Virginia Woolf's London." *Literary Landscapes of the British Isles: A Narrative Atlas*. By Daiches and Flower. New York: Paddington, 1979. 69–89. Print.

Daldry, Stephen, dir. *The Hours*. Perf. Meryl Streep, Nicole Kidman, and Julianne Moore. Paramount, 2002. Film.

Daugherty, Beth Rigel. "'Readin', Writin', and Revisin'': Virginia Woolf's 'How Should One Read a Book?'" Rosenberg and Dubino 159–75.

——. "Taking a Leaf from Virginia Woolf's Book: Empowering the Student." Hussey and Neverow-Turk 31–40.

——. "Teaching *Mrs. Dalloway* and *Praisesong for the Widow* as a Pair." Gillespie and Hankins 175–82.

Daugherty, Beth Rigel, and Mary Beth Pringle, eds. *Approaches to Teaching Woolf's* To the Lighthouse. New York: MLA, 2001. Print. Approaches to Teaching World Lit.

Davidoff, Lenore. *The Best Circles: Society Etiquette and the Season*. London: Croom Helm, 1973. Print.

Davis, Laura, and Jeanette McVicker, eds. *Virginia Woolf and Her Influences: Selected Papers from the Seventh Annual Conference on Virginia Woolf*. New York: Pace UP, 1998. Print.

de Lauretis, Teresa. *The Practice of Love: Lesbian Sexuality and Perverse Desire*. Bloomington: Indiana UP, 1994. Print.

DeMeester, Karen. "Trauma, Post-traumatic Stress Disorder, and Obstacles to Postwar Recovery in *Mrs. Dalloway*." *Virginia Woolf and Trauma: Embodied Texts*. Ed. Suzette Henke and David Eberly, with Jane Lilienfeld. New York: Pace UP, 2007. 77–93. Print.

DeSalvo, Louise. *Virginia Woolf: The Impact of Childhood Sexual Abuse on Her Life and Work*. Boston: Beacon, 1989. Print.

Desnos, Robert. "Dream and the Cinema." R. Abel 283–85.

Dettmar, Kevin, and Jennifer Wicke, eds. *The Longman Anthology of British Literature: The Twentieth Century*. New York: Addison, 2003. Print.

DiBattista, Maria. "Joyce, Woolf, and the Modern Mind." *Virginia Woolf: New Critical Essays*. Ed. Patricia Clements and Isobel Grundy. London: Vision, 1983. 96–114. Print.

Dick, Susan. "Building It Round One: *Mrs. Dalloway*." *Virginia Woolf*. London: Arnold, 1989. 30–43. Print.

Dittrich, Lisa R., and Anne L. Farmakidis, eds. *The Humanities and Medicine: Reports of 41 U.S., Canadian, and International Programs*. Spec. issue of *Academic Medicine* 78.10 (2003): 951–1075. Print.

Doan, Laura, and Terry Brown. "Being There: Woolf's London and the Politics of Location." Barrett and Cramer, *Re: Reading* 16–21.

Dobrée, Bonamy. "Seen on the Stage." *Vogue* [London] late Dec. 1925: 64+; late April 1926: 51+; early Dec. 1926: 74+; late Dec. 1926: 42+; Print.

Donald, James, Anne Friedberg, and Laura Marcus, eds. *Close Up, 1927–1933: Cinema and Modernism*. Princeton: Princeton UP, 1998. Print.

Dowling, David. Mrs. Dalloway: *Mapping Streams of Consciousness*. Boston: Twayne, 1991. Print. Masterwork Studies.

Dubino, Jeanne. "Creating 'the Conditions of Life': Virginia Woolf and the Common Reader." Barrett and Cramer, *Re: Reading* 129–37.

Duffy, Michael, ed. *First World War.com: A Multi-media History of World War One*. 10 Apr. 2004. Web. 15 Jan. 2008.

Dulac, Germaine. "The Aesthetics, the Obstacles, Integral *Cinégraphie*." 1926. Trans. Stuart Liebman. R. Abel 389–97.

———. "The Essence of the Cinema: The Visual Idea." 1925. Trans. Robert Lamberton. *The Avant-Garde Film: A Reader of Theory and Criticism*. Ed. P. Adams Sitney. New York: New York UP, 1978. 36–42. Print.

———. "The Expressive Techniques of the Cinema." 1924. Trans. Stuart Liebman. R. Abel 305–18.

———, dir. *The Seashell and the Clergyman* [*La coquille et le clergyman*]. 1923. Light Cone, 2008. Film.

———. *The Smiling Madame Beudet* [*La souriante Mme Beudet*]. 1923. Light Cone, 2008. Film.

Dyer, Geoff. *The Missing of the Somme*. London: Phoenix, 1994. Print.

Dymond, Justine. "Virginia Woolf Scholarship from 1991 to 2003: A Selected Bibliography." *Modern Fiction Studies* 50.1 (2004): 241–79. Print.

Edmundson, Mark. *Why Read?* New York: Bloomsbury, 2004. Print.

Edwards, Lee R. "War and Roses: The Politics of *Mrs. Dalloway*." *The Authority of Experience: Essays in Feminist Criticism*. Ed. Arlyn Diamond and Edwards. Amherst: U of Massachusetts P, 1977. 160–77. Print.

Eliot. T. S. *The Waste Land*. Ed. Michael North. New York: Norton, 2001. Print.

Ellis, Sarah Stickney. *The Women of England: Their Social Duties and Domestic Habits*. London: Fisher, 1845. Print.

Ellmann, Richard. *James Joyce*. Rev. ed. New York: Oxford UP, 1982. Print.

Esslin, Martin. *The Theatre of the Absurd*. 1961. Garden City: Anchor, 1969. Print.

Evans, Hilary, and Mary Evans. *The Party That Lasted One Hundred Days: The Late Victorian Season: A Social Study*. London: Macdonald, 1976. Print.

Evans, Kim, dir. "Virginia Woolf's *Mrs. Dalloway*." Writ. and adapt. Evans and Gillian Greenwood. 21 Feb. 1988. *Modern World: Ten Great Writers*. Home Vision, 1988. Videocassette.

Evans, Martyn, and Ilora G. Finlay, eds. *Medical Humanities*. London: BMJ, 2001. Print.

Falcetta, Jennie-Rebecca. "Geometries of Space and Time: The Cubist London of *Mrs. Dalloway*." *Woolf Studies Annual* 13 (2007): 111–36. Print.

Farley, Lisa. "Learning from the Archive: Toward a Theory of Thoughtful Judgment." *Teaching through Testimony*, Part Two. Ed. Jacqueline Ellis and Edvige Giunta. Spec. issue of *Transformations: The Journal of Inclusive Scholarship and Pedagogy* 17.1 (2006): 70–84. Print.

Felman, Shoshana. "Psychoanalysis and Education: Teaching Terminable and Interminable." *Yale French Studies* 63 (1982): 21–44. Rpt. in *Contemporary Literary Criticism: Literary and Cultural Studies*. 4th ed. Ed. Robert Con Davis and Ronald Schliefer. New York: Addison-Wesley, 1998. 410–29. Print.

Felman, Shoshana, and Dori Laub. *Testimony: Crises of Witnessing in Literature, Psycho-analysis, and History*. New York: Routledge, 1992. Print.

Felski, Rita. "Modernist Studies and Cultural Studies: Reflections on Method." *Modernism/Modernity* 10.3 (2003): 501–17. Print.

Ferry, David. "In the Reading Room." *New Yorker* 15 Sept. 2003: 56. Print.

First Look Pictures. "Virginia Woolf's *Mrs. Dalloway*." Los Angeles: Overseas Film Group, 1996. Print. Preliminary production information.

Fleishman, Avrom. "Forms of the Woolfian Short Story." *Virginia Woolf: Revaluation and Continuity*. Berkeley: U of California P, 1980. 40–70. Print.

———. *Virginia Woolf: A Critical Reading*. Baltimore: Johns Hopkins UP, 1975. Print.

Flitterman-Lewis, Sandy. *To Desire Differently*. Expanded ed. New York: Columbia UP, 1996. Print.

Fox, Alice. *Virginia Woolf and the Literature of the English Renaissance*. Oxford: Clarendon, 1990. Print.

Freeman, Judi. "Bridging Purism and Surrealism: The Origins and Production of Fernand Léger's *Ballet Mécanique*." Kuenzli 28–45.

Freire, Paulo. *Pedagogy of the Oppressed*. 20th anniversary ed. Trans. Myra Bergman Ramos. New York: Continuum, 1996. Print.

Friedman, Susan Stanford. *Mappings: Feminism and the Cultural Geographies of Encounter*. Princeton: Princeton UP, 1998. Print.

Froula, Christine. "*Mrs. Dalloway*'s Postwar Elegy: Women, War, and the Art of Mourning." Froula, *Virginia Woolf* 87–126.

———. *Virginia Woolf and the Bloomsbury Avant-Garde: War, Civilization, Modernity*. New York: Columbia UP, 2005. Print.

Fuderer, Laura Sue. "Criticism of Virginia Woolf from 1972 to December 1990: A Selected Checklist." *Modern Fiction Studies* 38.1 (1992): 303–42. Print.

Fuegi, John, and Jo Francis. "The Making of *The War Within*." Gillespie and Hankins 206–17.

———, dirs. *The War Within: A Portrait of Virginia Woolf*. Flare, 1995. Film.

Fulker, Teresa. "Virginia Woolf's Daily Drama of the Body." *Woolf Studies Annual* 1 (1995): 3–25. Print.

Fulton, Lorie Watkins. "'A Direction of One's Own': Alienation in *Mrs. Dalloway* and *Sula*." *African American Review* 40.1 (2006): 67–77. Print.

Fussell, Paul. *The Great War and Modern Memory*. Oxford: Oxford UP, 1975. Print.

Gance, Abel. *J'accuse*. 1919. Flicker Alley, 2008. DVD.

Garnett, Angelica. Introduction. *Mrs. Dalloway*. By Virginia Woolf. London: Hogarth, 1990. vii–xv. Print.

Garvey, Johanna X. K. "Difference and Continuity: The Voices of *Mrs. Dalloway*." *College English* 53.1 (1991): 59–76. Print.

Gelfant, Blanche H. "Love and Conversion in *Mrs. Dalloway*." *Criticism* 8.3 (1966): 229–45. Print.

Giddens, Anthony. *The Consequences of Modernity*. Stanford: Stanford UP, 1990. Print.

Gilbert, Martin. *The First World War: A Complete History*. New York: Holt, 1994. Print.

Gilbert, Sandra, and Susan Gubar. *Letters from the Front*. New Haven: Yale UP, 1996. Print. Vol. 3 of *No Man's Land: The Place of the Woman Writer in the Twentieth Century*.

———. *The Madwoman in the Attic: The Woman Writer and the Nineteenth-Century Imagination*. New Haven: Yale UP, 1979. Print.

Gillespie, Diane F. "'Human Nature Is on You': Septimus Smith, the Camera Eye, and the Classroom." Davis and McVicker 162–67.

Gillespie, Diane F., and Leslie K. Hankins, eds. *Virginia Woolf and the Arts: Selected Papers from the Sixth Annual Conference on Virginia Woolf*. New York: Pace UP, 1997. Print.

Gillies, Mary Ann. *Henri Bergson and British Modernism*. Montreal: McGill-Queen's UP, 1996. Print.

Girouard, Mark. *Life in the English Country House: A Social and Architectural History*. New York: Penguin, 1980. Print.

Glaxo. Advertisement. *Punch* 29 Dec. 1920: n. pag. Print.

Glenny, Allie. *Ravenous Identity: Eating and Eating Distress in the Life and Work of Virginia Woolf*. New York: Palgrave, 2000. Print.

Gorris, Marleen. "The Lighter Side of Feminism." Interview by Robert Sklar. *Cineaste* 16.2 (1988): 26–28. Print.

———, dir. *Mrs. Dalloway*. Perf. Vanessa Redgrave, Natasha McElhone, Rupert Graves, and Michael Kitchen. First Look Pictures, 1998. Film.

Gottlieb, Laura Moss. *Index to the Virginia Woolf Miscellany, 1973–1998: The First Fifty Issues*. Rohnert Park: Sonoma State UP, 1998. Print.

Goudal, Jean. "Surrealism and Cinema." *La revue hebdomadaire* [Paris] Feb. 1925. Rpt. in Hammond 84–94.

Great Britain. War Office. Parliamentary Recruiting Committee. *Report of Publications Sub-Department*. Kew: National Archives. Print. War Office Catalog nos. 106/367.

The Great War and the Shaping of the Twentieth Century. Public Broadcasting Service. PBS, 1996. Television.

The Great War and the Shaping of the Twentieth Century. Public Broadcasting Service. PBS, 2004. Web. 22 Oct. 2008.

Greenfield, Lawrence A., and Tracy L. Snell. "Bureau of Justice Statistics Special Report: Women Offenders." *U.S. Department of Justice, Office of Justice Programs*. U.S. Dept. of Justice, 3 Oct. 2000. Web. 2 Mar. 2008.

Greenhalgh, Trisha, and Brian Hurwitz, eds. *Narrative Based Medicine: Dialogue and Discourse in Clinical Practice*. London: BMJ, 1998. Print.

Gregory, Adrian. *The Silence of Memory: Armistice Day, 1919–1946*. Oxford: Berg, 1994. Print.

Groen, Rick. "Mrs. Dalloway Moves Gracefully to the Screen." *Globe and Mail* [Toronto] 27 Feb. 1998: D1+. Print.

Guth, Deborah. "'What a Lark! What a Plunge!': Fiction as Self-Evasion in *Mrs. Dalloway*." *Modern Language Review* 84.1 (1989): 18–25. Print.

Haig and Unknown Soldier. 1920. *Getty Images*. Web. 22 Feb. 2008. Image no. 52782450.

Hammond, Paul, ed. *The Shadow and Its Shadow: Surrealist Writings on the Cinema*. 3rd ed. San Francisco: City Lights, 2000. Print.

Hankins, Leslie. "Abel Gance's *J'accuse* and Virginia Woolf's *Mrs. Dalloway*: Rereading a Modernist Novel by the Light of the Silver Screen." *J'accuse*. 1919. Restored ed. Flicker Alley, 2008. 14–17. DVD booklet.

———. "'Across the Screen of My Brain': Virginia Woolf's 'The Cinema' and Film Forums of the Twenties." *The Multiple Muses of Virginia Woolf*. Ed. Diane F. Gillespie. Columbia: U of Missouri P, 1993. 148–79. Print

———. "*Cinéastes* and Modernists: Writing about Film in 1920s London." Scott, *Gender* 809–58.

———. "'Colour Burning on a Framework of Steel': Virginia Woolf, Marleen Gorris, Eileen Atkins and *Mrs. Dalloway*(s). *Virginia Woolf in Performance*. Ed. Sally Greene. Spec. issue of *Women's Studies* 28.4 (1999): 367–77. Print.

————. "Complicating Adaptation: Virginia Woolf's 1925 Novel, *Mrs. Dalloway*, and Abel Gance's 1918–9 Film, *J'accuse*." *Selected Papers from the Eighteenth Annual Conference on Virginia Woolf*. Ed. Eleanor McNees and Sara Veglahn. Clemson: Clemson U Digital P, forthcoming. Print.

————. "The Doctor and the Woolf: Reel Challenges—*The Cabinet of Dr. Caligari* and *Mrs. Dalloway*." Hussey and Neverow-Turk 40–51.

————. "Iris Barry, Writer and *Cinéaste* in *The Adelphi*, *The Spectator*, the Film Society and the British *Vogue*: Forming Film Culture in London of the 1920s." *Modernism/Modernity* 11.3 (2004): 488–515. Print.

————. "Switching Sex and Redirecting Desire: The Surrealist Film, *Entr'acte*, and Woolf's *Orlando*." *Virginia Woolf Miscellany* 67 (2005): 25–26. Print.

————. "Tracking Shots through Film History: Virginia Woolf, Film Archives, and Future Technologies." Ardis and Scott 266–75.

————. "Virginia Woolf and Film—The Archival Turn: Bloomsbury, *Vogue*, *Anna Karenina*, and Judith Chaplin 'In an Extremely Well-Appointed Library.'" *The Edinburgh Companion to Virginia Woolf and the Arts*. Ed. Maggie Humm. Edinburgh: Edinburgh UP, forthcoming. Print.

————. "Virginia Woolf's 'The Cinema': Sneak Previews of the Holograph Pre-texts through Post-publication Revisions." *Woolf Studies Annual* 15 (2009): forthcoming. Print.

Hanlon, Mike, ed. *Trenches on the Web: Reference Library*. *WorldWar1.com*. Great War Soc., 15 Jan. 2000. Web. 15 Jan. 2008.

Hare, David. *The Hours*. New York: Miramax Books, 2002. Print.

Harper, Howard. "*Mrs. Dalloway*, the Film." Davis and McVicker 167–171.

Harper, Philip Brian. *Private Affairs: Critical Ventures in the Culture of Social Relations*. New York: New York UP, 1999. Print.

Harris, Jocelyn. "Clarissa Lives! Reading Richardson through Rewritings." *Approaches to Teaching the Novels of Samuel Richardson*. Ed. Lisa Zunshine and Harris. New York: MLA, 2006. 140–46. Print. Approaches to Teaching World Lit.

Harrison, Suzan. "Playing with Fire: Women's Sexuality and Artistry in Virginia Woolf's *Mrs. Dalloway* and Eudora Welty's *The Golden Apples*." *Mississippi Quarterly* 56.2 (2003): 289–313. Print.

Hartman, Geoffrey. "Memory.com: Tele-Suffering and Testimony in the Dot Com Era." *Raritan* 19.3 (2000): 1–18. Print.

Hawthorn, Jeremy. *Virginia Woolf's* Mrs. Dalloway: *A Study in Alienation*. London: Chatto, 1975. Print.

HD [Hilda Doolittle]."The Cinema and the Classics, I: Beauty." *Close Up* July 1927: 22–33. Rpt. in Donald, Friedberg, and Marcus 105–09.

————. "Projector, I." *Close Up* July 1927: 46–51. Rpt. in Scott, *Gender* 848–51.

————. "Projector, II.: *Chang*." *Close Up* Oct. 1927: 35–44. Print.

Hecht, Ben. *Thousand and One Afternoons in Chicago*. 1922. Chicago: U of Chicago P, 1992. Print.

Heine, Elizabeth. "The Significance of Structure in the Novels of E. M. Forster and

Virginia Woolf." *English Literature in Transition, 1880–1920* 16 (1973): 289–306. Print.

Henderson, Diana E. "Rewriting Family Ties: Woolf's Renaissance Romance." *Virginia Woolf: Reading the Renaissance.* Ed. Sally Greene. Athens: Ohio UP, 1999. 136–60. Print.

Henke, Suzette A. "Modernism, Trauma, and Narrative Reformulation." Scott, *Gender* 555–63.

———. "*Mrs. Dalloway*: The Communion of Saints." *New Feminist Essays on Virginia Woolf.* Ed. Jane Marcus. Lincoln: U of Nebraska P, 1981. 125–47. Print.

———. "'The Prime Minister': A Key to *Mrs. Dalloway.*" *Virginia Woolf: Centennial Essays.* Ed. Elaine K. Ginsberg and Laura Moss Gottlieb. Troy: Whitston, 1983. 127–41. Print.

———. "Virginia Woolf: The Modern Tradition." *The Gender of Modernism: A Critical Anthology.* Ed. Bonnie Kime Scott. Bloomington: Indiana UP, 1990. 622–28. Print.

Herman, Judith. *Trauma and Recovery.* New York: Basic, 1992. Print.

Hessler, John G. "Moral Accountability in *Mrs. Dalloway.*" 1978. Bloom, *Clarissa Dalloway* 126–36.

Hipp, Daniel. *The Poetry of Shell Shock: Wartime Trauma and Healing in Wilfred Owen, Ivor Gurney, and Siegfried Sassoon.* Jefferson: McFarland, 2005. Print.

Hoff, Molly. "The Pseudo-Homeric World of *Mrs. Dalloway.*" *Twentieth-Century Literature* 45.2 (1999): 186–209. Print.

———. "Woolf's *Mrs. Dalloway.*" *Explicator* 58.3 (2000): 148–50. Print.

———. "Woolf's *Mrs. Dalloway.*" *Explicator* 59.2 (2001): 95–98. Print.

———. "Woolf's *Mrs. Dalloway.*" *Explicator* 60.1 (2001): 31–33. Print.

———. "Woolf's *Mrs. Dalloway.*" *Explicator* 60.4 (2002): 205–07. Print.

———. "Woolf's *Mrs. Dalloway.*" *Explicator* 61.1 (2002): 37–39. Print.

Hoffman, Charles G. "From Short Story to Novel: The Manuscript Revisions of Virginia Woolf's *Mrs. Dalloway.*" *Modern Fiction Studies* 14.2 (1968): 171–86. Print.

Holtby, Winifred. "So Handy for the Fun Fair." Tater, *Women* 52–67.

———. *Virginia Woolf.* London: Wishart, 1932. Print.

Homan, Sidney. "*Waiting for Godot*: Inmates as Students and—Then—Teachers." *Approaches to Teaching Beckett's* Waiting for Godot. Ed. June Schlueter and Gnoch Brater. New York: MLA, 1991. 156–62. Print. Approaches to Teaching World Lit.

Hotchkiss, Lia M. "Writing the Jump Cut: *Mrs. Dalloway* in the Context of Cinema." *Virginia Woolf: Texts and Contexts: Selected Papers from the Fifth Annual Conference on Virginia Woolf.* Ed. Beth Rigel Daugherty and Eileen Barrett. New York: Pace UP, 1996. 134–39. Print.

Hovannisian, Richard G. "Case Study 1: The Armenian Genocide." *Teaching about Genocide: Issues, Approaches, and Resources.* Ed. Samuel Totten. Greenwich: Information Age, 2004. 95–109. Print.

Howard, Maureen. Foreword. *Mrs. Dalloway.* By Virginia Woolf. Orlando: Harcourt, 1981. vii–xiv. Print.

Hughes, Langston. *Selected Poems*. New York: Vintage, 1990. Print.

Hughes, Mary Joe. "Michael Cunningham's *The Hours* and Postmodern Artistic Re-Presentation." *Critique* 45.4 (2005): 349–61. Print.

Humm, Maggie. *Modernist Women and Visual Cultures*. New Brunswick: Rutgers UP, 2003. Print.

———. *Snapshots of Bloomsbury: The Private Lives of Virginia Woolf and Vanessa Bell*. New Brunswick: Rutgers UP, 2006. Print.

Hussey, Mark. Foreword. Prose vii–ix.

———, ed. *Major Authors on CD-ROM: Virginia Woolf*. Woodbridge: Primary Source, 1997. CD-ROM.

———. Preface. *Mrs. Dalloway*. By Virginia Woolf. Orlando: Harcourt, 2005. ix–xviii. Print.

———. *The Singing of the Real World: The Philosophy of Virginia Woolf's Fiction*. Columbus: Ohio State UP, 1986. Print.

———, ed. *Virginia Woolf and War: Fiction, Reality, and Myth*. Syracuse: Syracuse UP, 1991. Print.

———. *Virginia Woolf A to Z: A Comprehensive Reference for Students, Teachers, and Common Readers to Her Life, Works, and Critical Reception*. New York: Facts on File, 1995. Print.

Hussey, Mark, and Vara Neverow, eds. *Virginia Woolf: Emerging Perspectives: Selected Papers from the Third Annual Conference on Virginia Woolf*. New York: Pace UP, 1994. Print.

Hussey, Mark, and Vara Neverow-Turk, eds. *Virginia Woolf Miscellany: Proceedings of the First Annual Conference on Virginia Woolf*. New York: Pace UP, 1992. Print.

Huxley, Aldous. "Where Are the Movies Moving? Some Notes on the Potentialities of the Cinema in the Expression of Fantastic Themes and Extravagant Flights of Fancy." *Vogue* [London] early Dec. 1926: 76+. Print.

———. "Where Are the Movies Moving? The Brilliant Success of the Cinema in Portraying the Fantastic and Preposterous." *Vanity Fair* July 1925: 39+. Print.

Hynes, Samuel. *The Soldiers' Tale: Bearing Witness to Modern War*. New York: Penguin, 1997. Print.

Imperial War Museum. Poster collection. Imperial War Museum, London.

Imperial War Museum Collections. United Kingdom, n.d. Web. 1 Mar. 2008.

Indigo Girls. *Rites of Passage*. Sony, 2000. CD.

International Virginia Woolf Society. *International Virginia Woolf Society*. Univ. of Toronto, 13 Sept. 2008. Web. 24 Nov. 2008.

Jameson, Fredric. *Postmodernism; or, The Cultural Logic of Late Capitalism*. Durham: Duke UP, 1991. Print.

Jensen, Emily. "Clarissa Dalloway's Respectable Suicide." *Virginia Woolf: A Feminist Slant*. Ed. Jane Marcus. Lincoln: U of Nebraska P, 1983. 162–79. Print.

Johnson, Niall. *Britain and the 1918–19 Influenza Pandemic: A Dark Epilogue*. London: Routledge, 2006. Print.

Joyce, James. *The Dead*. Ed. Daniel R. Schwarz. Boston: Bedford, 1994. Print.

———. *Dubliners*. 1914. New York: Penguin, 1985. Print.

————. *Ulysses*. 1922. New York: Vintage, 1986. Print.

Joyes, Kaley. "Failed Witnessing in Virginia Woolf's *Mrs. Dalloway*." *Woolf Studies Annual* 14 (2008): 69–89. Print.

Kaplan, E. Ann. *Trauma Culture: The Politics of Terror and Loss in Media and Literature*. New Brunswick: Rutgers UP, 2005. Print.

Kaysen, Susanna. *Girl, Interrupted*. New York: Vintage, 1993. Print.

Kern, Stephen. *The Culture of Time and Space, 1880–1918*. Cambridge: Harvard UP, 1983. Print.

King, James. *Virginia Woolf*. New York: Norton, 1994. Print.

Kirklin, Deborah, and Ruth Richardson, eds. *Medical Humanities: A Practical Introduction*. London: Royal Coll. of Physicians, 2001. Print.

Kirkpatrick, B. J. *A Bibliography of Virginia Woolf*. 3rd ed. Oxford: Clarendon, 1980. Print.

Kirkpatrick, B. J., and Stuart N. Clarke. *A Bibliography of Virginia Woolf*. 4th ed. Oxford: Clarendon, 1997. Print.

Kirschner, Susan, and Paul Connolly. "Opening Questions: A Workshop in Writing to Read Virginia Woolf." Barrett and Cramer, *Re: Reading* 251–58.

Kitchen, Judith. *The House on Eccles Road: A Novel*. Saint Paul: Graywolf, 2002. Print.

Kolodny, Annette. "A Map for Rereading: Gender and the Interpretation of Literary Texts." *Feminist Criticism: Essays on Women, Literature, and Theory*. Ed. Elaine Showalter. New York: Pantheon, 1985. 46–62. Print.

Kuenzli, Rudolf, ed. *Dada and Surrealist Film*. Cambridge: MIT P, 1996. Print.

Kureishi, Hanif, writ. *Sammy and Rosie Get Laid*. Dir. Stephen Frears. Hallmark, 1997. Videocassette.

LaCapra, Dominick. *History in Transit: Experience, Identity, Critical Theory*. Ithaca: Cornell UP, 2004. Print.

Lambert, Elizabeth G. "Mrs. Dalloway Meets the Robot Maria." Gillespie and Hankins 277–82.

————. "Proportion Is in the Mind of the Beholder: *Mrs. Dalloway's* Critique of Science." Hussey and Neverow 278–82.

Lanchester, John. *Mr. Phillips: A Novel*. New York: Putnam, 2000. Print.

Landry, Lionel. "Caligarism; or, The Theatre's Revenge." Trans. Stuart Liebman. R. Abel 268–70. Print. Trans. of "Caligarisme ou la revanche du théâtre." *Cinéa* 28 Apr. 1922: 12.

Lane, Richard J. Mrs. Dalloway. Detroit: Gale, 2001. Print. Literary Masterpieces 11.

Lang, Fritz, dir. *Metropolis*. Babelsburg Studios, 1927. Film.

Latham, Jacqueline. "The Manuscript Revisions of Virginia Woolf's *Mrs. Dalloway*: A Postscript." *Modern Fiction Studies* 18.3 (1972): 475–76. Print.

Latimer, Tirza True. "Inversions, Subversions, Reversions: Did Relache Queer the Discourse?" *On-Stage Studies* 20 (1997): 65–82. Print.

Lawder, Standish. *The Cubist Cinema*. New York: New York UP, 1975. Print.

Lawrence, D. H. *Sons and Lovers*. Ed. Helen Baron and Carl Baron. Cambridge: Cambridge UP, 1992. Print.

———. "Tickets, Please." *The Complete Short Stories*. Vol. 2. New York: Viking, 1961. 334–46. Print.

Le Bon, Gustave. *The Crowd*. Mineola: Dover, 2002. Print.

Lee, Hermione. *Virginia Woolf*. New York: Knopf, 1997. Print.

———. *Virginia Woolf's Nose: Essays on Biography*. Princeton: Princeton UP, 2005. Print.

Leed, Eric J. *No Man's Land: Combat and Identity in World War I*. Cambridge: Cambridge UP, 1979. Print.

Leese, Peter. *Shell Shock: Traumatic Neurosis and the British Soldiers of the First World War*. New York: Palgrave, 2002. Print.

Lefebvre, Henri. *The Production of Space*. Trans. Donald Nicholson-Smith. Afterword by David Harvey. Oxford: Blackwell, 1991. Print.

Léger, Fernand. "*La Roue*: Its Plastic Quality." 1922. R. Abel 271–74.

———. "*Mechanical Ballet*: Film by Fernand Léger and Dudley Murphy, Musical Synchronism by Geroge Antheil." *Little Review* 10.2 (1924-25): 42–44. Print.

———. "A New Realism—The Object (Its Plastic and Cinematographic Value)." Trans. Rosamond Gilder. *Little Review* 11.2 (1926): 7–8. Print.

———. "Painting and Cinema." 1925. R. Abel 372–73.

Léger, Fernand, and Dudley Murphy, dirs. *Ballet mécanique*. 1924. *Unseen Cinema*. Image Entertainment, 2005. DVD.

Lehmann, John. *Virginia Woolf and Her World*. New York: Harcourt, 1975. Print.

Lehner, Ernst, and Johanna Lehner. *Folklore and Symbolism of Flowers, Plants, and Trees*. New York: Tudor, 1960. Print.

Leslie Stephen's Photograph Album. Smith College Libraries, 2003. Web. 3 Mar. 2008. Mortimer Rare Book Room, online exhibitions.

Levenback, Karen. *Virginia Woolf and the Great War*. Syracuse: Syracuse UP, 1999. Print.

Levenson, Michael, ed. *Cambridge Companion to Modernism*. Cambridge: Cambridge UP, 1999. Print.

———. Introduction. Levenson, *Cambridge* 1–8.

Lilienfeld, Jane. "Accident, Incident, and Meaning: Traces of Trauma in Virginia Woolf's Narrativity." Ardis and Scott 153–58.

Lippincott, Robin. *Mr. Dalloway*. Louisville: Sarabande, 1999. Print.

Lord, Catherine M. "The Frames of Septimus Smith: Through Twenty Four Hours in the City of Mrs. Dalloway, 1923, and of Millennial London: Art Is a Shocking Experience." *Parallax* 5.3 (1999): 36–46. Print.

Lorde, Audre. "Uses of the Erotic: The Erotic as Power." *Sister Outsider*. Freedom: Crossing, 1984. 53–59. Print.

Lord Mayor's Fund for Armenian Refugees. Advertisement. Drawing by Louis Raemaekers. *Times* [London] 3 July 1916: 3. Print.

Luckhurst, Roger. *The Trauma Question*. New York: Routledge, 2008. Print.

Lukács, Georg. "The Ideology of Modernism." *Realism in Our Time: Literature and the Class Struggle*. Trans. John Mander and Necke Mander. New York: Harper, 1962. 17–46. Print.

Lyotard, Jean-François. "Answering the Question: What Is Postmodernism?" Trans. Régis Durand. *The Postmodern Condition: A Report on Knowledge*. Trans. Geoff Bennington and Brian Massumi. Minneapolis: U of Minnesota P, 1984. 71–82. Print.

MacKinnon, Gillies, dir. *Regeneration*. Fox Video, 1998. Videocassette.

Majumdar, Robin, and Allen McLaurin, eds. *Virginia Woolf: The Critical Heritage*. London: Routledge, 1975. Print.

Marcus, Jane. *Hearts of Darkness: White Women Write Race*. New Brunswick: Rutgers UP, 2004. Print.

———. "Registering Objections: Grounding Feminist Alibis." *Reconfigured Spheres: Feminist Explorations of Literary Space*. Ed. Margaret R. Higgonet and Joan Templeton. Amherst: U of Massachusetts P, 1994. 171–93. Print.

Marcus, Laura. "The Great War in Twentieth-Century Cinema." Sherry, *Cambridge Companion* 280–301.

———. *The Tenth Muse: Writing about Cinema in the Modernist Period*. Oxford: Oxford UP, 2008. Print.

Marcuse, Herbert. "The Ideology of Death." *The Meaning of Death*. Ed. Herman Feifel. New York: McGraw, 1959. 64–76. Print.

Marsh, Nicholas. *Virginia Woolf: The Novels*. New York: St. Martin's, 1998. Print. Analysing Texts.

Martin, Ann. "Sleeping Beauty in a Green Dress: *Mrs. Dalloway* and Fairy Tale Configurations of Desire." *Virginia Woolf: Out of Bounds: Selected Papers from the Tenth Annual Conference on Virginia Woolf*. Ed. Jessica Berman and Jane Goldman. New York: Pace UP, 2001. 25–31. Print.

Marwick, Arthur. *The Deluge: British Society and the First World War*. New York: Norton, 1965. Print.

McBride, Dwight A. "Can the Queen Speak? Racial Essentialism, Sexuality, and the Problem of Authority." *Black Men on Race, Gender, and Sexuality: A Critical Reader*. Ed. Devon N. Carbado. New York: New York UP, 1999. 253–75. Print.

McDowell, Linda, and Joanne Sharp, eds. *Space, Gender, Knowledge: Feminist Readings*. Oxford: Oxford UP, 1997. Print.

McNaron, Toni A. H. "'The Albanians, or Was It the Armenians?': Virginia Woolf's Lesbianism as Gloss on Her Modernism." Neverow-Turk and Hussey 134–41.

McNees, Eleanor. "Colonizing Virginia Woolf: *Scrutiny* and Contemporary Values." Rosenberg and Dubino 41–58.

———, ed. *Virginia Woolf: Critical Assessments*. Vol. 3. London: Helm, 1994. Print.

Meisel, Perry. *The Absent Father: Virginia Woolf and Walter Pater*. New Haven: Yale UP, 1980. Print.

Mendelson, Edward. "The Death of Mrs. Dalloway: Two Readings." *Textual Analysis: Some Readers Reading*. Ed. Mary Ann Caws. New York: MLA, 1986. 272–80. Print.

Mepham, John. *Criticism in Focus: Virginia Woolf*. New York: St. Martin's, 1992. Print.

Mezei, Kathy, ed. *Ambiguous Discourse: Feminist Narratology and British Women Writers*. Chapel Hill: U of North Carolina P, 1996. 66–92. Print.

Mill, John Stuart. *The Subjection of Women*. Mineola: Dover, 1997. Print.

Miller, J. Hillis. "*Mrs. Dalloway*: Repetition as the Raising of the Dead." *Fiction and Repetition: Seven English Novels* By Miller. Cambridge. Harvard UP, 1982. 176–202. Print.

Minow-Pinkney, Makiko. *Virginia Woolf and the Problem of the Subject: Feminine Writing in the Major Novels*. Brighton: Harvester, 1987. Print.

Mirza, Heidi Safia. Introduction. *Black British Feminism: A Reader*. Ed. Mirza. London: Routledge, 1997. 1–28. Print.

Modernist Studies Association. *MSA Annual Conference*. Johns Hopkins Univ., n.d. Web. 8 Jan. 2009.

Moers, Ellen. *Literary Women*. Garden City: Anchor, 1977. Print.

Monte, Steven. "Ancients and Moderns in *Mrs. Dalloway*." *Modern Language Quarterly* 60.4 (2000): 587–616. Print.

Moran, Patricia. *Word of Mouth: Body Language in Katherine Mansfield and Virginia Woolf*. Charlottesville: UP of Virginia, 1996. Print.

Morgan, Geneviève Sanchis. "Elizabeth Dalloway Talks Back: Students and the *Mrs. Dalloway* Experience." Davis and McVicker 234–38.

Morrison, Toni. *Sula*. 1973. New York: Plume, 1982. Print.

———. "Virginia Woolf's and William Faulkner's Treatment of the Alienated." MA thesis. Cornell U, 1955. Print.

Mosse, George. *Fallen Soldiers: Reshaping the Memory of the World Wars*. New York: Oxford UP, 1990. Print.

Murphy, Bruce, ed. *Benét's Reader's Encyclopedia*. 4th ed. New York: Harper, 1996. Print.

Museum of London Picture Library. *Museum of London Prints*. Museum of London, n.d. Web. 3 June 2007.

Nava, Mica. "Modernity's Disavowal: Women, the City, and the Department Store." *Modern Times: Reflections on a Century of English Modernity*. Ed. Nava and Alan O'Shea. London: Routledge, 1996. 38–76. Print.

Neuman, Shirley. "*Heart of Darkness*, Virginia Woolf, and the Spectre of Domination." *Virginia Woolf: New Critical Essays*. Ed. Patricia Clements and Isobel Grundy. Totowa: Barnes, 1983. 57–76. Print.

Neverow-Turk, Vara, and Mark Hussey, eds. *Virginia Woolf: Themes and Variations: Selected Papers from the Second Annual Conference on Virginia Woolf*. New York: Pace UP, 1993. Print.

New York Times. "Featured Author: Virginia Woolf." *New York Times*. New York Times, 1999. Web. 1 Mar. 2008.

Nord, Deborah Epstein. *Walking the Victorian Streets: Women, Representation, and the City*. Ithaca: Cornell UP, 1995. Print.

Novack, Dennis H., Anthony L. Suchman, et al. "Calibrating the Physician: Personal Awareness and Effective Patient Care." *Journal of the American Medical Association* 278.6 (1997): 502–09. Print.

O'Dair, Sharon. "Beyond Necessity: The Consumption of Class, the Production of Status, and the Persistence of Inequality." *New Literary History: A Journal of Theory and Interpretation* 31.2 (2000): 337–54. Print.

Orr, Gregory. *Poetry as Survival.* Athens: U of Georgia P, 2002. Print.

Owen, Wilfred. *The Collected Poems.* New York: New Directions, 1965. Print.

Pace, David, and Joan Middendorf. "Decoding the Disciplines: Helping Students Learn Disciplinary Ways of Thinking." Center for Teaching and Learning, Otterbein College. 2 Sept. 2005. Workshop.

Parsons, Deborah L. *Streetwalking the Metropolis: Women, the City, and Modernity.* Oxford: Oxford UP, 2000. Print.

———. "Trauma and War Memory." *The Cambridge History of Twentieth-Century English Literature.* Ed. Laura Marcus and Peter Nicholls. Cambridge: Cambridge UP, 2004. 175–96. Print.

Pater, Walter. Preface. *Selected Writings of Walter Pater.* Ed. Harold Bloom. New York: Columbia UP, 1974. 17–22. Print. Excerpt from *The Renaissance: Studies in Art and Poetry.* By Pater. New York: Macmillan, 1899. ix–xvi.

Peace Pageant. 1919. *Getty Images.* Web. 22 Feb. 2008. Image no. 3347873.

Peele, Thomas. "Queering *Mrs. Dalloway.*" *Literature and Homosexuality.* Ed. Michael J. Meyer. Amsterdam: Rodopi, 2000. 205–21. Print.

Phillips, Kathy J. "Devouring the Lamb: Sex, Money, and War." Phillips, *Virginia Woolf* 1–51.

———. *Virginia Woolf against Empire.* Knoxville: U of Tennessee P, 1994. Print.

Poole, Roger. *The Unknown Virginia Woolf.* 1978. 3rd ed. Atlantic Highlands: Humanities, 1990. Print.

"Posters and Art of WW1." *About.com.* New York Times, 2007. Web. 15 Jan. 2008.

Potter, Jane. "'Is Your Best Boy Wearing Khaki?' Publishing and Propaganda." *Boys in Khaki, Girls in Print: Women's Literary Responses to the Great War, 1914–1918.* Oxford: Clarendon, 2005. 52–87. Print.

Prose, Francine, ed. *The* Mrs. Dalloway *Reader.* Fwd. Mark Hussey. Orlando: Harcourt, 2004. Print.

Radstone, Susannah. "Trauma Theory: Contexts, Politics, Ethics." *Paragraph: Journal of Modern Critical Theory* 30.1 (2007): 9–29. Print.

Reid, Panthea. *Art and Affection: A Life of Virginia Woolf.* New York: Oxford UP, 1996. Print.

Reid, Su, ed. Mrs. Dalloway *and* To the Lighthouse. London: Macmillan, 1993. Print. New Casebooks.

Rich, Adrienne. "Compulsory Heterosexuality and Lesbian Experience." *Adrienne Rich's Poetry and Prose.* Ed. Barbara Charlesworth Gelpi and Albert Gelpi. New York: Norton, 1975. 203–23. Print.

Richardson, Dorothy. "Continuous Performance: Dorothy Richardson." Donald, Friedberg, and Marcus 150–209.

———. "So I Gave up Going to the Theatre." *Close Up* July 1927: 34–37. Rpt. in Scott, *Gender* 851–52.

Richter, Harvena. "The *Ulysses* Connection: Clarissa Dalloway's Bloomsday." *Studies in the Novel* 21.3 (1989): 305–19. Print.

Rivers, W. H. R. "The Repression of War Experience." *Lancet.* 2 Feb. 1918: 173–77. *Brigham Young University Library.* Web. 1 Mar. 2008.

Robinson, David. *Das cabinet des Dr. Caligari.* London: British Film Inst., 1997. Print.

Roof, Judith. "Hocus Crocus." Ardis and Scott 93–102.

———. "The Match in the Crocus: Representations of Lesbian Sexuality." *Discontented Discourses: Feminism / Textual Intervention / Psychoanalysis*. Ed. Marleen Barr and Richard Feldstein. Urbana: U of Illinois P, 1989. 100–16. Print.

Rose, Gillian. *Feminism and Geography*. Minneapolis: U of Minnesota P, 1993. Print.

Rose, Phyllis. *Woman of Letters: A Life of Virginia Woolf.* New York: Oxford UP, 1978. Print.

Rosenberg, Beth Carole. *Virginia Woolf and Samuel Johnson: Common Readers*. New York: St. Martin's, 1995. Print.

Rosenberg, Beth Carole, and Jeanne Dubino, eds. *Virginia Woolf and the Essay*. New York: St. Martin's, 1997. Print.

Ruotolo, Lucio P. *The Interrupted Moment: A View of Virginia Woolf's Novels*. Stanford: Stanford UP, 1986. Print.

Ruttmann, Walter, dir. *Berlin: Symphony of a Great City*. Fox, 1927. Film.

Sassoon, Siegfried. "Working Party." *The Penguin Book of First World War Poetry*. 2nd ed. Ed. Jon Silkin. New York: Penguin, 1981. 123–24. Print.

Saxton, Ruth. "The Female Body Veiled: From Crocus to Clitoris." Saxton and Tobin 95–122.

Saxton, Ruth, and Jean Tobin, eds. *Woolf and Lessing: Breaking the Mold*. New York: St. Martin's, 1994. Print.

Schaefer, Josephine O'Brien. "The Great War and 'This Late Age of World's Experience' in Cather and Woolf." Hussey, *Virginia Woolf and War* 134–50.

Schiff, James. "Rewriting Woolf's *Mrs. Dalloway*: Homage, Sexual Identity, and the Single-Day Novel by Cunningham, Lippincott, and Lanchester." *Critique* 45.4 (2004): 363–82. Print.

Schlack, Beverly Ann. *Continuing Presences: Virginia Woolf's Use of Literary Allusion*. University Park: Pennsylvania State UP, 1979. Print.

Schnapp, Jeffrey. "Crash (Speed as Engine of Individuation)." *Modernism/Modernity* 6.1 (1999): 1–49. Print.

Schröder, Leena Kore. "*Mrs. Dalloway* and the Female Vagrant." *Essays in Criticism* 45.1 (1995): 324–46. Print.

Scott, Bonnie Kime, ed. *Gender in Modernism: New Geographies, Complex Intersections*. Urbana: U of Illinois P, 2007. Print.

———. Introduction. *Mrs. Dalloway*. 1925. By Woolf. Orlando: Harcourt, 2005. Print.

Searles, Susan. "'Accesses of Emotion—Bursting into Tears': Why All the Crying in Virginia Woolf's *Mrs. Dalloway*?" Neverow-Turk and Hussey 112–18.

Seldes, Gilbert. "The Abstract Movie." *New Republic* 15 Sept. 1926: 95–96. Rpt. in Scott, *Gender* 844–47.

Shakespeare, William. *Cymbeline. The Complete Works of Shakespeare*. Ed. George Lyman Kittredge. Boston: Ginn, 1936. 1333–76. Print.

Shay, Jonathan. *Achilles in Vietnam: Combat Trauma and the Undoing of Character*. New York: Simon, 1995. Print.

Sherry, Vincent, ed. *The Cambridge Companion to the Literature of the First World War*. Cambridge: Cambridge UP, 2005. Print.

————. *The Great War and the Language of Modernism*. New York: Oxford UP, 2004. Print.

Shields, E. F. "The American Edition of *Mrs. Dalloway*." *Studies in Bibliography* 27 (1974): 157–75. Print.

Showalter, Elaine. *The Female Malady: Women, Madness, and English Culture, 1830–1980*. New York: Penguin, 1985. Print.

————. *A Literature of Their Own: British Women Novelists from Brontë to Lessing*. London: Virago, 1978. Print.

Silver, Brenda R. *Virginia Woolf: Icon*. Chicago: U of Chicago P, 1999. Print.

————. *Virginia Woolf's Reading Notebooks*. Princeton: Princeton UP, 1983. Print.

Simmel, Georg. "The Metropolis and Mental Life." *The Sociology of Georg Simmel*. Ed. Kurt Wolff. New York: Free, 1964. 409–24. Print.

Simpson, Kathryn. "The Paradox of the Gift: Gift-Giving as a Disruptive Force in 'Mrs. Dalloway in Bond Street.'" *Woolf Studies Annual* 11 (2005): 53–75. Print.

————. "'Queer Fish': Woolf's Writing of Desire between Women." *Woolf Studies Annual* 9 (2003): 55–82. Print.

Sizemore, Christine Wick. *Negotiating Identities in Women's Lives: English Postcolonial and Contemporary British Novels*. Westport: Greenwood, 2002. Print.

————. "The 'Outsider-Within': Virginia Woolf and Doris Lessing as Urban Novelists in *Mrs. Dalloway* and *The Four-Gated City*." Saxton and Tobin 59–72.

Smith, Laura A. "Who Do We Think Clarissa Dalloway Is Anyway? Re-Search into Seventy Years of Woolf Criticism." Neverow-Turk and Hussey 215–21.

Smith, Patricia Juliana. *Lesbian Panic: Homoeroticism in Modern British Women's Fiction*. New York: Columbia UP, 1997. Print.

Snaith, Anna. "'I Wobble': Narrative Strategies: Public and Private Voices." *Virginia Woolf: Public and Private Negotiations*. New York: St. Martin's, 2000. 63–87. Print.

————. *Virginia Woolf: Public and Private Negotiations*. London: Palgrave, 2000. Print.

Sontag, Susan. *"Illness as Metaphor" and AIDS and Its Metaphors*. New York: Doubleday, 1990. Print.

————. *Regarding the Pain of Others*. New York: Farrar, 2003. Print.

Sparks, Elisa Kay. *Links for Woolf's* Mrs. Dalloway. *Clemson University*. Clemson Univ. n.d. Web. 1 Mar. 2008.

Spater, George, and Ian Parsons. *A Marriage of True Minds: An Intimate Portrait of Leonard and Virginia Woolf*. New York: Harcourt, 1977. Print.

Spengler, Birgit. "Michael Cunningham Rewriting Virginia Woolf: Pragmatist vs. Modernist Aesthetics." *Woolf Studies Annual* 10 (2004): 51–79. Print.

Spilka, Mark. "On Mrs. Dalloway's Absent Grief: A Psycho-Literary Speculation." *Contemporary Literature* 20.3 (1979): 316–38. Print.

————. *Virginia Woolf's Quarrel with Grieving*. Lincoln: U of Nebraska P, 1980. Print.

Sprague, Claire. "Multipersonal and Dialogic Modes in *Mrs. Dalloway* and *The Golden Notebook*." Saxton and Tobin 3–14.

Squier, Susan Merrill. "Tradition and Revision: The Classic City Novel and Virginia Woolf's *Night and Day*." *Women Writers and the City: Essays in Feminist Literary Criticism*. Ed. Squier. Knoxville: U of Tennessee P, 1984. 114–33. Print.

———. *Virginia Woolf and London: The Sexual Politics of the City*. Chapel Hill: U of North Carolina P, 1985. Print.

Stam, Robert. *Literature through Film: Realism, Magic, and the Art of Adaptation*. Oxford: Blackwell, 2005. Print.

Steele, Elizabeth. *Virginia Woolf's Literary Sources and Allusions: A Guide to the Essay*. New York: Garland, 1983. Print.

Stetz, Margaret Diane. "*Quartet in Autumn*: New Light on Barbara Pym as Modernist." *Arizona Quarterly* 41.1 (1985): 24–37. Print.

Strick, Joseph, dir. *Ulysses*. British Lion Films, 1967. Film.

Strom, Adam. "Teaching about the Armenian Genocide." *The Armenian Genocide: Cultural and Ethical Legacies*. Ed. Richard G. Hovannisian. New Brunswick: Transaction, 2007. 239–44. Print.

Sullivan, Andrew. *Love Undetectable: Notes on Friendship, Sex, and Survival*. New York: Knopf, 1998. Print.

Sumner, Rosemary. *A Route to Modernism: Hardy, Lawrence, Woolf*. New York: St. Martin's, 2000. Print.

Tambling, Jeremy. "Repression in *Mrs. Dalloway*'s London." *Essays in Criticism* 39.2 (1989): 137–55. Print.

Tate, Trudi. *Modernism, History, and the First World War*. Manchester: Manchester UP, 1998. Print.

———. "*Mrs. Dalloway* and the Armenian Question." *Textual Practice* 8.3 (1994): 467–86. Print.

———, ed. *Women, Men, and the Great War: An Anthology of Stories*. Manchester: Manchester UP, 1995. Print.

Thomas, Sue. "Virginia Woolf's Septimus Smith and Contemporary Perceptions of Shell Shock." *English Language Notes* 25.2 (1987): 49–57. Print.

Thomson, David. "Britain at War, 1914–18." *England in the Twentieth Century, 1914–1963*. By Thomson. New York: Penguin, 1970. 36–59. Print.

Tibbetts, John C. "So Much Is Lost in Translation." *Film Genre 2000: New Critical Essays*. Ed. Wheeler Winston Dixon. Albany: State U of New York P, 2000. Print.

To the Young Women of London. 1915. *Keep the Home Fires Burning: Documents from the British Home Front, 1914–1918*. 1991. Imperial War Museum, London. Print.

Trombley, Stephen. *All That Summer She Was Mad: Virginia Woolf: Female Victim of Male Medicine*. New York: Continuum, 1981. Print.

Trotter, David. *Cinema and Modernism*. Oxford: Blackwell, 2007. Print. Critical Quarterly Book Ser.

Turvey, Malcolm. "The Avant-Garde and the 'New Spirit': The Case of *Ballet mécanique*." *October* 102 (2002): 102–37. Print.

"2,500,000 Posters: Their Success as Recruiting Agents." *Daily Chronicle* [London] 24 June 1915: 3. Print.

Tylee, Claire M. *The Great War and Women's Consciousness: Images of Militarism and Womanhood in Women's Writing, 1914–1964*. Iowa City: U of Iowa P, 1990. Print.

United States. Bureau of Justice Statistics. *More Than a Quarter Million Prison and Jail Inmates Are Identified as Mentally Ill. U.S. Department of Justice, Office of Justice Programs*. U.S. Dept. of Justice, 11 July 1999. Web. 2 Mar. 2008.

———. Copyright Office. 17 USC. Ch.1. Oct. 2007. Web. 20 Oct. 2008.

Unter, Jennifer. "Virginia Woolf's Clarissa and Zora Neale Hurston's Janie: Images of Women in Literature." *Mount Olive Review* 6 (1992): 56–60. Print.

Vickroy, Laurie. "A Legacy of Pacifism: Virginia Woolf and Pat Barker." *Women and Language* 27.2 (2004): 45–50. Print.

Vidor, King, dir. *The Big Parade*. MGM, 1925. Film.

Virilio, Paul. *Speed and Politics: An Essay on Dromology*. Trans. Mark Polizzoti. New York: Columbia UP, 1986. Print.

Wachman, Gay. *Lesbian Empire: Radical Crosswriting in the Twenties*. New Brunswick: Rutgers UP, 2001. Print.

———. "Pink Icing and a Narrow Bed: *Mrs. Dalloway* and Lesbian History." Gillespie and Hankins 344–50.

Walker, Nancy A. *The Disobedient Writer: Women and Narrative Tradition*. Austin: U of Texas P, 1995. Print.

Walkowitz, Judith. *City of Dreadful Delight: Narratives of Sexual Danger in Late-Victorian London*. Chicago: U of Chicago P, 1992. Print.

Wang, Ban. "'I' on the Run: Crisis of Identity in *Mrs. Dalloway*." *Modern Fiction Studies* 38.1 (1992): 177–91. Print.

Webb, Caroline. "Life after Death: The Allegorical Progress of *Mrs. Dalloway*." *Modern Fiction Studies* 40.2 (1994): 279–98. Print.

Weimer, Maryellen. *Learner-Centered Teaching: Five Key Changes to Practice*. San Francisco: Jossey-Bass, 2002. Print.

Weintraub, Stanley. *A Stillness Heard Round the World: The End of the Great War: November 1918*. New York: Dutton, 1985. Print.

Weiser, Barbara. "Criticism of Virginia Woolf from 1956 to the Present: A Selected Checklist with an Index to the Studies of Separate Works." *Modern Fiction Studies* 18.3 (1972): 477–86. Print.

West, Rebecca. *Return of the Soldier*. New York: Penguin, 1998. Print.

White, Mimi. "Two French Dada Films: *Entr'acte* and *Emak Bakia*." *Dada Surrealism* 13 (1984): 37–47. Print.

Whitehall Cenotaph. 1919. *Getty Images*. Web. 22 Feb. 2008. Image no. 3164400.

Whitworth, Michael. *Virginia Woolf*. Oxford: Oxford UP, 2005. Print.

Wicke, Jennifer. "*Mrs. Dalloway* Goes to Market: Woolf, Keynes, and Modern Markets." *Novel: A Forum on Fiction* 28.1 (1994): 5–23. Print.

Wiene, Robert, dir. *The Cabinet of Dr. Caligari*. Goldwyn, 1919. Film.

Williams, Lisa. *The Artist as Outsider in the Novels of Toni Morrison and Virginia Woolf*. Westport: Greenwood, 2000. Print.

Williams, Raymond. "Culture Is Ordinary." *Conviction*. Ed. Norman MacKenzie. London: MacGibbon, 1959. 74–92. Print.

Williams, Wendy Patrice. "Falling through the Cone: The Shape of *Mrs. Dalloway* Makes Its Point." Hussey and Neverow 210–13.

Wilson, Elizabeth. *The Sphinx in the City: Urban Life, the Control of Disorder, and Women*. Los Angeles: U of California P, 1991. Print.

Wilson, Jean Moorcroft. *Virginia Woolf, Life and London: A Biography of Place*. New York: Norton, 1987. Print.

Winter, Jay. *Remembering War: The Great War between Memory and History in the Twentieth Century*. New Haven: Yale UP, 2006. Print.

———. *Sites of Memory, Sites of Mourning: The Great War in European Cultural History*. Cambridge: Cambridge UP, 1995. Print.

Winter, Jay, and Blaine Baggett. *The Great War and the Shaping of the Twentieth Century*. New York: Penguin, 1996. Print.

Wolfe, Jesse. "The Sane Woman in the Attic: Sexuality and Self-Authorship in *Mrs. Dalloway*." *Modern Fiction Studies* 51.1 (2005): 34–59. Print.

Wolff, Janet. "The Invisible Flâneuse: Women and the Literature of Modernity." *Theory, Culture and Society* 2.3 (1985): 37–46. Print.

Wollaeger, Mark. "Woolf, Postcards, and the Elision of Race: Colonizing Women in *The Voyage Out*." *Modernism/Modernity* 8.1 (2001): 43–75. Print.

Wood, Andelys. "Walking the Web in the Lost London of *Mrs. Dalloway*." *Mosaic* 36.2 (2003): 19–32. Print.

Woolf, Leonard. Preface. 1953. *A Writer's Diary*. By Virginia Woolf. New York: Harcourt, 1981. vii–x. Print.

Wright, G. Patton. "Note on Editorial Method." *Mrs. Dalloway*. 1925. By Virginia Woolf. London: Hogarth, 1990. 173–218. Print. Definitive Collected ed.

Wright, Nathalia. "*Mrs. Dalloway*: A Study in Composition." *College English* 5.7 (1944): 351–58. Print.

Wussow, Helen M. *The Nightmare of History: The Fictions of Virginia Woolf and D. H. Lawrence*. Bethlehem: Lehigh UP, 1998. Print.

Wyatt, Jean. "Avoiding Self-Definition: In Defense of Women's Right to Merge (Julia Kristeva and *Mrs. Dalloway*)." *Women's Studies* 13.1-2 (1986): 115–26. Print.

———. "*Mrs. Dalloway*: Literary Allusion as Structural Metaphor." *PMLA* 88.3 (1973): 440–51. Print.

Yeats, W. B., ed. *The Oxford Book of Modern Verse, 1892–1935*. New York: Oxford UP, 1960. Print.

Zwerdling, Alex. "*Mrs. Dalloway* and the Social System." Zwerdling, *Virginia Woolf* 120–43.

———. *Virginia Woolf and the Real World*. Berkeley: U of California P, 1986. Print.

INDEX OF NAMES

Modern Language Association of America

Approaches to Teaching World Literature

Eliot's Middlemarch. Ed. Kathleen Blake. 1990.

Eliot's Poetry and Plays. Ed. Jewel Spears Brooker. 1988.

Shorter Elizabethan Poetry. Ed. Patrick Cheney and Anne Lake Prescott. 2000.

Ellison's Invisible Man. Ed. Susan Resneck Parr and Pancho Savery. 1989.

English Renaissance Drama. Ed. Karen Bamford and Alexander Leggatt. 2002.

Works of Louise Erdrich. Ed. Gregg Sarris, Connie A. Jacobs, and
James R. Giles. 2004.

Dramas of Euripides. Ed. Robin Mitchell-Boyask. 2002.

Faulkner's The Sound and the Fury. Ed. Stephen Hahn and Arthur F. Kinney. 1996.

Fitzgerald's The Great Gatsby. Ed. Jackson R. Bryer and Nancy P. VanArsdale. 2009.

Flaubert's Madame Bovary. Ed. Laurence M. Porter and Eugene F. Gray. 1995.

García Márquez's One Hundred Years of Solitude. Ed. María Elena de Valdés and
Mario J. Valdés. 1990.

Gilman's "The Yellow Wall-Paper" and Herland. Ed. Denise D. Knight and
Cynthia J. Davis. 2003.

Goethe's Faust. Ed. Douglas J. McMillan. 1987.

Gothic Fiction: The British and American Traditions. Ed. Diane Long Hoeveler
and Tamar Heller. 2003.

Grass's The Tin Drum. Ed. Monika Shafi. 2008.

Hebrew Bible as Literature in Translation. Ed. Barry N. Olshen and
Yael S. Feldman. 1989.

Homer's Iliad *and* Odyssey. Ed. Kostas Myrsiades. 1987.

Hurston's Their Eyes Were Watching God *and Other Works.* Ed. John Lowe. 2009.

Ibsen's A Doll House. Ed. Yvonne Shafer. 1985.

Henry James's Daisy Miller *and* The Turn of the Screw. Ed. Kimberly C. Reed and
Peter G. Beidler. 2005.

Works of Samuel Johnson. Ed. David R. Anderson and Gwin J. Kolb. 1993.

Joyce's Ulysses. Ed. Kathleen McCormick and Erwin R. Steinberg. 1993.

Works of Sor Juana Inés de la Cruz. Ed. Emilie L. Bergmann and Stacey Schlau. 2007.

Kafka's Short Fiction. Ed. Richard T. Gray. 1995.

Keats's Poetry. Ed. Walter H. Evert and Jack W. Rhodes. 1991.

Kingston's The Woman Warrior. Ed. Shirley Geok-lin Lim. 1991.

Lafayette's The Princess of Clèves. Ed. Faith E. Beasley and
Katharine Ann Jensen. 1998.

Works of D. H. Lawrence. Ed. M. Elizabeth Sargent and Garry Watson. 2001.

Lazarillo de Tormes *and the Picaresque Tradition.* Ed. Anne J. Cruz. 2009.

Lessing's The Golden Notebook. Ed. Carey Kaplan and Ellen Cronan Rose. 1989.

Mann's Death in Venice *and Other Short Fiction.* Ed. Jeffrey B. Berlin. 1992.

Marguerite de Navarre's Heptameron. Ed. Colette H. Winn. 2007.

Medieval English Drama. Ed. Richard K. Emmerson. 1990.

Melville's Moby-Dick. Ed. Martin Bickman. 1985.

Metaphysical Poets. Ed. Sidney Gottlieb. 1990.

Miller's Death of a Salesman. Ed. Matthew C. Roudané. 1995.

Milton's Paradise Lost. Ed. Galbraith M. Crump. 1986.

Milton's Shorter Poetry and Prose. Ed. Peter C. Herman. 2007.
Molière's Tartuffe *and Other Plays.* Ed. James F. Gaines and
    Michael S. Koppisch. 1995.
Momaday's The Way to Rainy Mountain. Ed. Kenneth M. Roemer. 1988.
Montaigne's Essays. Ed. Patrick Henry. 1994.
Novels of Toni Morrison. Ed. Nellie Y. McKay and Kathryn Earle. 1997.
Murasaki Shikibu's The Tale of Genji. Ed. Edward Kamens. 1993.
Nabokov's Lolita. Ed. Zoran Kuzmanovich and Galya Diment. 2008.
Poe's Prose and Poetry. Ed. Jeffrey Andrew Weinstock and Tony Magistrale. 2008.
Pope's Poetry. Ed. Wallace Jackson and R. Paul Yoder. 1993.
Proust's Fiction and Criticism. Ed. Elyane Dezon-Jones and
    Inge Crosman Wimmers. 2003.
Puig's Kiss of the Spider Woman. Ed. Daniel Balderston and Francine Masiello. 2007.
Pynchon's The Crying of Lot 49 *and Other Works.* Ed. Thomas H. Schaub. 2008.
Novels of Samuel Richardson. Ed. Lisa Zunshine and Jocelyn Harris. 2006.
Rousseau's Confessions *and* Reveries of the Solitary Walker. Ed. John C. O'Neal
    and Ourida Mostefai. 2003.
Scott's Waverley Novels. Ed. Evan Gottlieb and Ian Duncan. 2009.
Shakespeare's Hamlet. Ed. Bernice W. Kliman. 2001.
Shakespeare's King Lear. Ed. Robert H. Ray. 1986.
Shakespeare's Othello. Ed. Peter Erickson and Maurice Hunt. 2005.
Shakespeare's Romeo and Juliet. Ed. Maurice Hunt. 2000.
Shakespeare's The Tempest *and Other Late Romances.* Ed. Maurice Hunt. 1992.
Shelley's Frankenstein. Ed. Stephen C. Behrendt. 1990.
Shelley's Poetry. Ed. Spencer Hall. 1990.
Sir Gawain and the Green Knight. Ed. Miriam Youngerman Miller and
    Jane Chance. 1986.
Song of Roland. Ed. William W. Kibler and Leslie Zarker Morgan. 2006.
Spenser's Faerie Queene. Ed. David Lee Miller and Alexander Dunlop. 1994.
Stendhal's The Red and the Black. Ed. Dean de la Motte and Stirling Haig. 1999.
Sterne's Tristram Shandy. Ed. Melvyn New. 1989.
Stowe's Uncle Tom's Cabin. Ed. Elizabeth Ammons and Susan Belasco. 2000.
Swift's Gulliver's Travels. Ed. Edward J. Rielly. 1988.
Teresa of Ávila and the Spanish Mystics. Ed. Alison Weber. 2009.
Thoreau's Walden *and Other Works.* Ed. Richard J. Schneider. 1996.
Tolstoy's Anna Karenina. Ed. Liza Knapp and Amy Mandelker. 2003.
Vergil's Aeneid. Ed. William S. Anderson and Lorina N. Quartarone. 2002.
Voltaire's Candide. Ed. Renée Waldinger. 1987.
Whitman's Leaves of Grass. Ed. Donald D. Kummings. 1990.
Wiesel's Night. Ed. Alan Rosen. 2007.
Works of Oscar Wilde. Ed. Philip E. Smith II. 2008.
Woolf's Mrs. Dalloway. Ed. Eileen Barrett and Ruth O. Saxton. 2009.
Woolf's To the Lighthouse. Ed. Beth Rigel Daugherty and Mary Beth Pringle. 2001.
Wordsworth's Poetry. Ed. Spencer Hall, with Jonathan Ramsey. 1986.
Wright's Native Son. Ed. James A. Miller. 1997.